Popular Music in Theory

UNIVERSITY PRESS OF NEW ENGLAND
publishes books under its own imprint and is the publisher for Brandeis University Press, Dartmouth College, Middlebury College Press, University of New Hampshire, Tufts University, Wesleyan University Press, and Salzburg Seminar.

Wesleyan University Press
Published by University Press of New England, Hanover, NH 03755
© 1996 by Keith Negus

First published in 1996 by Polity Press in association with Blackwell Publishers Ltd.
First U.S. edition 1997

Printed in Great Britain

5 4 3 2 1

ISBN 0–8195–6310–2

Library of Congress Catalog Card Number: 96–61301

CONTENTS

INTRODUCTION

This book has been written as a systematic attempt to outline, explain and provide a critical introduction to some of the major theoretical issues and debates in the study of contemporary popular music. It is intended for students, researchers and teachers in the broad interdisciplinary area of popular music studies, and particularly for those who are taking courses and classes in sociology, cultural studies and media and communication studies.

One of my aims is to highlight how academic study and intellectual debate connect with, inform and can help our understanding of and perhaps participation in many everyday activities in which music is a central part. Despite the fact that we often respond to music in an immediate and spontaneous manner, there are numerous occasions when theoretical understanding informs daily experiences of and discussions about popular music: for example, if you have ever argued about the manipulative influence of the recording industry, or discussed whether a particular music is 'authentically' black, gay, Latin or Irish; when you hear someone dismiss a certain musical style as repetitive and standardized while embracing other sounds as challenging and complex; if you are familiar with the claim that some songs can communicate a radical political message whereas televised charity events do little more than make money for rich pop stars. If you have discussed, thought about or listened to arguments about these types of issues then you will already be familiar with some of the theoretical debates I will be discussing in this book.

Not only does theory and analysis guide how music is experienced and understood, it also has an impact on how it is created and distributed and the attempts that are made to control it. Again there are numerous everyday examples of this occurring: when a particular type of music is played in supermarkets to encourage the purchase of goods, or when different types of music are piped into bars and restaurants to make people drink more quickly or linger longer over their meals; when music is composed as a national anthem, chosen for political rallies or performed at religious ceremonies, or when certain types of music and instruments are banned from performance in public places; when a symphony is placed on a film soundtrack, rap put on a computer game and a mambo chosen for a commercial. In all of these situations the actions of the numerous people involved are guided by theoretical reasoning and analysis.

In approaching these types of issues I will be critically surveying a range of theoretical writings on popular music and highlighting and assessing their relative merits, while also proposing some arguments of my own and pointing to directions for further study and research. In an attempt to cover a range of themes and issues, I have divided up the chapters of this book within a framework made up of single-word titles, a design which might be construed as implying rather grand intentions. However, they have been named as a way of signalling specific themes and identifying significant issues which, in my experience, have been and continue to be a focus of major research activity and debate among those engaged in the study of popular music. In this way I hope that the chapter titles are reasonably self-explanatory, although I will make a few remarks about the way I have organized them. In Chapter 1 I start by considering how different writers have characterized the audiences for popular music (which in recent times has frequently been as active, creative and oppositional) and then provide an immediate contrast to this in Chapter 2 by focusing on approaches to the music industry (often portrayed as mechanistic, exploitative and conservative). These first two chapters are set up in this way so as to emphasize a series of dichotomies that have often separated discussions of musical production and consumption (commerce/creativity, determinism/free will, constraining/liberating), and which have also formed an uneasy division in a range of studies of cultural activity. The chapters which follow then seek gradually to break down this distinction by emphasizing the relationships and social processes that are stretched across or which come in between production and consumption. Hence, in subsequent chapters I seek to highlight how cultural identity, historical change, geographical location and political processes have a significant influence on how music is produced, distributed and consumed. One of my aims throughout these chapters is to balance summarizing other authors' work and illustrating issues with an attempt gradually to introduce more speculative arguments that I hope will provoke debate outside of these pages. Hence, while the chapters of this book can be approached individually or dipped into (and I have tried to make them relatively self-contained), there is a certain logical sequence which assumes a degree of familiarity with preceding chapters.

What I have written here should not be taken as a definitive or comprehensive account of the subject, nor is it an attempt to establish intellectual boundaries. Instead, I would like it to be treated as a starting point, as a source of questions and commentaries rather than as a source of answers and solutions. This book is intended mainly for students and researchers who wish to find ways of assessing, drawing points out from and arguing with a range of literature that can be found in this area of study. But, it is also a book that you should approach critically and argue with. Hence, in many places I have tried to leave the discussion deliberately open (most of the issues and debates here are far from resolved anyway).

While this book has been written as an introduction to various issues and not with the intention that it should be taken as embracing a unified or complete overall argument, there is one main theme that weaves throughout: that of mediation. I will be dealing with this issue in a more specific and detailed way in Chapter 3. Here I want to make just a few general introductory remarks.

Although mediation has often been used in an elusive way and is sometimes a vaguely defined concept, it is one that I am using to stress how popular music cannot be known in any neutral, immediate or naively experiential way. I am using the idea of mediation to stress that human experiences are grounded in cultural activities which are understood and given meaning through particular languages and symbol systems. These are, in turn, constituted within particular social circumstances and subject to different types of political regulation. We may, somewhere deep inside, 'feel' and 'know' music in a quite profound way – I wouldn't want to deny that this is possible and that it happens all the time, and I don't think that many people who love and are continually moved by music would want to refuse this possibility either. However, as soon as we try to communicate and share this experience we are caught up in language and culture – the range of concepts, communicative actions and social practices that we must use to formulate, convey and exchange meanings with other people. If this sounds a little abstract at the moment, I hope that it becomes gradually clearer throughout the book.

One of the implications of adopting this approach is that popular music cannot be understood with *mirrors*. By that I mean that music cannot simply *reflect* a society, an individual's personality or life, a nation, a city or 'the age we live in'. That word, reflection, is one that slips very easily into both academic discourse and everyday conversations about popular music. But no music can be a mirror and capture events or activities in its melodies, rhythms and voices. The world, a society, an individual life, or even a particular incident, is far too complex for any cultural product (book, film or song) to be able to capture and spontaneously 'reflect'. Hence, my general point is that music is created, circulated, recognized and responded to according to a range of conceptual assumptions and analytical activities that are grounded in quite particular social relationships, political processes and cultural activities.

As a central theme of the following chapters is that of mediation, I should acknowledge that this book is itself heavily mediated by my own background and experience of living in Britain and observing and listening from a particular position at a specific time. On this issue, a number of points are worth highlighting. First, I have found it occasionally impossible to avoid using the term 'we'. I have already been doing this in a type of 'we the human race' manner. This is, of course, a highly ideological and rhetorical way of writing that can be used to signify membership of a particular group ('us') and also as a way of including or implicating you, the reader, in what I am writing ('we all think or know this – don't we?'). In this book I am using 'we' in a more restricted sense to refer to 'those of us studying popular music'.

On this issue, though, I need to make a further point. A number of people who are studying popular music will quite justifiably feel that their interests have been neglected. In particular, this book contains little direct engagement with formal musicology, an area of knowledge and technique which for a sociologist has to be approached over one of the great disciplinary divides. Despite its usefulness, and in spite of my best efforts, I am simply not conversant enough with the discipline to include substantial musicological references. However, I will be drawing on musicology and making reference to various musical styles, texts and genres as and when they relate to the specific social theories and issues I am covering.

A further point, and related to this, concerns the use of the term 'popular music', a label which really needs qualifying. The theoretical issues with which this book deals are mainly about *recorded* popular music, made since the phonograph, and mostly during the latter half of the twentieth century. Unlike film studies, an occasionally close academic ally, which can confine itself to the moving image *media*, popular music studies is broader and vaguer in scope and intentions. The moving image media can be traced to particular social and technological developments within a particular period of history, and this provides a boundary for study in a way which has no parallel in popular music studies.

My final point in these caveats is that most of what I have written here is based on articles written in or translated into the English language. It is a bias that is hard to overcome without great linguistic competence, but it is one that suggests that there is perhaps a great need for Anglo scholars to engage in a systematic way with writings from outside of this orbit. There is, then, as should be clear by now, far more to be said about popular music than is contained in this book. It is very much an introduction and, as such, as I have already mentioned, it should be taken as a starting point for further research and debate. It is only through constant critique and dialogue that a broader and more inclusive range of approaches to and knowledge about popular music can be developed and put on the agenda in this area of study.

Many of the ideas and arguments that I am putting forward in this book have evolved through several years of thinking and talking about music, and it would be difficult, and probably tedious for any reader, to acknowledge where all of these thoughts might have started life and the type of transformations they have been through on the way. Here I would like to confine my thanks to those who have made a particular and tangible contribution. First I would like to thank Patria Román Velázquez, who has been a constant companion, endured every chapter in the story and provided a continuous and much appreciated blend of constructive critique, noisy argument, encouragement and emotional support. I have been greatly influenced by many of her ideas and observations. Mike Pickering has given me much food for thought during the many conversations that we have had while the book was taking shape and he carefully read and provided very useful comments on the chapters in draft form. Dave Harker has subjected early drafts of most of the chapters to his characteristically scathing but comradely critique. His scribbled comments and general observations have helped me clarify many points, and often given me a good laugh. Paul du Gay has continued to be a source of encouragement and ideas; his critical distance from something called 'popular music studies' has been a useful antidote during some of my more barking moments.

Many other people have made useful suggestions, observations or criticisms in response to drafts or ideas that I was trying to work through at particular moments. Here, strictly in alphabetical order, I would like to thank Gavin Barber, Martin Cloonan, Sara Cohen, Niall Farrall, Eamon Forde, Simon Frith, Dave Hesmondhalgh, Charles Leech, Toru Mitsui, Jonathan Morrish, Rosa Saucedo Saucedo, Annabelle Sreberny-Mohammadi, John Street, Philip Tagg, Sarah Thornton and Masahiro Yasuda. I would also like to acknowledge the easy-going, friendly and supportive environment that has been created and maintained over the years by everyone who has contributed to the International Association for the Study of Popular Music (IASPM). Last, but not least, I would like to thank John Thompson at Polity Press for asking me to write this book and for his helpful suggestions, critical comments, patience and encouragement. Some sections of Chapter 3 originally appeared in an essay published by *The Sociological Review* (Vol. 47, No. 2, 1995) and I am grateful for their permission to reuse these here.

CHAPTER ONE
AUDIENCES

With so many people participating in numerous musical events around the world at any one time, a chapter that attempts to introduce theories about music audiences will inevitably be highly selective. After all, the audiences for popular music can range from the thousands of people who gather in stadiums to witness performances by well-known bands and singers (and perhaps the additional millions who might be receiving transmissions of such events on radio and television) to those dancing to music at a wedding or birthday party. Music audiences can include people engaging in devotional activity, the crowds hearing a cacophony of different melodies and rhythms as they pass through a shopping mall and someone listening to a cassette tape on a Walkman while cycling through the countryside.

If you add to this the fact that before the introduction of recorded music at the end of the nineteenth century much of this activity was not even possible – the audiences for music always listened, looked and danced in the presence of performing musicians – then you will realize that any approach to music audiences could encompass a wide variety of historically changing and geographically variable experiences and activities.

This modest introductory chapter does not even begin to attempt to address such complexity and diversity. Instead, my main concern here is with how the audiences for music have been theorized in the years since the development of modern recording technology, and in particular since the growth of the associated media technologies of radio and the moving image in the latter part of the twentieth century. Furthermore, the audience theorizing on which I will be focusing in this chapter is concerned mainly with the issue of 'reception' – that is, with how people receive, interpret and *use* music as a cultural form while engaging in specific social activities. This has been one of the most influential strands of reasoning in studies of popular music since the 1970s and this chapter is intended as a critical summary and assessment of this particular approach.

In adopting such a focus, for many years the theorists of music audiences have been concerned with the activities of young people. During the 1950s the focus was on the 'teenager'. In the 1960s the terms of reference shifted to a concern with the problems of 'youth', which in turn led to numerous writings about youth subcultures. During the 1980s and into the 1990s there has been a broader interest in fans and music scenes in general.

In tracing the development of theories about popular music and young audiences I shall be recounting a tale about an increasingly 'active' audience. This is a theoretical trajectory which offers a direct challenge, but which also owes an enduring debt, to the critique of popular music listening proposed by Theodor Adorno. I shall therefore start this chapter by giving some details about Adorno's approach to the audiences for popular music.

Adorno's children: the regression of listening

Adorno wrote about music and culture between the 1920s and the 1960s. He was a member of a group of predominantly German Jewish scholars who have become known as the Frankfurt School, and his thought is frequently riven with a pessimism that is derived partly from observing a period of considerable political turmoil. Adorno had lived through the futile bloodshed of the 1914–18 war, the failure of the working-class revolutions that had spread across Europe after the Russian revolution of 1917 and the growth of fascist parties from the 1920s. When the Nazi party seized power in 1933 Adorno had to flee Germany, and eventually relocated in the United States.

Adorno was also living at a time when technological changes had led to the improvement and increasing popularity of recorded music on the phonograph disc and when radio broadcasting and the introduction of sound in cinema had provided opportunities for commercial marketing and political propaganda. While the Nazi party were making maximum use of these media technologies in Germany, Adorno arrived in the United States to find the same media being used to produce and distribute forms of commercial culture. Adorno was thus writing at a formative moment in the development of the modern communication technologies and mass media that have had a major impact on the production, distribution and consumption of popular music.

In exile, Adorno made a connection between what he had observed in Germany and then in the United States and developed an argument in which the domination and manipulation of the people (who are reduced to 'masses') became explicitly connected to the production and dissemination of a particular form of culture (produced as 'mass culture'). In pursuing this argument, Adorno was concerned with how forms of culture could contribute to authoritarian forms of domination and thwart any prospects for political critique or emancipatory social change. I will be giving more details about what Adorno had to say about the production of popular music as mass culture in the next chapter; here I want to outline what he had to say about consumption.

For Adorno, the popular music that was being distributed by the music industries as 'mass culture' required the listener to make very little effort. He argued that it led to 'de-concentrated listening' in which listeners rejected everything that was not familiar and 'regressed' to the point where they began to 'behave like children' (1991: 44–5). One particularly 'child-like' type of consumption that Adorno identified was what he called 'quotation listening.' By this he meant that, instead of listening to music and attempting to grasp an entire piece of work as a whole, the regressive listener dwelt upon the most obvious fragments of melody. In doing so audiences adopted a 'musical children's language' and listened to different works 'as if the symphony were structurally the same as a ballad' (1945: 213).

Such listening was not because of the inherent stupidity of listeners but due to the way in which the recording and publishing industries had promoted standardized, repetitive music: songs that encouraged audiences to make no effort when listening to music. Adorno (1976) referred to the very successful category of 'easy listening', arguing that this was clear evidence that music was deliberately being created to encourage distracted audience activity. He asserted that such sounds were made up of the most familiar harmonies, rhythms and melodies that had a 'soporific' effect on social consciousness. Not only was this music generating a sleep-inducing form of diversion and distraction, Adorno claimed that in doing so it prevented people from reflecting on their position in the world. In their leisure time, the regressive listeners were pacified by music that merely provided a temporary escape from the boredom of the factory, assembly line or office.

Adorno maintained that music, like other art forms, should have the potential to provoke listeners to think critically about the world. However, the popular music that was produced for the purpose of entertainment led merely to passivity. It was a type of music that made people accept the status quo and engendered obedience towards authoritarianism. Popular music, argued Adorno, was indeed responsible for contributing to social passivity, as audiences regressed to a 'child-like' state and were thus easily manipulated by the adult authority of capitalist corporations and fascist states.

Adorno's listeners: alone in the bedroom and lost in the crowd

It is Adorno's somewhat despairing view of passive music listening that subsequent theorists have sought to challenge. Of particular relevance to some of the theorists who followed him, and to many everyday discussions about music consumption, are 'two types' of music listener that Adorno identified. The first type was the person who was lost in the crowd, the type of human being who was easily manipulated by the collectivity. The second was the obsessive individual. This was the type of person who was alienated from the people around them and not fully integrated into social life.

For Adorno, during the 1940s, the collective experience was most visible during popular forms of dancing such as the jitterbug. Adorno argued that this flamboyant and jerky form of dancing was ritualistic and an act of 'compulsive' mimicry. Those who danced to the jitterbug were losing their individuality, responding to the music by 'whirring around' like fascinated insects. Observing with distaste, Adorno remarked that people dancing the jitterbug were engaging in a 'stylized' type of dancing that had 'convulsive aspects reminiscent of St. Vitus's dance or the reflexes of mutilated animals' (1991: 46).

Such comments displayed a poor understanding of how the body and dancing have been employed throughout history and across the world to respond to music. Yet similar words have often been used to condemn dancing to popular music, whether to the charleston, rock-'n'-roll, disco or techno music. Such fears have often managed to combine a distaste for overt expressions of sexuality, a fear of 'civilized' behaviour being corrupted by 'primitive' rhythms (usually overtly racist) and a concern that young people are being manipulated by forms of crowd psychology.

In contrast to this, Adorno identified the opposite type of music listener. This he characterized as

> the eager person who leaves the factory and occupies himself with music in the quiet of his bedroom. He is shy and inhibited, perhaps has no luck with girls and wants to preserve his own special sphere . . . at the age of 20 he is still at the stage of the boy scout working on complicated knots just to please his parents. (1991: 46–7)

This is an image of the alienated, poorly socialized loner in *his* bedroom (it is a gendered type). This person takes solace in the illusion of intimacy that is created through music and prefers this to social contact with other people. Over forty years after Adorno wrote this, such an image was often used to caricature the male fans of The Smiths and the other melancholic guitar rock bands that followed them. As one journalist wrote in a review of the first album by the British band Suede: 'This is music for the boys who don't dance, who prefer an evening's self-pitying wallow in their bedroom' (Gill, 1993: 16).

The two types that Adorno identified have not been used simply as caricatures, as in the quote just cited, but have frequently reappeared to justify the anxieties of concerned moral guardians. The obsessive individual has often been identified as the young fan of heavy rock music, listening alone in a small town bedroom, estranged from family and friends, neurotic and prone to irrational, suicidal or aggressive behaviour brought about through intense and prolonged exposure to this music. More socially integrated, but just as manipulated by the products of the music media, are the amorphous crowds of ravers who gather in fields and large warehouses and who lose their individuality in a sea of waving arms and trance-like swaying bodies. Both of these images were conjured up and then used as a cause for social concern by religious leaders, parents and social workers during the 1980s and 1990s. Both are remarkably similar to the types identified by Adorno forty years earlier.

These are rather despairing and quite condescending views of the social activities that accompany the reception of popular music. And it is these images of the audiences for popular music that have been challenged by writers who have developed theories about the 'active' reception of music. Not long after Adorno was writing about these types of listeners, the identification of the 'teenage' consumer in the USA and Britain provided a focus for the development of a less manipulative model of popular music consumption.

The active minority against the majority

In an article first published in 1950, David Riesman (1990) reported on research he had conducted on the listening habits of teenagers and made a distinction that was to have an enduring influence on later studies. The distinction Riesman made was between two groups of music listeners: a *majority* group and a *minority* group. Riesman's theory forms a link between Adorno's arguments and the ideas of later subcultural theorists.

Having interviewed groups of teenagers in Chicago, Riesman reported that most of the young people to whom he had spoken formed a majority group that had undiscriminating tastes in popular music. They were the audience for the large radio stations and the well-known 'name' bands. These were young people who paid attention to the star singers and who listened to 'the hit parade'. Members of this majority group were not very concerned about how music was produced and their listening habits were fairly indiscriminate. Music and performers were principally a subject for superficial everyday conversation and gossip.

In contrast, the minority group adopted a more critical and questioning posture. Riesman found this group to be composed of discriminating active listeners. This audience had developed quite elaborate and sophisticated standards of music listening and appreciation. Members of the minority group involved themselves in detailed technical discussions about the composition and performance of music. In contrast to the majority, members of the minority group tended to dislike the name bands and big stars and were dismissive of most of the music that could be heard on the radio.

Instead, these listeners preferred what they considered to be 'uncommercialized', unadvertised less-known bands.

Riesman found that members of the minority group had developed their own 'private language' as an exclusive way of talking about the music and musicians that they liked. However, they stopped using this vocabulary when it was adopted along with 'their' music by the majority group, perceiving this to involve a process of commercial exploitation. Hence, members of the minority group were explicitly positioning themselves against and above the tastes of the majority group.

The distinction that Riesman made was between an *active*, hip and rebellious minority and a *passive*, undiscriminating and conformist majority. Such a way of dividing listeners partly retains Adorno's assumptions about passive and indiscriminate music consumption, but it adds an additional, more active and engaged minority group. Not *all* music consumption is passive, although *most* of it still is. This is a distinction that has been used by numerous music fans throughout the world for many years to differentiate themselves from other listeners, and it is a division that was developed further in academic writing during the 1960s.

The young generation

In a book first published in the early 1960s, Stuart Hall and Paddy Whannel (1964) recast this distinction in generational terms. For these two writers, the minority group was what they referred to as the 'younger generation'. This was identified as the 'creative minority' within the social structure of British society, as Hall and Whannel emphasized the 'generation gap' which had been created between older people and those who had come into their teens during the late 1950s and early 1960s.

Hall and Whannel argued that this younger generation were beginning to challenge the staid conventions and 'puritan restraints' of bourgeois morality. As they did so they developed a 'subculture' that combined new attitudes to sexual relationships and linked this to various expressions of anti-establishment radicalism. The ideas and attitudes of the subculture were often directly connected with musical consumption, in particular the listening to and participation in folk, blues and rock music.

Hall and Whannel observed that the use of music by young audiences was a contradictory combination of what they referred to as the 'manufactured' and the 'authentic'. Like Adorno, they argued that commercial interests were attempting to exploit and manipulate musical preferences and activities. But at the same time they suggested that young people were also creating products that 'expressed' their own interests and which communicated these to other members of the young class. This was apparent in the music of The Who, a band whose recording *My Generation* – with its constant refrain of 'talking 'bout my generation' – was emblematic of Hall and Whannel's description of pop music as symbolically affirming a spirit of rebellion and independence.

Although embracing some of the sentiments of such a song in their analysis, Hall and Whannel ultimately remained unconvinced about the wider potential of such generational tensions. Like Riesman, who had found both active and passive musical audiences, they suggested that while teenage culture was an 'area of self expression for the young' it was also a 'lush grazing pasture for commercial providers' (Hall and Whannel, 1964: 276). In making this distinction they argued that there was a tension between the attempts at manipulation by the commercial providers and the responses and interpretations of the audience. Such a distinction, between an active young minority who were creating a 'subculture' and a passive older conservative majority, was then integrated into a more theoretically developed subcultural theory.

Subculture and style

Subcultural theory was first introduced in studies of crime and so-called deviant behaviour, initially by sociologists in the United States, as far back as the 1930s. During the 1940s and 1950s writers such as Howard Becker (1973), who studied dance musicians, sought to understand how the social activities associated with music involved the active adoption of alternative value systems (as opposed to 'deviant' or 'dysfunctional' behaviour). From the late 1960s and during the 1970s this approach began to be applied to youth subcultures.

In giving a brief introduction to this approach here I am going to avoid skating across the many details of different studies and focus on one of the most influential accounts, that of Dick Hebdige (1979). Titled *Subculture*, and covering the appearance of punk in Britain and the subcultural styles that preceded it, Hebdige's book has had a great influence on later theoretical approaches to music audiences.

In developing his theory of subcultures, Hebdige drew on Raymond Williams's conception of culture as 'ordinary'. Against a classical and conservative approach that had been concerned with culture as a standard of aesthetic excellence and which was derived from an 'appreciation' of European 'high' culture, Williams advocated a more 'social' approach to the term. This took culture to refer to 'a particular way of life which expresses certain meanings and values not only in art and learning but also in institutions and ordinary behaviour' (Williams, 1965: 56).

Following this less elitist and more anthropological approach to the concept, Hebdige set out to examine culture as a broad range of social activities, meanings, values, beliefs, institutions and commodities and to consider how these elements were related in 'a whole way of life'. He did this by focusing on one part of British culture, a subculture.

As the term implies, a subculture is a subdivision within a culture. However, in British subcultural theory, the term has been specifically employed to refer to groupings within subordinate cultures. Like other subcultural theorists (Clarke et al., 1981; Hall and Jefferson, 1976; Willis, 1977) Hebdige stressed that there was not simply one 'culture' in Britain. An individual's social experience, and hence their cultural activities, was shaped by a variety of specific factors, such as gender, ethnicity and age, with class being the most significant mediating influence. From this perspective, cultural life could be thought of as composed of a number of 'cultural configurations' which do not hold equal status and in which dominant and subordinate cultures are created along the broad divisions of class.

In this context, distinctive youth subcultures (such as the teddy boy, mod and punk) were seen to emerge as a 'response' to a subordinate social class position. Writing against conservative criminologists and concerned policy makers who viewed the activities of these groups as deviant anti-social behaviour, subcultural theorists argued that subcultures developed as a means by which groups in a subordinate class position attempted to contest the dominant system of values. Youth subcultures appeared as an attempt, through ritual and style (rather than conventional political activity), to resolve the problems and dilemmas that were encountered as a result of being in an inferior social class position.

In adopting this approach, Hebdige used the concept of *style* to refer to how various elements were combined to generate meaning and to signify and communicate a way of life to the surrounding world. He conceptualized the style of any subcultural group as made up of an 'ensemble' of bodily postures, mannerisms and movements, clothes, hair cuts, an 'argot' (way of speaking and choice of words), and specific activities that involved the use of music and various commodities. In focusing on the styles of subcultures Hebdige took the previous contrast between a majority and a minority and drew a distinction between subcultural styles and the styles of the 'mainstream'. This has become a key division within subcultural theory and an influential distinction that has been made in much writing on popular music.

Hebdige argued that subcultural styles can be distinguished from mainstream styles by the *intentional* way that they have been 'fabricated' by members of a subculture to actively construct a sense of difference from the conventional outfits worn by the 'average man or woman in the street'. The construction of a style involves the 'appropriation' of existing clothes, commodities, languages, images, sounds and behavioural codes. Through a process of repositioning and recontextualizing these are then reused to generate the meanings of a particular subculture. Hence, any element of a subcultural style could not be understood in isolation. Its meaning was generated *in relation* to other elements.

In observing how subcultures produced a sartorial and sonorial challenge to the conventional codes in the surrounding culture, Hebdige found a parallel in the 'radical aesthetic practices' of Dada and Surrealism (artistic movements that immediately followed the First World War in Europe). During this time artists such as André Breton and Marcel Duchamp had combined and juxtaposed conventionally incompatible elements in an attempt to subvert common sense and undermine bourgeois conventions. Hebdige drew an analogy between this and the aesthetic practices of audiences and performers during the punk era:

> Like Duchamp's 'ready mades' – manufactured objects which qualified as art because he chose to call them such, the most unremarkable and inappropriate items – a pin, a plastic clothes peg, a television component, a razor blade, a tampon – could be brought within the province of punk

(un)fashion . . . Objects borrowed from the most sordid of contexts found a place in punks' ensembles; lavatory chains were draped in graceful arcs across chests encased in plastic bin liners. Safety pins were taken out of their domestic 'utility' context and worn as gruesome ornaments through the cheek, ear or lip . . . fragments of school uniform (white bri-nylon shirts, school ties) were symbolically defiled (the shirts covered in graffiti, or fake blood; the ties left undone) and juxtaposed against leather drains or shocking pink mohair tops . . . (Hebdige, 1979: 106–12)

These visual 'disruptions' of existing conventions were accompanied by similar challenges to mainstream styles of dancing, music recording and performance. Dancing became a caricature of the 'solo' individualistic gyrating that had been developed to accompany rock music; punks adopted a blank robotic stilted shuffle or engaged in frenzied pogoing by jumping up and down on the spot.

The music was unpolished, informed by an amateur aesthetic that exposed its rough edges in opposition to the sophisticated well-produced studio music of popular singers such as Elton John and 'progressive rock' bands such as Genesis. Punk music was fast, uniform and based on a limited musical repertoire which relied upon repetitive drumming and a 'barrage of guitars'. The treble was turned up, the bass frequently buried in a muddy mix, and a mannered angry vocal style adopted in which words were screamed, snarled or shouted with lyrics that deliberately opposed the conventions of songwriting as poetry or romance. Hebdige claimed that punk combined music, dancing and visual style in such a way as to signify 'chaos' and 'noise' at various levels. This was a noise that interrupted and disrupted conventional ways of dressing, making music and dancing.

Hebdige made an important contribution to theories about the relationship between music, dressing and dancing by indicating how a wide range of visual codes and cultural practices are interrelated and brought together as a style and in opposition to other styles. He demonstrated how young people actively use a range of existing artefacts and in doing so give new meanings to old commodities (against the idea that the commodity will lead to one particular type of consumption).

As I have already indicated, Hebdige's theory drew on but also extended the ideas proposed by earlier writers who had sought to understand music audiences in terms of a majority and a minority. Hebdige's little book has been very significant: it has influenced the ideas of fans who present themselves as 'underground' or 'alternative'; it has influenced the musical and visual styles put together by musicians; it has influenced the way that journalists have written about subsequent styles of music; and it has provided a model for many subsequent academic research projects. With this in mind, I now want to introduce four criticisms of this type of subcultural approach to music audiences: its male bias; its elitism; the issue of the mainstream; the problem of homology.

Subcultures and gender: the boys on the street

Feminist writers were quick to spot the ways in which subcultural theory had tended to marginalize the cultural activities of girls and women. As Angela McRobbie (1980) observed, it was the teddy boy who adopted the clothes of the Edwardian gent; the skinhead's exaggerated working-class boots and braces were male; it was the female punks who wore the traditionally 'feminine' suspenders. When it came to the issue of gender, the spectacular subcultures did not look quite so 'oppositional'. McRobbie argued that, by emphasizing the highly visible, 'masculine' and public forms of cultural expression that they had observed displayed on the 'street', subcultural theorists had neglected the visual styles and musical practices of girls and women. Furthermore they had neglected the way that the musical activities of girls were often more home-oriented and less immediately visible.

By romanticizing the public appearance of subcultures, male theorists had overlooked the very real dangers that are posed to girls and women on the street. With its connotations of female prostitution, 'excessive loitering on street corners might be taken as a sexual invitation to the boys' (McRobbie and Garber, 1991: 5). More than this, the street is a public site from which many women feel excluded due to the way in which such connotations are directly connected to the possibilities of sexual and physical violence. As a result, girls and women are often forced to negotiate 'different leisure spaces' that have been marginalized or rendered 'invisible' from the perspective of subcultural theory.

McRobbie and Garber suggested that these are more likely to be found within a web of family relationships, friendship networks and off-street sites such as a youth club. On this point, subcultural theory completely neglected the consumption of music in the home. Hebdige did not even acknowledge the home as a site for the combination of a style *before* going out into public. Nor did he consider the domestic context of listening within the dynamics of a variety of family relationships.

In pointing to these neglected issues, McRobbie (1994) raised the question of whether there are any differences between the way that men and women, or boys and girls, consume and use popular music. She suggested that theorists of youth culture should be more attuned to the way that musical activities intersect with gender codes, differing attitudes to sexuality and changing modes of femininity and masculinity. (Such issues do not just arise in consumption and will be pursued in more detail in Chapter 4).

The elitism of subculture theory

For Gary Clarke (1990), Hebdige's theory was elitist and Adorno's influence still present, detected in the casual way in which the vast majority of audience members were ignored. Clarke argued that, by setting up a distinction between an active subculture and the undifferentiated passive mainstream, the practices of the vast majority of people who listen to popular music were dismissed. In a similar way Larry Grossberg has noted that subcultural styles have never been quite so spectacular in North America, and as a result this approach has led to 'the great mass of rock-'n'-roll fans who refuse not only any particular subcultural identity but, often, any visible sense of style as otherness' being 'written out of the history of pop music' (Grossberg, 1987: 149).

In addition, the focus of this type of subcultural theory was on the aesthetic strategies of the members of subordinate classes. Hebdige was concerned with their 'art' rather than any explicitly political activities; it was in this aspect that 'opposition' was located. The 'solutions' offered by subcultures were ultimately portrayed as a form of 'symbolic resistance'. Yet many punks were active within a contradictory array of anarchist and socialist political organizations. Punk audiences frequently participated in anti-racist struggles, particularly the Rock Against Racism movement, which was attempting to engage in political activity that was far more than symbolic resistance (Gilroy, 1987; Widgery, 1986).

The subcultural minority and the mainstream

In his critique, Clarke (1990) asked whether the subcultures that were readily visible to the observing academic were in any way oppositional or alternative to the mainstream. For Dave Laing (1985) they were certainly not, and Hebdige was mistaken in his assumptions that punk was separate from mainstream styles. The error that Hebdige had made, according to Laing, was to interpret punk simply as a subculture. In contrast to Hebdige, Laing argued that punk was primarily punk *rock*, a music genre that existed alongside other music genres. This was firmly part of the 'all-male-guitar-dominated rock' tradition. Far from being outside, it was part of the mainstream, as the style and commercial success of bands like The Stranglers and The Clash bore out (Laing, 1985).

Since Hebdige was writing there has been a proliferation of music genres associated with different youth groups, each with its own stylistic codes and conventions. There has also been a growth of leisure practices that are associated with music consumption (video viewing, karaoke singing, computer game playing, for example). As a consequence, a further theoretical issue has been concerned with whether the concept of an undifferentiated mainstream is a useful way to refer to the majority of the music audience.

For Sarah Thornton (1995) it is not, and the mainstream is an uncritically received idea that has been used by various music enthusiasts to distinguish their own 'uncommercial' and 'hip' tastes from those whom they perceive to be corrupted by commerce and the mass media. This has then been re-presented even more uncritically by academics, such as Riesman with his minority group and Hebdige with his subculture. In contrast, Thornton suggests that the mainstream is not an undifferentiated majority and that the use of this concept conceals a diversity of discriminating practices that are occurring among various musical crowds and taste publics. These may well be labelled subcultures by the media, but they are far from innocent. Through a case study of British rave clubs in the late 1980s and early 1990s, Thornton argues that audiences are not spontaneous subcultures. Instead, they are carefully created by commercial-oriented club owners who use flyers, magazines, telephone calls and posters to 'deliver a particular crowd to a specified venue on a given night. To a large degree, then, club crowds come pre-sorted and pre-selected' (Thornton, 1995: 22). Although acknowledging that club goers are both 'active and creative', Thornton's main argument is that their activities and distinctions are usually a 'phenomena of the media' (1995: 116). While the club owners are organizing clubbers by 'delivering' them to a venue, their identity is being given by the 'communications media', who 'create subcultures in the process of naming them and draw boundaries around them in the act of describing them' (1995: 162).

In place of the voluntarism and spontaneity of Hebdige's subculture, Thornton presents a more calculated process in which the media and commercial interests have been building a subcultural audience for their products since the beginning. Unlike Hebdige, Thornton is more critical of the self-definitions presented by members of subcultures. Setting out to understand how audiences imagine themselves and draw boundaries around their own social world, she argues that the activities of young 'clubbers' consist in acquiring various media products and accumulating cultural knowledge and employing these as a form of 'subcultural capital' (a concept drawn from Pierre Bourdieu (1986) which rests on an analogy with the use of economic capital). Subcultural capital is used by aspiring youth groups as a way of gaining status and to differentiate their own preferences and activities from those of other social groups.

Similar ideas about how audiences use musical knowledge as a form of 'symbolic capital' (Roe, 1990) have been pursued by a number of researchers who, considering how audiences think of their own lives in relation to different types of music, have found that patterns of music purchasing and listening vary from place to place and according to education, social class, race, gender and age. Such differences have also shown how preferences for genres, songs and artists are employed as markers of 'distinction' – as a way of indicating a sense of affiliation to and a distance from other individuals, peer groups and classes (Ala et al., 1985; Bourdieu, 1993; Lewis, 1991; Roe, 1985, 1990; Roe and von Feilitzen, 1992; Trondman, 1990). Such activities involve a more conformist struggle for status seeking and recognition rather than any alternative gestures of opposition or resistance.

The contrast that this approach establishes with the subcultural theory of Hebdige takes me back to Hall and Whannel's point that audiences seem to receive what they want, need and can creatively use, yet at the same time they also get what they are given. Popular music seems to provide opportunities for conformist aspirational status seeking and for more rebellious oppositional activities. Such contrasting conclusions may have been reached because different cultural practices were observed and then interpreted at distinct historical moments (Hebdige in the late 1970s, Thornton at the end of the 1980s), in which case a further issue might be whether certain music audiences are more oppositional, creative and spontaneous than others (and other audiences more manipulated and constructed by media and commercial interests from the start). With the dynamics of commercial manipulation and spontaneous creativity so intricately interwoven and changing over time, the argument about whether music audiences are oppositional and spontaneous, or conformist and manipulated, seems set to continue.

From subcultures to scenes

An alternative perspective, and an attempt to move away from the idea of subcultures, has been suggested by Will Straw (1991) with his development of the concept of a 'music scene'. Although this term has been used for many years by music fans and deployed casually in a number of academic studies, Straw has attempted to apply to it a degree of conceptual rigour. Arguing against the idea of a musical 'community' that is stable and rooted in a specific place, Straw suggests that a scene 'is that cultural space in which a range of musical practices coexist, interacting with each other within a variety of processes of differentiation, and according to widely varying trajectories of change and cross-fertilization' (1991: 273).

Although at first sight this may appear vague, Straw shows how such an approach can be applied by elaborating on these points in relation to the alternative rock and dance music scenes in North America. Through this he shows how scenes can have variable 'logics' and how the participants in a scene develop different ways of understanding temporal and spatial change. Straw argues that such logics are directly connected to the commercial circulation of music recordings. So, for example, the alternative rock scene is understood by its participants in relation to a canon of music recordings (usually albums) that encode a particular sense of historical time and geographical place. Dance has a faster temporal logic, organized more usually around single tracks rather than albums, and operates within and across different spaces that connect together urban locations from where important dance music has emerged.

Straw contends that music scenes are not necessarily oppositional or disruptive subcultures, but neither are the practices of the people who make up a particular scene simply shaped by the music industries. He suggests that scenes do not spontaneously emerge from a particular group, class or community, but from various 'coalitions' and 'alliances' which have to be actively created and maintained. It is through such practices that specific boundaries are erected and social divisions drawn. Straw points out that both the alternative rock and dance scenes are notable for creating boundaries in relation to class, race, gender and age.

Straw's concept provides a framework for thinking about musical audiences that is looser and more fluid than theories of subculture. However, it affords relatively little indication of the dynamics that might be involved. It is not clear how scenes emerge and what social processes might contribute to the establishment of audience alliances – unlike Hebdige's analysis of the intentional construction of a style in an attempt to create meanings in opposition to the mainstream and conventional. On this point, the rather abstract model of a scene as sketched by Straw seems to tell us little more than that people form musical taste groupings around particular genres of music. It doesn't really indicate how such musical preferences might lead to the formation of 'alliances' which are anything more than shared consumption habits.

Homology and the internationalization of subcultural styles

Straw's concept of the scene has been proposed as an attempt to move away from the idea of a necessary relation between social location and musical consumption. It is a challenge to the assumption of a 'homology' – the idea that all of the parts that go to make up a style (most notably dress, dancing and music) form a unity that expresses the 'whole way of life' of the subcultural group (Hebdige, 1979; Willis, 1990).

Although Hebdige acknowledged that the relationship between experience, expression and signification may be 'disrupted', his general argument was that the punk subculture emerged as a response to very specific social circumstances. In addition, while Hebdige certainly presented far more than a straightforward 'reflection' theory (the participants actively create their style as a response to specific social conditions), this approach does leave two problems. One pertains to the direction of the implied causality in Hebdige's homology. The other issue concerns what we are to make of subcultural styles that have 'moved out' from the initial location of their first appearance. I shall deal with each in turn.

In presenting a theory of how the punk subcultural style emerged as a response to a subordinate class position, Hebdige tended to produce a one-sided causal theory of homology. In emphasizing how audiences reconstructed the texts (clothing, music and body movements), he neglected the way that 'texts construct their own appropriate audiences' (Grossberg, 1992: 41). This point can be pursued further by returning to Laing's argument about punk rock.

In maintaining that punk was not outside a mainstream, Laing (1985) stressed that it was first and foremost a music genre rather than a subculture. By doing this Laing sought to challenge Hebdige by placing music as central to any understanding of punk, arguing that the activities of its fans and performers were shaped by its character as a music genre rather than a subculture. Laing suggested that, rather than subcultures spontaneously generating their own sounds and visual conventions, the emergence of a new music genre can create the conditions *for* subcultural activity. From this perspective it is the music that provides the impetus for groupings of people actively to come together and create a style. In contrast to Hebdige's account of subcultural style which treated the music as one (rather unimportant) element, Laing suggests that the music is far more significant in providing the preconditions and impetus for any subculture to form in the first place.

The other point, about subcultures moving away from their local origins, can be pursued by asking a more general question about punk: how are we to make sense of the internationalization of this particular way of dressing, dancing and making a noise? What does a subcultural style mean as it has moved from its authentic point of origin and been adopted in different parts of the world? What do the sounds and visuals of punk style mean as they are exhibited in the clubs of San Francisco, on the streets of Tokyo or on the beaches of Rio?

One response might be to assert that this process merely involves acts of imitation and commercial exploitation; the original was an authentic example of cultural expression whereas subsequently punk has become a commodified fashion. This would certainly seem a plausible argument when considered in relation to the appearance of the punk look in shopping malls, on TV comedy programmes and on tourist postcards.

However, the punk style and way of making music has also been adopted to register similar forms of social disaffiliation and to disrupt dominant conventions in comparable, but more politically charged ways to those described by Hebdige. The sounds and images of punk were transformed and reappropriated by many musicians and audience members in the Stalinist states of Central and Eastern Europe during the 1980s. Punk noises and visuals were used to register a sense of distance from and opposition to political repression and to challenge state-promoted culture (such as officially sanctioned rock bands). Punk styles of music and dress were adopted to register opposition in Hungary, Czechoslovakia, Poland and the German Democratic Republic. These were often greeted with censorship, physical assault, sanction and detention (Ryback, 1990) – a historical echo that is not too far away from the actions of local government during the 1970s in Britain which banned particular artists from performing, audiences from meeting and recordings from distribution (Savage, 1991; Cloonan, 1993).

The sounds, words and images that have been distributed via the media and music industries can be used in different ways and provide possibilities for a variety of conformist or oppositional activities. But they are not *necessarily* always going to take on the same form or fit neatly into subcultural categories. There is, then, more than a 'homology' connecting social experience and musical expression.

Creative audiences and imaginative fans

A number of writers have responded to the criticisms of subcultural theory that I have just outlined by focusing on the audiences for music in less exclusive terms. Here I shall refer to two authors who have made contributions to this area of study, Lisa Lewis and Iain Chambers.

Lisa Lewis has carried out studies of the viewers of MTV and the activities of fans at concerts and at various public 'fan events' (1990).

In her own work, and by drawing together writers for a collection of articles (Lewis, 1992), Lewis has thoroughly challenged the types of listeners identified by Adorno and the focus on hip minorities by subcultural theorists. Like Joli Jensen (1992), she has suggested that fans are neither regressive, obsessed, alienated individuals nor a manipulated collective mass. Instead, fans are imaginative, discriminating people who are capable of making a number of fine distinctions and who actively participate in creating the meanings that become associated with popular music. Fans contribute an integral element to how we understand popular music and particular artists. Lewis suggests that fans create communities with a collective shared sense of identity that is built around their appreciation of a particular performer. Such groups produce important 'reservoirs of knowledge' that contribute directly to the meanings attributed to performers.

This is relevant to the most obvious subcultural styles (Hebdige clearly shows how a large part of the meaning of punk came from the activities of its audiences), but Lewis's argument is also relevant to the teenage and pre-teenage fans of pop performers such as Take That, New Kids on the Block, Menudo, and The Osmonds. Here again the activities and appearance of the fans became an integral part of how the identity of the performers was understood. But such connections are also relevant to a wide range of performers. How could we understand the enduring popularity of Bob Dylan, for example, without reference to the legions of highly intelligent people who have followed him around for years and who have continued to find profound meanings in some of his most banal and wilfully ironic utterances?

Like Lewis, Iain Chambers's (1985, 1994) work can be read as a refutation of Adorno's thesis that the activities of listeners can be explained as manipulated by the recording industry. Chambers argues that record companies, radio stations and the music press are unable to control the meanings of the texts and technologies that they produce and distribute. While the industries might have a direct impact on how music is produced, they are unable to control the way it is used by audiences.

Like Hebdige, but less concerned to find easily identified subcultures, Chambers argues that the commodities of the music industry are actively transformed as they are 'appropriated' by various groups and individuals and then used for the expression of individual identities, symbolic resistance, leisure pursuits and forms of collective and democratic musical creativity in everyday life. Chambers draws examples from the 1960s when hippies used music in festivals, anti-war demonstrations and various 'happenings' that were associated with the counter-culture, and develops his narrative through to the middle of the 1980s when vinyl records, turntables, tape machines and mixing equipment were reused to create the distinctive styles of rap and hip-hop.

In narrating a predominantly British history, Chambers (1985) has emphasized the diversity of pop styles and the constant changes that popular music had undergone since the middle of the 1950s. He has also highlighted how music has been central to audiences' and listeners' lives, frequently having a direct impact on the surrounding society and culture. This might range from individual expressions of sexuality through dancing in a disco, to large-scale musical events that attempt to contribute to the creation of cultural and political solidarity with oppressed people in another part of the world.

This is the complete antithesis of Adorno's model of passive easy listening, individual alienation and mass manipulation. It is a theory about diversity, plurality and the *active* individual and collective participation in musical practices – a social activity during which the texts and technologies of popular music continually provide opportunities for a wide range of people to participate in aesthetic, political and cultural activity.

Drawing on similar theoretical traditions to Hebdige, Chambers has emphasized the way that popular music is 'polysemantic' – it has many meanings. The music industry cannot simply churn out standardized products with a sole meaning and only one possible use. Instead, many possibilities are made available at the same time, and it is ultimately the audience who are able to 'appropriate' these and determine which will predominate. For Chambers popular music can provide insights into how people receive and then actively use cultural forms in different ways throughout everyday life, not just in the rare and exclusive moments of subcultural style formation.

Popular music in everyday life

Chambers's work can be read as an attempt to move beyond a concern with exclusive subcultures and to consider how music is experienced across 'the immediate surfaces of everyday life' (1985:

211). However, his approach still retains many of the assumptions of subcultural theory. Like subcultural theorists, Chambers argues that powerful new sounds emerge from the margins and challenge existing musical conventions. He also privileges the idea of resistance, characterizing music as 'an important counter-space in our daily lives' which can escape from or challenge various socially enforced routines and categories (1985: 209).

In these respects, Chambers has not pursued music very far across the surfaces of daily life and still seems to be searching for the extraordinary moments identified by subcultural theorists. In contrast to such an approach, research conducted in Sweden suggests that much music listening takes place *within* existing conventions and routines rather than contrary to them. Following empirical studies of children and young people (a broad age group between three and 24 years old) Celia von Feilitzen and Keith Roe found that, 'depending on age, 75–90 per cent of all music listening occurs in connection with some other parallel activity' (1990: 62). Unlike that of subcultural theorists, this research focused less on public display and more on the home and domestic context. Von Feilitzen and Roe found that the most common activities that accompanied music were waking up, eating, homework and housework. Such findings support Simon Frith's (1983) criticism of subcultural theory, and his argument that music is more frequently a background to other activity than a central part of any 'counter-space' or 'cultural struggle'.

However, if we pursue this theme too far we will be led to a dichotomy: music as foreground or music as background. Such a distinction can be misleading, implying that music can be identified as central/foreground or peripheral/background, when more often it is an integral *part* that should be understood in relation to other very particular cultural practices and activities. Such an approach has been pursued in much folk-music scholarship that has been carried out concurrently with the growth of subcultural theory. As Mike Pickering has observed of this strand of research, the aim has been to get close to 'the lived realities of popular song in vernacular milieu' (1990: 38). Via studies of particular musical events and performances, and through tracing the way songs have been actively used and transformed as they have endured through time (Pickering and Green, 1987), such research has sought to understand the 'localised usage of song, as it is assimilated into the fabric of everyday life' (Pickering, 1990: 38). A similarly more open and less subculturally exclusive approach to the use of music in everyday life has also featured in more recent studies by Ruth Finnegan and Sara Cohen in Britain, Susan D. Crafts, Daniel Cavicchi and Charles Keil in the United States and Jocelyne Guilbault in the Caribbean. These researchers have been particularly significant in pushing the study of audiences into a broader approach to music as an integral part of everyday life.

Through a study of amateur musicians in Milton Keynes, Finnegan (1989) has highlighted how musical consumption is an integral element of everyday musical production. Finnegan's anthropological study focused on musical practices grounded in a specific town, where she found much creativity as local musicians invested considerable effort in acquiring instruments, rehearsing, recording and performing. Finnegan suggested that 'consumption' was central to the way in which musicians created their own identities and sounds by imitating and learning from existing recordings. Hence her study sought further to undermine the idea that consumption is passive (and directly in contrast to the idea that production is more active) by highlighting how becoming a musician involves consuming as well as producing music.

Like Finnegan, Cohen has studied music making in an English city. Her research has been focused on the way that music is part of everyday social relations and interactions in Liverpool, from the devoted audiences for unknown rock bands to the various groups of people who seek to claim The Beatles as their own (1991a, 1995a). A particularly interesting, and unusual, case study is Cohen's account of how music fits into the life of 88-year-old Jack Levy. Through an anthropological study that starts with the details of one person's unique experience, Cohen (1995b) shows how music can be closely connected with memory – both of past events in an individual life and also in the historical memory of being Jewish in England. She highlights how music is often an integral part of many social gatherings of the Jewish community, but also provides a tangible and tactile connection to family and friends through the exchange of music recordings. Cohen evokes the idea of Liverpool Jews living in a 'circle', one part of which is formed by the exchange of music recordings. She quotes Jack recalling that 'somehow those records came around. And one person got hold of one, and it was passed all around.' Jewish records and songs became part of the circle and part of the process of defining it (Cohen, 1995b: 437).

Here Cohen gives an indication of how people of varying ages are joined together through quite specific 'musical circles' – created through the *circulation* of songs and recordings that is far removed from the logic of youth-oriented subcultures and scenes. The concept of musical circles, which remains slightly underdeveloped in Cohen's study, may provide a useful metaphor for exploring some of the quite tangible ways in which albums, compact discs and cassettes are used to create connections with other people that are defined through the circulation of music.

Like Cohen's work, the research conducted by Susan D. Crafts, Daniel Cavicchi and Charles Keil (1993) for their 'Music in Daily Life Project' has involved detailed study of the musical activities of people who span a broad range of social backgrounds and who are between the ages of four and 83. In their book they recount how music is important for children as lullabies, for dancing and as an accompaniment to outdoor activities, and focus on older people who have gained significant religious and military experiences in association with music. The authors also provide details of how people use various types of music as a mood enhancer and for the emotions that it generates.

While this material is presented with little theoretical framing or discussion, as George Lipsitz has written in his Foreword, the research clearly shows that 'people listen across the spectrum of genre categories, and very few individuals identify themselves as interested only in one kind of music' (Crafts, Cavicchi and Keil, 1993: xiii). This research suggests that musical preferences do not simply correspond to market research categories and cannot 'easily be clustered into subcultures'. However, there is more than an implicit theory of free market individualism on offer in this book. Charles Keil acknowledges this explicitly when he writes that 'each person is unique. Like your fingerprints, your signature, and your voice, your choices of music and the ways you relate to music are plural and interconnected in a pattern that is all yours, an "idioculture" or idiosyncratic culture in sound' (Crafts, Cavicchi and Keil, 1993: 2).

Unlike Cohen, who uses one individual's experience to show how music listening leads into and is part of a range of social relationships, this book simply ignores the characteristics that individual musical activities (or 'signatures and fingerprints') might share with other people and atomizes musical preference into a plurality of unique individual choices.

Finally in this section I shall mention Jocelyne Guilbault's study of zouk in the Caribbean. In this research Guilbault also starts from individual experiences but she then relates these to her broader concern with how 'various cultures respond to the same music' (1993a: xvii). Focusing mainly on the islands of Martinique, Guadeloupe, St Lucia and Dominica, she shows how zouk has generated a complex of responses and interpretations. Some people love the music as a way of unwinding and relaxing, for its sense of freedom and youthful vibrancy, for providing a feeling of home or for contributing to pride and unity among people. Others hate it for its banality and monotony, for its alienating impact on young people and for being a thoroughly 'degenerate music'. As we begin to hear echoes of Adorno arguing with Chambers, Guilbault provides a sophisticated analysis of such contrasting ideas by relating these musical meanings to various geographical, generational, gender and class divisions. She also shows how the interpretation of the music changes as it becomes more popular around the world as a result of commercial tie-ups with the recording industries of France. Although zouk is a focus for marking social divisions when relatively confined to the islands, as its popularity spreads it begins to provide a sense of home and a proud 'we' feeling for different people, both on the islands and among those dispersed from the islands.

Guilbault, like Cohen, indicates how music is closely related to cultural identity. She also shows how the meaning of music changes (both at home and away) as it moves out from its point of origins – just as the meaning of punk changed for different audiences as it moved out from Britain to other parts of the world. These four studies are notable in many ways. Here I want to identify four reasons why I consider them to be important in relation to the general discussion in this chapter:

- The activities associated with 'consumption' and the idea of the 'audience' is by no means straightforward. The practices of musicians are those of both 'consumers' and 'producers'. Rock musicians learn riffs from recordings and perform these on equipment purchased as consumers, yet can very soon be playing concerts and making their own recordings as producers. Likewise, many rap musicians have started out as consumers of existing recordings, turntables and mixing equipment in the process of becoming the new producers.

- The audiences for music are composed of more than just young people. As I have already indicated, research since the 1950s has been characterized by an overemphasis on young people (now only a small part of the world-wide audience for various popular musics) and an overobservation of the public activities and styles of the street and the club. It should be fairly obvious that such an orientation privileges a very specific type of activity and person and neglects an enormous amount of musical activity engaged in by a variety of other audiences across the world.
- These studies indicate that the activity of music audiences does not fit neatly into many existing theoretical models or commercial music marketing categories (look in your own music collection, no matter how large or small, and see if you agree). The research above shows that individual tastes are eclectic and that the mixture of music in many people's lives is lived *across* commercial and scholarly categories. Musical activity cannot be contained within the discrete boundaries proposed by theories of subculture, nor by the music industry's segmentation of social life into marketing categories or taste publics.
- The same musical genre or piece of music may be enjoyed and engaged with in completely different ways. Quite different audience experiences and activities are associated with listening to the same music in a performance event in stadiums, while driving or jogging with a Walkman or while dancing to a juke box in an open-air bar. These studies suggest that the meaning of music is very hard to tie down, and indicate that we could learn much about music audiences by studying the same music in different contexts and among different people.

Conclusion: the active audience and the industry

I started this chapter with Adorno's model of a passive and manipulated audience and, through a discussion of theories that made a distinction between a passive majority and an active minority, I have concluded with a consideration of theories about a great variety of different activities. As the writers I have been discussing in the latter part of this chapter have shown, behind the simple terms 'audience' and 'consumption' there lurk a wide range of behaviours, creative activities and discriminating practices.

However, some critics have raised questions about where such theoretical orientations might lead and asked: do music audiences confront so many possibilities? Are we all so free in our choices and spontaneously creative when experiencing music or using recorded music products? Do theories of the active audience provide merely an uncritical celebration of the free market ideology of consumer capitalism?

These were the types of questions that a number of theorists started asking in the early 1990s, not only those thinking about popular music (Thornton, 1995) but writers studying other media and cultural forms where ideas about the active audience had grown in popularity (Curran, 1990; Frith, 1991; Morley, 1993). The questions concerned how 'active' audiences actually are and how 'open' to interpretation and different use the texts and technologies might be. Pondering these points in relation to similar debates about the audiences for television, David Morley observed that being active is not the same thing as having power and influence; for viewers and listeners to 'reinterpret meanings is hardly equivalent to the discursive power of centralised media institutions to construct the texts that the viewer then interprets' (Morley, 1993: 16). Morley asked whether the activities of viewers and listeners might be limited by being directed towards certain 'preferred' meanings and social uses.

In raising this question Morley was drawing on an earlier model of 'encoding/decoding' that had been formulated by Stuart Hall (1980). Hall had suggested that, while media texts could be interpreted in various ways, such possibilities were limited and that audiences were directed towards particular meanings. Audiences then had to adopt particular strategies in relation to this; viewers could accept the dominant meaning, negotiate and only partially accept this or they could develop an independent interpretation. Hall thus made a schematic distinction between audience activity based around dominant, negotiated and oppositional interpretations of media texts – a contrast with the assumption of one 'effect' or the idea of numerous 'polysemantic' possibilities that has informed much of the active audience theory discussed in this chapter.

Hall was referring to news and current affairs programming, and I do not want to leap straight from an analysis of television viewing to popular music reception; there are vast differences in the way that the two cultural forms are received and used. This model also has its problems, not least the difficulty of identifying what the preferred meaning might be and where it might be found in the encoding–decoding process. However, Morley has suggested that Hall's ideas might provide a way of taking a fresh look at the issue in order to ask a number of more critical questions about the activity of audiences. For example, in what ways do performers and the music industries direct fans to certain 'preferred' meanings? How do musical technologies and texts 'encode' particular meanings, uses and interpretations and how do audiences then actually 'decode' these? Do some forms of music encourage a more 'passive' acceptance of dominant societal codes while others provide possibilities for more 'oppositional' activity? Surely there are many differences in the activities of audiences for rock, rap, country, classical, jazz, folk, easy listening, film soundtracks and stage musicals – how does audience activity vary and what impact does the place of audience activity have on the use of music? Are the groups of people singing in karaoke boxes more 'active' than the audiences applauding at concerts or the individuals listening alone on their personal stereos?

Such questions are particularly important in light of the way that music *has* been used in a deliberate attempt to influence human behaviour. Buried away in many business magazines and management journals are reports of behavioural studies which seek to understand how 'functional music' can be used to manipulate the buying patterns of supermarket shoppers, the eating habits of patrons in restaurants, the well-being of passengers waiting in airports and the productivity of workers in factories, shops and offices (see, for example, Bruner, 1990; Lanza, 1994; MacLeod, 1979; Milliman, 1982).

Simon Jones and Thomas Schumacher (1992) have pointed out that since the 1950s (the moment when audiences seem to start becoming more active) this functional music has been used in more and more situations: on passenger ships and airlines, in sports stadiums, zoos, hospitals, public parks, cemeteries, health clinics, bars, swimming pools and hotel lobbies. This has been integrated into quite particular environments and given specific sound levels depending on whether that environment is a restaurant, an airport, a clothing store or a children's toy shop.

Companies such as the Muzak Corporation and their clients have been spending vast amounts of money on acquiring copyrights to songs, employing arrangers to modify well-known pieces of music and then profiling and monitoring the behaviour of various 'audiences' (Jones and Schumacher, 1992; Lanza, 1994). The Muzak Corporation's own research suggests that they are effective – that their music programming can make us purchase more or work harder. So, how imaginative or resistant can an active audience be in such circumstances?

While clearly showing that audiences for popular music are not passive dupes, most of the arguments about active audiences tend to ignore the influence of the music (and muzak) corporations. This they do despite the fact that the 'audience' features prominently in the commercial strategies of such corporations. After all, if audiences are so active and can create their own 'oppositional' messages and meanings without giving in to any 'preferred' ideas, why do entertainment corporations spend so much money on promotion, marketing and advertising? Why are the audiences for star performers the subject of extensive market research, analysis and carefully targeted marketing?

As Morley observed, being active is not the same as having power and influence. Theories about the active audience tend to evade the issue of *how* the activities of consumption might be shaped by the industries involved, how musical products and visual styles are made available for 'appropriation' in the first place and how they may limit the opportunities for creative use and interpretation available at any one time. Following Morley's argument, it might be suggested that, while audiences have historically been physically separated or dislocated from most of the *sites* of musical production, they are not separate from the *processes* of musical production. The contribution of active audience theory has been to challenge Adorno by showing how audiences are not easily stupefied and contribute much to producing the meanings of popular music. But, perhaps we should now follow Adorno's tracks back into the world of musical production and start asking further questions about the relationships *between* the music industries and the audiences.

CHAPTER TWO
INDUSTRY

Whether in the words of academic theorists, journalists, fans or musicians, the music industry frequently appears as villain: a ruthless corporate 'machine' that continually attempts to control creativity, compromises aesthetic practices and offers audiences little real choice. Such an image will be featuring in the first part of this chapter. In the latter part, however, I will move on to tell an additional story about the activity of the human beings who inhabit the machine. In doing this I will be highlighting the different perspectives that can be gained from examining the *macro* relations at a more abstract corporate level and the *micro* day-to-day activities within the industry. I will suggest that it is misleading to assume something about one from the other. The work of people in the industry should not be dismissed as the activities of automated cogs in a machine, cynical bureaucrats or well intentioned but gullible puppets. However, in recognizing the contribution that people within the industry make to popular music, we should not lose sight of the transnational corporations they work for, and how these operate on the global commercial stage in a manner that has initially provoked the use of non-human metaphors. The industry needs to be understood as both a commercial business driven by the pursuit of profit and a site of creative human activity from which some very great popular music has come and continues to emerge. The problem is trying to bring the two together: most theorists have tended to come down on the side of the corporate machine or the human beings.

The culture industry: standardization and pseudo-individuality

The corporate control argument can be traced back to the writings of Theodor Adorno, who challenged the view of those who believed that the arts were independent of industry and commerce by proposing that popular music was produced by a 'culture industry' that was little different to the industries that manufactured vast quantities of consumer goods. All products were made and distributed according to rationalized organizational procedures and for the purpose of profit maximization. Adorno, writing with Max Horkheimer, characterized the culture industry as an 'assembly-line' and referred to the 'synthetic, planned method of turning out its products (factory-like not only in the studio but, more or less, in the compilation of cheap biographies, pseudo-documentary novels, and hit songs)' (Adorno and Horkheimer, 1979: 163).

In developing this argument further Adorno drew on the terminology employed in books that offered guidance to those who wanted to write hit songs. He observed that aspiring commercial songwriters were advised that their melodies and lyrics should fit rigid formulas and patterns. He also noted that the songs which became successful over time were often referred to as 'standards', a category that clearly draws attention to their formulaic character (Adorno, 1976: 25). From the 'plan' to the details, songs were based around the repetition of 32-bar sequences, regularly recurring refrains, choruses and 'hooks' – another term indicative of the industry's intentions of angling to hook the listener. This was done for quite explicitly commercial reasons, so that the song would imprint itself on the mind of the listener and then be purchased in its commodity form. Adorno argued that commercial song publishers were like the fascist propagandists who were attempting to spread their message across Europe; both were only interested in the 'title, the beginning of the text, the first eight bars of the refrain and the close of the refrain, which is usually anticipated as a motto in the introduction' (1989: 55).

For Adorno, the writing of a song had become a mechanical operation motivated purely by commercial gain and social manipulation. An instrumental approach to the composition of music had led to songs being rationalized to the point that the elements could be substituted for each other, just like the cogs in a machine.

Despite his continual emphasis on rational standardization and while frequently using the metaphor of an assembly-line, Adorno also noted that 'producing hit songs still remains at the handicraft stage' (1990: 306). In making this observation he suggested that the standardization that occurs in songwriting is not simply the same as the 'standardization of motor car and breakfast cereals' (1990: 306). The composer was not physically located on a rationally organized factory assembly-line. Instead, the pressure to adhere to formulas was induced by the need to compete for attention in a commercial market where standard patterns were more easily distributed, promoted and recognized.

Adorno was highly critical of what he referred to as 'pseudo-individuality', a phrase that he used to refer to how the culture industry disseminated products that made claims to 'originality'. For Adorno the deception of pseudo-individuality was most commonly perpetrated during the improvisations that were a characteristic of jazz. He argued that when jazz performers engaged in 'free improvisation' this was merely a conceit; Adorno's point was that 'what appears as spontaneity is in fact carefully planned out in advance with machinelike precision' (1967: 123).

Such deceptions were neither inevitable nor intrinsic to jazz, but due to the way that this musical form had been subject to the administration of the culture industry. Although noting that jazz provided occasional possibilities for 'real improvisation' that might be practised by 'oppositional groups, which . . . engage in such things out of sheer pleasure' (1967: 123), Adorno argued that such possibilities were no longer relevant because 'the formal elements of jazz have been abstractly pre-formed by the capitalist requirement that they be exchangeable as commodities' (1989: 52). Like other forms of music, once jazz had left its origins and been subject to the culture industry it had lost any authentic link to non-commodified forms of expression. Whatever its potential might have been as sonorial and social 'interference', jazz had been reduced to the most easily understood banal melodies and the most trivial of rhythms. For Adorno, jazz, as coopted and standardized by the culture industry, had become little more than a series of musical mannerisms.

Adorno observed a similar process occurring to many forms of music. For example, he argued that the performance of 'sacrosanct traditional music' had 'come to resemble commercial mass production' (1973: 10) and that the consumption of opera had become an act of recognition, similar to the identification of the refrains and hooks of a hit song. Instead of understanding an opera in its totality, Adorno (1976) contended that the listener was encouraged to react to its pseudo-individualized and abstracted 'unique' elements. The medium of radio was threatening to do the same thing to a Beethoven symphony. Adorno (1945) argued that as Beethoven's music had been commodified for recording and radio broadcasting so it had been radically altered. Important motifs that were developed within the context of a total symphonic composition had been reduced to little more than easily identifiable 'trade marks'.

For Adorno (1973), the distinction between 'classical' and 'popular' was misleading. He maintained that what was called 'classical' was a music that had been commodified and packaged in the same way as jazz and hit songs; it was simply another 'arbitrary category' of popular music. The relevance of Adorno's comments, made in the 1940s, can be observed in retail stores in the 1990s, where the jazz, rock, soul and classical sections are arranged together within one store and where (like other parts of the store) the classical sections are dominated by personalities, such as Luciano Pavarotti, and compilations, such as *Puccini's Greatest Hits*.

Hence, Adorno argued that there were two basic ways in which the culture industry commodified and standardized music. First, it provided the context within which hit songs were produced. People were employed specifically to compose music that generated the maximum amount of revenue for the company in the market (the practice that contemporary recording contracts attempt to enforce). Second, forms of music that may not have had their origins strictly 'within' the modern culture industry were subsequently subjected to its industrial commercial logic.

Cooptation and corporate control

Like Adorno, Steve Chapple and Reebee Garofalo (1977) were concerned with how capitalist corporations turned popular music into a commodity. However, unlike Adorno – who could see no value in the popular music that was produced under capitalism – these writers did catch glimpses of potential. Like many intellectuals who have written about popular music since the late 1960s, Chapple and Garofalo are members of a generation who grew up with rock-'n'-

roll and believed in the radical social potential of popular music when connected to youthful rebellions against authoritarianism or when harnessed to political campaigns (such as the Civil Rights Movement and the protest against the US army's involvement in Vietnam). Popular music thus does provide numerous possibilities for individual or collective expression and for communicating and engendering social solidarity (as writers such as Hebdige, Chambers and Lewis suggested in the last chapter). However, for Chapple and Garofalo, as soon as such possibilities appear they are either not realized or are severely restricted due to the impact of the corporations which exert control over the music industry.

In putting this argument, Chapple and Garofalo have emphasized that historically, throughout the twentieth century, a few companies have been responsible for the majority of recorded music that has been manufactured and distributed in the United States. Their central proposition is that this concentration of ownership among a few major companies which control access to the means of recording and reproducing popular music enables capitalist corporations to 'colonize leisure'. In the process artists and the recording industry staff involved in producing music are integrated into an entertainment business which is 'firmly part of the American corporate structure' (Chapple and Garofalo, 1977: 300). This argument then leads to the conclusion that any critical effect of commercially recorded popular music or any creative possibilities which might arise during production are lost, absorbed and 'coopted' by a ruthless and exploitative commercial system.

Dave Harker has put forward a similar argument when considering the production and distribution of popular songs. In agreement with Chapple and Garofalo, he notes that 'the committed artist is in an invidious position in capitalist society' (1980: 211). If this commitment is not simply to the system and success within it, but guided by a radical desire to use the available channels of production and communication to create alternatives, then the artist must confront the sort of constraints outlined by Adorno and Chapple and Garofalo; they must come up with a standard product that will not offend their corporate patrons who control access to the routes of communication with the public. For Harker this inevitably leads to the compromising of ideals and the silencing of any dissenting voices. Harker suggests that this has not only affected the work of potentially critical songwriters such as Bob Dylan and John Lennon, whose lyrics offered little more than empty slogans or a vague politics of 'us' and 'them', but also impacted on the audience, who seem to suffer a similar fate. Such an observation is summed up in Harker's blunt assertion that, 'under capitalism, it will remain the case that most artists (if not most of the audience) will have to be content to succumb to the commercial sausage machine, and be compensated with cash' (1980: 111).

In developing these arguments Chapple and Garofalo and Harker have drawn attention to how the music industry has systematically exploited the music made by black performers. This is a theme that has been developed more thoroughly by Nelson George, a writer who has been concerned about the impact of the record industry on the music and cultural identities of black performers. For George (1988), the white-dominated industry has been directly responsible for transforming black forms of expression into a commodity and for contributing to 'the death of rhythm and blues'.

George has argued that the social and political possibilities that emerged with and which were allied to the rhythm and blues styles created by black musicians (such as the struggle for economic self-determination and the movement for civil rights which were part of the 'rhythm and blues world') were destroyed when subject to commercial packaging and corporate promotion mechanisms. Tracing the fate of rhythm and blues throughout the twentieth century, George, like Chapple and Garofalo, has emphasized the rationalization and restructuring of the record industry which gained momentum during the late 1960s. This has been decisive. It has ripped apart the connections that were being established between black musicians, independent black and white businesses and the black community. In their place it has instituted the 'conglomerate control of black music' in which black artists are forced into adopting a 'crossover mentality' to reach a mass white audience.

The same type of argument has been put by Peter Manuel about the impact of corporate control on Latino artists. Manuel has focused on salsa music as a form of political and cultural expression, what he has characterized as 'a vehicle of working class barrio identity' for the Latins of New York and Puerto Ricans (1991: 160). Like the theorists above, he contends that salsa's radical potentials were lost as it was transformed into a bland apolitical genre by an industry that was more concerned with producing easy listening Spanish-language music.

Like Chapple and Garofalo, Harker and George, Manuel argues that forms of music lose their radical political potential when coopted by the music business. Like Adorno, he maintains that this process leads to standardization and stylistic conservatism as sounds are 'decontextualized, depoliticized' and 'aimed at a homogenous mass audience' (1991: 165). The record companies, under pressure from parent corporations and radio sponsors, are forced to 'promote homogeneity at the expense of ethnic diversity' (1991: 172).

Both George and Manuel raise important issues about ethnic and racial identity, claiming that black and Latin musicians have been forced to compromise their social identity, altering their music and, in George's argument, their visual appearance to appease the interests of the music corporations. Both writers maintain that black and Latin artists have been forced away from communicating with their own communities, and redirected towards a wider white market. This raises important questions about the way that popular music is connected to issues of race, racism and ethnicity, subjects that will be covered in more detail in Chapter 4. At this point, I want to stay with the general argument about the music industry and the question about the impact of corporate ownership. I want to deal with this in more detail in relation to three common themes around which the above arguments often revolve: 1) independents versus majors; 2) commerce versus creativity; 3) production determining consumption. Not all of the writers I have just referred to pursue all of these particular issues in detail, but these are three themes that are often employed to support the argument about the degree of power and control exerted by the music industry.

Independents versus majors

Chapple and Garofalo, Harker, George and Manuel all draw on the notion of a dynamic between independents and majors to explain one of the ways that cooptation occurs. This argument is based on the idea that the small independent companies ('indies') are more aware of and receptive to new sounds. As these companies start finding, recording, producing and selling new types of music and as their recordings start gaining popularity and generating new audiences, so they begin to pose a threat to the market dominance and degree of control of music making enjoyed by the big corporations. This leads to a tension that is resolved by the absorption of the independents, who are coopted via processes of amalgamation, joint venture or complete buy-out. In the process the large corporations regain or increase their share of the music market and the independents lose their autonomy and become integrated into the financial, marketing and distribution networks of the major corporations.

This is a persuasive argument that has been used by many writers to explain different changes in popular music, including the growth of rhythm and blues (Gillett, 1983), the emergence of rock-'n'-roll (Chapple and Garofalo, 1977), the appearance of salsa (Manuel, 1991), the impetus for punk rock (Laing, 1985), and the sounds from different parts of the world that came to be marketed as 'world music' (Wallis and Malm, 1992). All of these musical trends have been observed to emerge due to the imagination of independent record companies. All have also been lamented for becoming formula based, bland and losing something of their initial creative vitality when the big corporations became involved.

There is much evidence to suggest that many independent companies (such as Atlantic, Fania, Sun, Casablanca, Tommy Boy, Factory, Sub Pop) have made a significant contribution to the production and distribution of important types of new music that would otherwise perhaps not have broken through due to the conservatism of the major corporations. However, it can be misleading to over-romanticize the plight of the independent company. As I have pointed out elsewhere (Negus, 1992), vast numbers of independent companies are making recordings not because of a commitment to an alternative cultural or political agenda, but, in Harker's terms, due to their commitment to the system and their own financial success within it. As Simon Frith (1983) has observed, the term independent is something of a misnomer, particularly as many of these small companies act as 'talent spotters' for the major companies. Because of this the relationship between independents and majors has been characterized as one of 'symbiosis' rather than tension (Burnett, 1990).

There are many types of independent company and numerous relationships have been established between small companies and major corporations. Instead of a binary opposition between indies and majors, I have argued that it might be better to recast these distinctions in terms of a 'web of major and minor companies' within which majors are 'split into semi-autonomous working groups and label divisions, and minor companies connected to these by complex patterns of ownership, investment, licensing, formal and informal and sometimes deliberately obscured relationships' (Negus, 1992: 18).

However, David Hesmondhalgh (1996) has suggested that there is still a value in retaining the notion of independence and not subsuming all the companies as minors. Not all small companies are simply small entrepreneurs, argues Hesmondhalgh. Some are attempting to create genuine alternatives. But they are faced with a situation whereby if they want to communicate their music to a wider audience then they have to do this through the capitalist system, and cope with the pressures to compromise as best they can. Because of this, Hesmondhalgh has suggested that it may well be useful to retain some notion of an independent (or 'alternative') company.

Stephen Lee (1995) has also argued that in studying popular music we should retain the idea of an independent company, and pursued this himself via a historical case study of Wax Trax! records. Tracing the company's life from its formation in 1981, and having gained access to the label's financial records and interviewed staff, Lee maintains that in the case of Wax Trax! the relationship between majors and independents was one of continual interaction (rather than competition). He suggests that as the independents become more commercially successful their business practices tend to shift towards those of the majors, while the musical interests of the majors shift towards the small companies in acknowledgement of their success with new musical styles and novel working practices.

In the case of Wax Trax! Lee argues that the dynamics of this process lead independents gradually to abandon any ideological commitments they may have started with in favour of economic objectives. Although often guided by an alternative belief system which informs the production of music for particular 'niche markets' (gay, industrial, dance, etc.), Lee contends that such activities are not conducted with any 'critical distance' from the business practices of the majors. In this case he suggests that 'the company's employees lacked the necessary means to critique or resist the seemingly implicit 'logic' of the market ... their efforts to establish a different space at the edges of the social formation began not exterior to the system, but well within it' (1995: 25).

Lee's study implies that the notion of 'independence' works as a belief system that defines different working practices and values to that of the majors, while at the same time providing a way of positioning a small company within an 'alternative' niche market – the latter seemingly contradicting the former. Although highlighting the dilemmas and contradictions that are faced by small companies, and although catching glimpses of passing potentials for alternative cultural practices, Lee ultimately adds a further twist to the cooptation argument by implying that so-called independent companies are not only firmly within the system (rather than outside of it) but that their 'ideology' of independence deludes them into believing that this is not the case or avoidable.

Lee's discussion is based on a study of one company. Further research would be needed before it could be concluded that all small companies operate in such a naive way and that the process of incorporation is so inevitable. On this point, it might be useful to compare the fate of a company like Wax Trax! with that of Virgin. When Virgin was purchased by EMI in 1992 it had become an important and influential 'independent' company with a reputation for working with artists in a more 'alternative' manner than some of the majors, while also achieving commercial success. Virgin was not sold to EMI in dire financial straits but because it presented a sound investment to the major and because Richard Branson wanted to raise capital to expand his airline business. This was not the romantic tale of 'indie' naiveté and major cooptation, and suggests that there may well be a wide range of different working relations and dynamics that occur as major and minor companies engage in joint ventures, merge or are bought out.

Whatever the range of economic dynamics between minor companies and major corporations, the difficult aesthetic questions remain. Are independent companies necessarily any more creative than the major corporations? Do independent companies provide more scope for artistic creativity than the large corporations? Such questions lead to a further division, that between commerce and creativity.

Commerce and creativity

The idea of a conflict between creativity and commerce has also been used to illustrate the power of the music industry and has informed numerous everyday claims about how musicians 'sell out' to the system. On one side are the heroes – the musicians, producers and performers (the creative artists); opposing them are the villains – record companies and entertainment corporations (the commercial corrupters and manipulators).

This opposition has been implicit in many of the studies mentioned so far, and has often been employed as an organizing principle to explain the dynamics of the music industry (Stratton, 1982a, 1982b). Sara Cohen (1991a) has illustrated this tension in an ethnographic study of 'unknown' rock bands in Liverpool. During her research she found that the bands she observed continually experienced a conflict between commerce and creativity. For example, financial negotiations with various managers, agents and record companies directly generated antagonism, competition and arguments among band members; musicians were annoyed that the press reviewed their music by referring to their lack of success (commercial criteria) rather than the intrinsic quality of their music (creative judgements). In addition, band members considered the prospect of earning extra cash from cabaret work as 'prostituting themselves for money' (Cohen, 1991a: 50).

Such sentiments led Cohen to make a distinction between two types of bands. First were bands that expressed 'cultural opposition or resistance to hegemony' and responded 'to commercialism by expressing its alienating effects in their music'. In contrast, Cohen found bands who adopted a 'capitalistic attitude' and in doing this 'took on commercial values and ambitions and constructed their music accordingly' (1991a: 196). Such an opposition is familiar in the British music press, where this distinction has for many years been regularly employed to define the good and bad and to distinguish between the true and false in a range of popular musics.

Frith has rejected such a tension as a 'cliched opposition' (Frith, 1991: 106) and provided a number of pointers to the way in which 'commerce' and 'creativity' are not opposing but far more closely interwoven. In work first published in the late 1970s, Frith quoted the rock musician Manfred Mann saying that 'the more people buy a record, the more successful it is – not only commercially but artistically' (1978: 202). From this point of departure, Frith developed a strand of reasoning about the fusing of art and commerce in rock music. He argued that, for Britain's 'original rock stars' in the 1950s (referring to Tommy Steele and Cliff Richard), art and commerce were not antagonistic but 'integrated' (1978: 164). He suggested further that during the 1960s the professional rock musician achieved a unique situation in which art and commerce were complementary. Against those who saw rock as outside of commerce, its radical potential continually being threatened by corporate capital, Frith argued that rock was an integral part of the commercial system and concluded that there was 'less conflict between art and commerce in rock than in any other mass medium' (Frith, 1983: 83).

By 1987, in collaboration with Howard Horne, Frith had extended this argument to the point where, through an analysis of the influence of British art schools, the romantic inspired critiques of pop (which had posited a commerce–creativity conflict) had actually become 'part of the pop process itself'. A fusing had been taking place in which 'art categories' had been 'dissolved by commerce' and 'commercial categories' had been 'dissolved by art' (Frith and Horne, 1987: 180). Frith and Horne claimed that 1980s British pop culture had come to be dominated by a 'market – art school sensibility' in which 'creativity, commentary and commerce have become indistinguishable' (1987: 69).

In making these observations, Frith was not simply celebrating the industry as a bastion of creativity that was giving audiences what they wanted. His arguments were directed against those who thought that rock was a form of 'folk' or 'community' music that had been outside of the industry and then subsequently commodified. Frith's point was that rock had not appeared from outside of the system of capitalist production at all, but had gained its popularity by being part of cultural commodity production at a moment when creativity and commerce had fused, reaching a mutually enhancing synthesis in the production and consumption of this genre of popular music.

However, if the argument about a conflict between commerce and creativity is clichéd, then Frith's contrasting idea that there is no tension and that the two are complementary too easily sweeps aside the sentiments of rock musicians and fans who *do* express their experience of record companies in these terms. Even millionaire singer George Michael appeared in a British courtroom in 1994 accusing the Sony Corporation of being more interested in his commercial value than in his artistic creativity. If those of us who study popular music are to take seriously the vocabularies of participants, as Harker (1980) once requested, then the use of clichés or received ideas in discussions about the music industry cannot simply be dismissed as artistic conceit or audience naiveté. Cohen's band members might have been using well travelled clichés, but they were also employing the vocabulary at their disposal to express their dissatisfaction with existing circumstances and their desire for a form of musical expression that could be free from commercial constraints. From the knowing perspective of academic theory, commerce versus creativity may be a clichéd argument, but from the perspective of the participants of music scenes these ideas are part of the way in which they make sense of what is happening to them.

Perhaps a way of pursuing this issue further would be to examine the tensions about 'commerce' and 'creativity' more carefully in specific contexts, without assuming that there will always be the same dynamics in different places. Frith's concern, after all, was with the fusing of commerce and creativity within specific genres at particular moments, 1960s–70s Anglo-American rock and 1980s British art-school-designer pop. Cohen's account was of rock bands in Liverpool during the 1980s. Both Frith, with Manfred Mann and Cliff Richard, and Cohen, with her bands who were trying to make a living and obtain recording contracts, drew on the participants' own views and showed that at different times and places rock was experienced as both a fusing of and a tension between creativity and commerce.

Frith and Cohen's work raises a number of questions for future research and discussion. Is it always self-evident that those of us who use these terms know what we mean by 'commerce' and 'creativity'? What is non-commercial music and is it always creative? Is non-creative music always commercial? As the terms are frequently the subject of dispute, it might also be useful to ask more questions about the conflicts over these terms, the arguments about what is commercial and what is creative. These are questions I have started to pursue in my own work when studying staff within the music industry.

Ordering the commercial and creative

Like other writers who have studied the music industry (Burnett, 1990; Chapple and Garofalo, 1977; Frith, 1983; Hirsch, 1972) I found much uncertainty among personnel involved in producing music. Neither business executives, fans, the musicians themselves nor journalists can predict what is going to be commercially successful or what new musics are going to be critically acclaimed. Because of this, record companies develop various strategies and working practices to try and deal with uncertainty. These vary from time to time and place to place. In the 1960s and 1970s Chapple and Garofalo found that some companies were trying to follow and manipulate what they thought were 'predictable', but elusive, cyclical trends (the recurrence of ever new teenage idols, for example). Other companies attempted to 'sign the musicians felt to be the most talented' in anticipation of their potential popularity (Chapple and Garofalo, 1977: 177). In my own work I found companies adopting very particular cultural-aesthetic strategies to deal with this uncertainty. In analysing these I have argued that in many cases the struggle is not *between* commerce and creativity but about what is *to be* commercial and creative (Negus, 1992, 1995).

One of the problems faced by record company staff is that the length of time between an artist signing a recording contract and the subsequent recordings, videos and promotional materials being released can be anything between six months to two years. In addition, record companies are not just being judged according to 'commercial' criteria by shareholders. The company's roster of artists and way of working with these artists is being assessed 'creatively' by key opinion formers (DJs, journalists, broadcasters) who influence fans, and also by successful artists who might be thinking about signing a new record contract, hence bringing both revenue and prestige to the company.

Faced with these dilemmas, companies strategically establish a series of aesthetic and commercial hierarchies. Potentially commercial music is ordered and certain categories of music are prioritized over others. During my research in Britain (Negus, 1992) I found this to be apparent in the way in which white, male, guitar-dominated rock bands were being prioritized as long-term commercial propositions and accorded considerable investment. In contrast, soul and dance music was being treated in a less strategic and more ad hoc manner. As these priorities were established, a naturalistic 'organic' set of creative practices were accorded a privileged position over more 'synthetic' combinatorial approaches to popular music. These *creative* practices were then inscribed into the *commercial* priorities of the record companies, so that rock was prioritized over soul, albums over singles, and the self-contained 'live' guitar bands over the loosely structured 'studio' keyboard groups.

Although such commercial and creative values were being strategically prioritized and produced together at this time, this did not lead to a fusing of commercial and creative impulses. Instead it led to continual disputes. One of the most notable divisions was between artist and repertoire (A & R) staff and marketing staff. A & R staff tended to adopt the belief that the more 'organic' ways of creating music would be most popular, while marketing staff believed that the adoption of a more self-conscious 'synthetic' aesthetic practice would produce the strongest combination of elements for successful popular music. Such disputes did not simply arise due to the occupational rivalry between different departments within the industry, but were directly informed by wider discourses and divisions over gender and race within British culture. Unlike in the United States, at the time of my study there were few senior female or black staff within the major record companies. In fact, there were few senior personnel with a knowledge and expertise in dealing with musics other than guitar rock music (Negus, 1992). The judgements about what would be most creative and commercial within the industry were thus not self-evident rational criteria determined by a knowledge of markets, but informed by a number of assumptions about the importance and authenticity of rock music, against which personnel working with female and black performers had actively to struggle.

The determinations of production

My argument is that there is not simply *a* type of music that naturally fits the commercial imperatives of the record industry. There are not only conflicts *between* commerce and creativity, there are disputes about what *is* creative and what *is to be* made commercial. Hence, although there is a 'market' for music, what becomes commercially successful on this market does not do so due to a spontaneous process in which 'the markets decide'. Neither does what is made available on the market simply coincide with what the public 'wants'. As the writers who have put the corporate control thesis have argued, not everyone has equal access to the means of creating and distributing music. The ability to control access to production facilities, manufacturing plants and distribution networks means that the large major corporations have far more influence than the smaller companies or enterprising individuals. The large companies also have far greater resources from which to generate profits and offset any investment in unsuccessful recordings. The smaller companies must perform financial balancing acts between their day-to-day running costs and revenue gained from the sales of recordings.

Since its origins at the end of the nineteenth century in Europe and the United States, the recorded music industry has been continually dominated by a few major corporations. For most of this time, between five and eight companies have accounted for about 70 per cent of the recorded music legally distributed and sold (Gronow, 1983; Chapple and Garofalo, 1977). Since the beginning of the 1990s, six major recording companies have controlled the means by which approximately 80 to 85 per cent of recordings sold in the world are produced, manufactured and distributed. These companies are Sony Music Entertainment, Electrical and Musical Industries (EMI), the Music Corporation of America (MCA), Polygram Music Entertainment, the Bertelesmann Music Group (BMG) and Warner Music International (see Burnett, 1990; Laing, 1992; Negus, 1992). While the continual merger and acquisition activity that has characterized the entertainment industry since the end of the 1980s would suggest that the company names that occupy this line-up may change during future years, there is unlikely to be a significant rise in the number of major companies which are competing over this market share.

As subdivisions of large transnational corporations, the major record labels are part of companies that have a range of interests and sources of income and which are able to withstand economic slumps and market changes far better than firms that only produce music. It is on account of this that it has been argued that the compromise and the 'sell out' to the system occurs; small companies that are trying to offer a radical alternative and individual creative artists simply find the economic pressures so great that they are ultimately coopted and made to perform in the interests of the big corporations.

From this perspective the prospects can also be bleak for audiences. In the last chapter I discussed the active audience theories proposed by writers who argued that the possibilities for radical forms of cultural expression are not coopted by the corporations but occur 'after' the influence of the industry as subcultures and fans reuse and 'appropriate' cultural commodities. Active audience theorists such as Dick Hebdige and Iain Chambers consider that such activities can provide genuinely oppositional and creative opportunities not because they are in any naive way pure or outside social mediation, but because they are not simply 'manufactured' or manipulated by the culture industry. However, for Frith such accounts merely romanticize activities that often involve little more than 'the shadowboxing of consumers'. In making this point, Frith has argued that it is misleading to draw a distinction between music as a commodity and music as a form of 'human expression'. He has claimed that 'what music means – what we hear as authentic – is already determined by the technological and economic conditions of its production; it does not exist in any ideal or innocent state' (Frith, 1988b: 130).

Whereas Chapple and Garofalo, George and Manuel do catch glimpses of a broader set of meanings and the passing potential of music being used as a means of radical expression (whether in the Latin barrios, the black rhythm and blues world or the white counter-culture), Frith seems to perceive no such possibilities. Despite the numerous ways in which music has been used, and although once writing about audiences using musical technologies as 'weapons in their continuous guerrilla war against the cultural power of capital and the state' (1986: 278), Frith has argued that the 'relations of cultural production determine the possibilities of cultural consumption' (1988a: 5).

Here Frith uses the concept of determinism, the idea that human activity in one area of life (in this case consumption) is an effect of or a response to powerful forces elsewhere (i.e., in production). Hence, he argues that what music 'means' and the 'possibilities of consumption' are 'determined' by the 'technological and economic conditions of its production'.

One response to such a position might be to acknowledge that Frith is right to the extent that what 'we hear' may well have come to us from the studios, factories and distribution systems of the music industry. But, how we actually *listen* to the sounds, words and images and what these *mean* and how we then *use* these in our lives can surely be no more 'determined' than the language we have available to speak with will determine what we are going to say. It is one thing to concede that our choices as audiences are clearly limited and that our scope for musical activity *is* influenced by some broad (hard to predict or identify) boundaries, but it is quite another to declare that music's more experiential dimensions – what we 'hear' and what music 'means' – is so clearly 'determined'.

The issue of determination – the way that 'external' forces shape human behaviour and the way that powerful human practices condition the behaviour of other people – is one that has preoccupied philosophers and theorists in the human and physical sciences for centuries. This is what makes the question Frith is addressing so important and his claim (that production *determines* consumption) so contentious.

To be fair to Frith, it is important to note that, in making this argument, he was opposing what he considered to be a celebratory and 'populist' tendency among active audience theorists who he judged were ignoring processes of production in a rather naive and cavalier fashion (1991). He was also stressing the power of production as part of a broader critique of writers who have treated rock music as a form of folk or community expression that is independent from industry and commerce (Frith, 1981). However, there has been a tendency in Frith's adoption of the corporate control argument to extend his claims beyond rock music and to suggest that there is no popular musical activity that is outside of the industrialized relations of record production. This is very apparent when he argues that

> The industrialization of music cannot be understood as something that happens *to* music, since it describes a process in which music itself is made ... Twentieth-century popular music means the twentieth-century popular record; not the record of something (a song? a singer? a performance?) which exists independently of the music industry, but a form of communication which determines what songs, singers and performances are and can be. (Frith, 1988a: 12)

This might be a reasonable claim to the extent that, if the focus of study is on the recorded sounds that have been distributed by the music industry, then this would seem a plausible starting point (it is a position I took for my own account of the discovery and development of artists in the music industry in Britain (Negus, 1992)). It *is* within the networks that branch out from and around the music industry where the majority of recorded popular music is made.

But I would question Frith's general claim that 'twentieth-century popular music means the twentieth-century popular record.' This seems to imply that there is no 'popular music' any-where in the world in the twentieth century that is 'outside' of this process of industrialized record production. This accords a very powerful capacity to the music industry to create the history of twentieth-century popular music.

Against Frith's certainty I would suggest that a further series of issues need to be addressed before we can equate the products of the music industry with twentieth-century popular music history. I would argue that it may be useful to make a distinction between types of twentieth-century music that exist independently of the music industry, if only as a starting point for some detailed histori-cal and geographical research. One point that Frith skates over here is the issue of who has *access* to this recorded history. As research by Peter Golding (1994) and Cees Hamelink (1995) has indicated, vast numbers of people in the world do not have daily access to the technologies of the mass media and communication (books, news-papers, telephones, radio receivers, televisions and record players) which are taken for granted by many people in Western Europe and North America. While the recorded popular song is undoubtedly hegemonic (Laing, 1986), it seems likely that there are vast numbers of people on this planet who, without Walkmans, CD players or portable stereos, are hearing musical sounds that have very little to do with the 'twentieth-century popular record'.

I have taken issue with Frith here because I believe that his argument denies the possibility of a history that is outside of the commodified production of popular music. In doing this it leads to what he acknowledges is a pessimistic theory (1988b) that presents capital as all-powerful. But it also disempowers the activities of all the people who are, if not making music that is entirely independ-ent, at least struggling towards the possibility of some form of critical distance from the commercial machine. As I have also noted, it is in addition an approach which evades the way in which sounds in some parts of the world are simply ignored by the recorded music industry.

In general, and despite its value in highlighting the power ex-erted over production, there is a tendency for the corporate control argument to lead to a fatalistic despair about the way that capital is able directly to determine how popular music is produced and consumed. In addition, there seems little prospect of change. Un-able to locate any radical potential or creative activity that is not coopted or determined in production (and not sharing the active audience theorist's belief in the power of appropriation), the 'cooptation' argument then works itself into a theoretical corner from which there seems little escape. Apart from a revolutionary socialist transformation of the entire capitalist system, which only Harker (1980) seems explicitly to advocate, we are left with vague postscripts about the potential of rock as 'people's music' (Chapple and Garofalo, 1977) or the hope that the shadow-boxing of consumers might give way to a 'material struggle for a piece of the new musical action' (Frith, 1988b: 130).

In making this last observation, Frith has vaguely offered a suggestion that the possibilities for optimism might lie within the 'material conditions' of production rather than among the shadows of consumption. At this point, then, it might be useful to start peering more closely at the activities that are going on within the music machine.

Transmissions: from artist to audience

From Adorno's 'assembly-line' to analogies with a 'sausage machine' (Harker, 1980) and 'production line' (Ryan and Peterson, 1982), one of the most enduring images of what goes on inside the recording industry has involved variations on a transmission model of products being shifted from artists to audience. This was formally theorized as a 'systems model' by Paul Hirsch (1972), who drew on organizational theory, studies of news production and research from industrial manufacturing to develop a 'filter-flow' model of music production.

For Hirsch, the process started with the selection of 'raw materials', which are drawn from the universe of potential recordings. These are then admitted to a 'creative subsystem' where they are filtered by producers and record company policy makers to the 'business sectors' of the industry and then through regional promoters and the media until finally reaching the public. At each stage record industry gatekeepers are engaged in selecting and rank ordering the products as they pass through the system.

Hirsch has argued that this system has been developed as a way of 'ordering potential chaos' (1970). Rather than having complex feedback mechanisms or trying to undertake market research on what had not yet been released to the public, the music industry was organized in such a way that each step would contribute to 'predetermine' what the audience will eventually get. Hence, in this model, the 'people's choice' will ultimately involve merely selecting from what is available – the final step in a process of selection and rank ordering.

This is a one-way transmission model that portrays recording industry personnel as little more than bureaucratic administrators merely involved in selecting, classifying and rank ordering a vast quantity of completed items which then flow through the system to the public. Although Hirsch considered that each step in the system was 'value added', by this he meant that there would be an 'increased probability of a successful outcome as the product is favourably processed at each stage . . . the product itself does not undergo change as it flows through the system' (1970: 7).

While Hirsch usefully highlighted how record companies develop 'preselection' strategies to deal with the uncertain commercial prospects for their products, he gave little indication of how this influenced the composition of music, lyrics and images. According to this model, the workers in the industry, such as A & R staff, producers, stylists and promotion people, do not seem to be doing very much with the 'product' other than making selections and filtering these to the next step in the system.

One of the main limitations of this model, particularly in relation to the contemporary music industry, is its emphasis on music as a 'raw material' that is then processed through a system to the public. Since Hirsch was writing, recording corporations have been increasingly organizing their activities around the 'exploitation of rights' rather than the 'manufacture of a product'. As Frith has argued, this means that on many occasions the sounds, words and images of popular music do not necessarily need to be 'sold to the public at all. The musical commodity can circulate within the media, generating income from the exploitation of performing rights alone' (Frith, 1987: 73). The work of music-business workers has become increasingly based around circulating the sounds and images of popular music across a range of media texts and entertainment items (films, adverts, videos, books, magazines). It is no longer so easy, if it ever was, to isolate and identify one piece of 'raw material' as a product that is being processed through the system.

The production of culture perspective:
systems, cycles and variables

While Hirsch tended to privilege the artistic creators of the 'raw material' that will be passed through the system, those adopting the 'production of culture perspective' have been explicitly opposed to the idea that cultural artefacts are simply the work of individual artists. One of the starting points for this approach is Howard Becker's theories of the 'worlds' within which art is produced (1974, 1976). Becker had argued that works of art could be understood by conceptualizing them as 'the result of the co-ordinated activities of all the people whose co-operation is necessary in order that the work should occur as it does' (1976: 41).

Taking Becker's formulations about the 'collective' practices of artistic production as his starting point, Richard Peterson advocated the adoption of a 'production of culture perspective' which he suggested should examine how 'elements of culture are fabricated' in locations, among occupational groups and within social milieus for whom 'symbol-system production is most self-consciously the centre of activity' (Peterson, 1976: 10).

Peterson's central concern was to explain how 'collaborative production' is coordinated. For Becker the production of works of art was coordinated by shared 'conventions' and 'consensual definitions' that were arrived at as various people formed, were attracted by, were recruited to and inhabited different 'art worlds': it was often the cultural life and social values of the art worlds that created the conditions for creative collaboration (Becker 1974, 1976). For Peterson and his followers it is more formal criteria.

Peterson developed his approach in a case study of country music jointly written with John Ryan. Employing a familiar mechanical metaphor, this essay considered the work of 'a number of skilled specialists [who] . . . have a part in shaping the final work as it goes through a series of stages which, superficially at least, resemble an assembly line' (Ryan and Peterson, 1982: 11).

Ryan and Peterson traced the progress of country music songs (which are more suited to this type of analysis than most soul, rock and rap music) through a 'decision chain' of discrete activities which involved writing, publishing, recording, marketing, manufacture, release and consumption. At each stage a number of choices were confronted and a number of modifications might be made to the songs. The 'problems of collaborative creation' were ultimately solved by the numerous specialists involved in the production of a country music recording coordinating their activities according to a 'product image'. This involved different staff using their judgement to shape 'a piece of work so that it is most likely to be accepted by decision makers at the next link in the chain' (Ryan and Peterson, 1982: 25). According to Ryan and Peterson all of the personnel involved in the country music chain adopt a rather pragmatic, strategic and commercially oriented approach which is organized around a 'product image'. This enables them to collaborate without having to share a common world.

Such an approach draws on the 'professional' ideas of senior record company executives who often explain that their organizations work in these terms – united in shared, commercially defined goals which override personal and departmental divisions. Useful as this approach might be in indicating how popular music can be produced through the adherence to a few routine working practices and shared goals based around a particular product image, there are numerous accounts in popular biographies and the trade and consumer press which indicate that music is frequently produced through conflict and a total lack of consensus or shared goals. Producers may be in dispute with artists, artists and producers together might be disagreeing and withholding recordings from A & R staff, A & R staff may in turn be in conflict with marketing staff, and promotion staff may demand that A & R staff tell their producers to go and remix a track because it is not suitable for radio play (Negus, 1992).

Hence, while many staff do have some notion of a 'product image' as a professional ideal, this idea may be contested, challenged and transformed as popular music is produced rather than simply acting as an organizing principle. In my own work (1992) I found that many staff referred to what they were doing in a more fragmentary and less unified way as part of 'a jigsaw' in which their own interests were focused on just one piece of the picture. Although Ryan and Peterson do acknowledge that staff *contribute* to rather than simply *filter* musical products, they do not acknowledge that this can then lead to a change in the product image as it moves along the 'decision chain'. In contrast, I have suggested that the pieces of the jigsaw often do not come together and the process is often not successful because it is continually being changed as it is being put together (Negus, 1992). My point, in drawing on the metaphors used by music industry personnel, is to argue that the contribution of different recording industry personnel does not merely involve 'filtering' or contributing to an identifiable 'product image'. Instead, it entails actively intervening and changing the sounds and images as they are being put together.

While the general production of culture 'perspective' has been concerned with how collaborative production is coordinated, a more formal 'model' has been developed from Peterson's attempts to identify the factors which 'constrain' or 'facilitate' the production of cultural products (Peterson, 1982). This has become formalized as six classes of 'variable' which operate alone or in combination to influence the production of culture: technology, law, market, industry structure, organizational structure and occupational careers. This model has been employed and applied to explain the disputes between music licensing organizations (Ryan, 1985) and also the quantitative relationship between the number of competing firms and amount of 'product diversity', measured in terms of the number of recordings available on the market (Burnett, 1990).

Although this model pays greater attention to the way that various occupational groups contribute to popular music, and acknowledges the potential tensions between these different interests, there is a tendency for the production of culture model to reduce the work of industry personnel to a system of business and management strategies, shared goals, structural variables and statistical patterns and to stay within formal institutionalized definitions. Based on the 'assumption that culture-producing organizations behave as any other type of organization' (Ryan, 1985: 5) and treating the 'systems' of production and consumption as 'mainly separate' (Burnett, 1990: 75), it is still based on 'a transmission model of communication' which approaches 'culture as a product that is created, disseminated and consumed' (Jensen, 1984: 104).

In her critique of the production of culture approach, Joli Jensen has argued that culture is not simply a 'product' which is ' "processed" like soap by organizational, technical, and economic "factors" ' (1984: 110). Instead, culture should be seen much more broadly as the means through which people create meaningful worlds in which to live. These 'worlds' are constructed through interpretations, experiences and activities through which material is 'created in connection with its consumption' (Jensen, 1984: 111).

Jensen's critique takes me in two further directions from the models of the music industry that I have just outlined, and informs my own approach to the industry. First, Jensen's emphasis on culture as more than simply a 'product' moves me from the 'production of culture' to what I shall shortly be referring to as the 'culture of production'. Second, against a model of production determining consumption or the activities of consumption being separate from production, Jensen advocates an approach which might attempt to understand the connections, interactions and overlaps *between* production and consumption. This latter approach has been pursued by Antoine Hennion and Jean Vignolle.

The mediations of production: reaching out and feeling the audience's pulse

Hennion and Vignolle have approached the recording industry from a similar starting point to the researchers above who take the production of popular music to involve 'collective creation' (Hennion, 1983). However, they have provided an analysis which challenges the unidirectional transmission model and attempted to move within formal and institutional definitions to the meanings and interpretations adopted by participants within the recording industry.

Based on observation in studios and a consideration of the work of personnel in French record companies, Vignolle has suggested that the conventional distinctions between 'creation' and 'execution' (a 'product' that is then filtered or processed) are misleading as the two become completely intermingled and occur simultaneously in popular music. He has argued that no point in the process has 'an absolutely fixed logical or chronological order of precedence' (Vignolle, 1980: 88). All of the people involved in the process, from the producers and studio staff to the marketing and promotion people, become involved in a 'collective process which is partly determined by each of them, but on which all are dependant as well' (1980: 89).

This interactive aspect has also been emphasized by Hennion, who notes that the final 'mixture is the fruit of continuous exchange of views between the various members of the team' (Hennion, 1983: 161). This immediately suggests a more complex and mediated approach to the way in which record industry personnel become involved in producing popular music. It is a conscious attempt to move away from viewing the record industry as a 'closed structure' (Vignolle, 1980: 97) towards one that is stretched across or situated between a series of mediations that connect together artists and audiences (Hennion, 1989).

However, when both writers theorize what is involved in this interactive relationship their conclusions tend to result in another consensual organizing principle, albeit a rather mysterious one. In explaining the relationship between artistic producers and consumers, Vignolle has suggested that record industry personnel 'project back to the audience a condensed ideal-type version of its own image'. In this way, record company staff do not require any specialist skills, but a more intuitive 'way of being-with-an-audience, the rules of which cannot be learnt anywhere or formally drawn up by the organization' (Vignolle, 1980: 95).

Hennion has reached similar conclusions when describing record industry personnel as 'representatives of a kind of imaginary democracy established by pop music; they do not manipulate the public so much as feel its pulse' (1983: 191). Despite moving away from simple transmission models and stressing the connections between production and consumption, the process of composing and recording popular music is ultimately reduced to empathy and intuition rather than organizational formulae, conventions and structural variables. If Peterson's theory draws on the 'professional' principles of higher management, then Hennion and Vignolle have adapted a strand of reasoning which can be found among various younger personnel in record companies who stress the subjective 'feel' they have for the job and the way in which it cannot be rationalized. Although I have also drawn on the working beliefs of recording industry personnel (and like the writers just mentioned also run the risk of uncritically re-presenting the participants' own unreflexive accounts), I have also tried to approach notions of empathy and intuition more critically in terms of the ideas, values and cultural practices which guide their work.

The culture of production

In my own research on the music industry I have attempted to make a further contribution to the studies outlined so far by adopting an approach which, shifting the terms of the 'production of culture' perspective, and partly for brevity, I will call the 'culture of production.' I am not offering this as yet another 'model' but as an additional way of approaching the production of popular music. My focus has been on the cultural practices of personnel that cannot simply be explained by reference to the determining influence of corporate capital or according to formal organizational criteria (job descriptions, occupational hierarchies, etc.). In pursuing this I have drawn on Raymond Williams's (1965) writings about culture as involving a 'whole way of life' and Stuart Hall's (1991, 1994) emphasis on culture as the means through which people create meaningful worlds in which to live. Hence, my argument is that in studying the music industry we need to do more than understand culture as a 'product' that is created through technical processes and routine practices. Culture, from this perspective, should be understood more broadly as the constitutive context within and out of which the sounds, words and images of popular music are made and given meaning.

In adopting this approach I have focused on recording industry personnel as 'cultural intermediaries', a term drawn from Pierre Bourdieu which refers to a class of workers engaged in 'occupations involving presentation and representation' and those involved in 'providing symbolic goods and services' (Bourdieu, 1986: 359). I have adopted this concept to emphasize that music industry workers are not simply filtering 'raw materials' or making decisions about a 'cultural product' that is passing along a chain. Instead, as Hennion and Vignolle have argued, they occupy a position *between* the artist and audience. As cultural intermediaries, recording industry personnel are constantly contributing to the production of and then reorganizing, circulating and *mediating* the words, sounds and images of popular music to audiences across a range of entertainment media and cultural texts (recordings, videos, advertisements, broadcasts, books, magazines, computer games and various merchandise).

Bourdieu has argued that the cultural intermediaries who work in 'the newest sectors of cultural and artistic production' occupy a position where 'jobs and careers have not yet acquired the rigidity of the older bureaucratic professions' (Bourdieu, 1986: 151). Entry into these jobs is often via networks of connections and shared values and life experiences formed among members of this group rather than the meritocracy of recruitment through formal qualifications. Because of this, cultural intermediaries do not work as gatekeepers who filter products according to organizational conventions, but as mediators who blur a number of formal distinctions associated with working life. This is very apparent in the music industry where staff blur a number of conventional distinctions:

1) *Work and leisure/production and consumption* – attending concerts and clubs and listening to, viewing and assessing a wide range of music products at 'home' and during their 'leisure' hours while simultaneously producing them at 'work'
2) *Personal taste and professional judgement* – many people have been recruited by the music industry because of their taste in and collections of music; the personal preferences of music industry workers inform the amount of time, energy and commitment devoted to particular acts and can be an important influence on who gets a recording contract (Negus, 1992)
3) *Artist, administrator and audience* – these distinctions are very clear cut in the filter-flow model and production of culture perspective, yet are constantly blurred in the day-to-day worlds of the music business. They can be observed in the movement of key taste makers and consumers (such as DJs and fanzine writers) into the industry and the way that singers, musicians, disc jockeys and managers are often working simultaneously as employees of recording companies.

In emphasizing the way that the production of popular music takes place *across* the webs of companies that make up the music industry, my approach has been to try and get at the informal cultural worlds being lived and remade on a daily basis. I have attempted to move away from purely formal and organizational definitions to look at the cultural context and wider social relationships within which these workers are situated, and to ask what formally defined 'constraints' and 'variables' might mean for those involved. I have also approached vague notions of empathy and intuition in a more critical way by examining the ideas, values and practices which music industry workers adopt to give meaning to and guide their work.

Earlier in this chapter I briefly referred to how particular aesthetic preferences, working beliefs and race and gender divisions form an integral part of the 'culture of production' within the British music industry. In the past these have contributed to the marginalization of women into specific occupations (most notably secretarial and public relations) and restricted the opportunities for staff with a knowledge of rhythm and blues and soul music (often leading to the deprioritizing of the recordings produced by Britain's black musicians). Such dynamics have had a direct impact on the way that music has been produced and distributed. But such issues are not explicable in terms of organizational variables or simply the control exerted by the corporations. During the time of my study, these were integral aspects of the 'culture of production' that constituted the context *within* which popular music was being made.

In concluding this chapter with a brief outline of the approach to the music industry that I developed in my previous book, *Producing Pop* (Negus, 1992), I am not intending that this be taken as a straightforward alternative to the theoretical perspectives presented earlier in this chapter. Instead, I intend it as a contribution to the continual dialogues and growth of research and knowledge in this area of study.

In an attempt to move away from transmission models and mechanical metaphors and to shift attention from what I consider to be an overemphasis on the determining power of the corporations, I have, like Hennion and Vignolle, argued that music industry staff are *mediators* between artists and audiences. By adopting this approach I do not mean to imply that no power is being exerted, that no exploitation takes place and that the work of these intermediaries is as influenced by the activities of audiences as it is by the decisions of senior executives within corporations. However, I would like to allow for the possibility that the corporations might not be all-powerful and that, at certain moments, committed artists, oppositional audiences and perhaps music industry personnel might be able to produce sounds and communicate ideas that do more than simply generate profits for the major entertainment corporations.

Conclusion: between corporate control and creative autonomy

In the first part of this chapter I outlined arguments about how the culture industry and music corporations coopt and commodify creative and cultural expression. From the perspective of this corporate control position, all of the cultural activity found by researchers such as myself and Hennion and Vignolle might be dismissed as irrelevant. Like Frith's shadow-boxing consumers, we might have found a lot of activity as people contribute to the production of recordings, make videos, promote performers and intervene between artists and audiences, but this might just be the phantom activities of workers who are really corporate puppets but denying this as part of a common-sense belief in their own creative autonomy. To return to David Morley's (1993) point, they may be *active* but they may not exert power and influence. After all, there *is* much evidence to suggest that artists are systematically exploited by incompetent record industry employees, that music industry personnel often have little choice in whom they sign and work with and that compromise and cop-out frequently replaces any commitment to artists. Yet there is also evidence to suggest that many record company staff do enjoy a degree of autonomy, find spaces to give opportunities to new imaginative artists and make a significant contribution to the production of popular music.

Again, I conclude this chapter with more questions. If the corporations are so powerful then how does so much great music get produced? If the staff in the industry are so autonomous and creative then why is so much standardized and routine music produced? How do we theorize the relationship between the corporate machine and the human activity?

In the remainder of this book I shall be slowly moving away from such dichotomies and in particular from the division I have set up by organizing the first two chapters of this book around a distinction between audience (equals consumption) and industry (equals production). I will be suggesting that equally significant social processes intervene between and across the production-consumption of popular music. Rather than arguing about whether production determines consumption or whether audiences can subvert the power of corporate controlled production, I shall be moving on to consider some of the ways that popular music is mediated by a series of technological, cultural, historical, geographical and political factors. It is these additional influences that contribute to the dynamism and changing nature of popular music styles and which make this such a fascinating subject of study. But it is also these broader social processes that continually frustrate our attempts to develop neat theoretical models about popular music, and which continually leave us with more questions than answers.

CHAPTER THREE
MEDIATIONS

In the last chapter I concluded with the idea that the recording industry is not merely the site of production, nor can it simply be characterized as an inhuman machine which processes the raw material of popular music through a series of inputs and outputs. Instead, various workers are involved in putting together the sounds, words and images of popular music and distributing these across a range of texts and technologies. In doing this, I argued, recording industry staff act as intermediaries, constantly *mediating* the movements between artists, audiences and corporations. In this chapter I will be developing the idea of mediation further by considering in more detail how the print, radio and televisual media come in between and influence the production and consumption of popular music.

I will start by briefly giving more details about what I mean by mediation, a concept that I am introducing as a way of starting to think about the processes that connect production and consumption. Drawing on Raymond Williams's (1976) discussion of the etymology and changing historical use of the word, but simplifying slightly, I want to identify three distinct senses of the term mediation: 1) the idea of coming in between, or of intermediary action; 2) a means of transmission, an agency that comes in between reality and social knowledge; 3) the idea that all objects, particularly works of art, are mediated by social relationships.

I will take each of these slightly different, but overlapping, meanings in turn and then explain how I am using them in combination to refer to the mediation of popular music in this chapter and in the book more generally.

1) *Mediation as intermediary action* In the last chapter I discussed the activity of recording industry personnel by referring to them as cultural intermediaries who intervene between production and consumption, between corporation and consumer and between artists and audience. Mediation in this sense of intermediary action refers to the practices of all the people who intervene as popular music is produced, distributed and consumed. This includes staff within record companies, but it also refers to disc jockeys, journalists, video directors, revenue collectors for copyright organizations and retail staff in record shops. As Williams (1976) has argued, such an idea of intermediary action should not be taken to imply a neutral process of conciliatory activity. Although intermediaries are often presented in such a way, as I have stressed in my work elsewhere, the cultural intermediaries in the music industry are frequently engaged in disputes with each other, with their corporate bosses and with recording artists. Such conflicts have a direct impact on how popular music is produced (Negus, 1992).

In some respects my use of the concept of cultural intermediary shares features with the metaphor of the gatekeeper which was adopted in studies of news organizations in the United States. This was initially used to refer to how personnel such as editors could open a 'gate' and then admit certain news stories and exclude others. The concept was central to Paul Hirsch's filter-flow model of the 'raw materials' of popular music passing through the music industry (Chapter 2) and has been used by a number of writers to characterize the work of personnel within the music business (Frith, 1983; Street, 1986; Wallis and Malm, 1984).

The concept of the gatekeeper is useful for indicating how music business personnel control access to resources such as finance, recording facilities, tours and venues and how staff in international departments perform a gatekeeping action when deciding which artists will release recordings in overseas territories. However, I prefer to characterize staff as intermediaries to stress that there is not a one-way 'flow' of material through various industry 'gates'. Instead, there are a series of interactions and mediations as people in particular occupations connect together and play an active part in the production, distribution and social consumption of popular music.

2) *Mediation as transmission* This refers to the way that media technologies have been used for the distribution of the sounds, words and images of popular music. At least six types of communication media have played an important part in the transmission of popular music.

From the peddlers of broadside ballads to the pluggers of sheet music to the numerous magazines that are now published for each genre, the *printed word* has been important in mediating knowledge and experience of popular music. Since commercial sound recording was introduced in 1877 popular music has been associated with a number of specific *sound carriers*, including the cylinder, discs of varying sizes and materials and the cassette tape and compact disc. Each has had an impact on how music has been created, distributed and listened to. *Radio* broadcasting provided a means for transmitting recorded music rapidly over distances and later enabled audiences to take music with them on the move. It continues to be one of the most influential transmission media alongside those of the *moving image* of film and television, which have been important over many years for distributing the images of recording artists. It was music video that brought together recorded image and music in one form and which, transmitted by more and more satellite services, is challenging radio as one of the main technological mediators of music. Facilitated by the development of digital storage techniques and satellites, *telecommunication technologies* are also playing an increasingly important part in mediating popular music by enabling phone-line musical composition between artists, computer networked dialogues among fans and the production of 'interactive' musical material by musicians. Finally, *musical instruments* have enabled different types of musical communication to take place. From early wind and string instruments through the introduction of the lute, piano, electric guitar, studio mixing desk, synthesizer and sampler, the technologies of sound production have had a significant impact on how musical messages have been created and received (for more detailed discussion, see Negus, 1992: chapter 2).

My point in briefly running through these technologies of mediation is to highlight how knowledge and experience of different types of music are closely related to forms of technological mediation – the *media* through and by which various sounds, words and images have been constituted, transmitted and received.

3) *Mediation of social relationships* The idea of the mediation of social relationships is implied in the two meanings of mediation given above, in terms of intermediary activity and technological transmissions that come in between people. However, the mediation of social relationships is more frequently understood as referring to how power and influence is exercised through such mediated relationships and how this has a direct impact on the creation and reception of manufactured objects, particularly works of art. From this perspective, the resulting works should therefore be judged critically in terms of how they may communicate a limited range of specific meanings which might ideologically privilege particular interests.

This approach to mediation draws on a tradition of Marxist analysis, with a particular issue concerning how human relationships and cultural forms are mediated by social class. An example of this approach can be found in Dave Harker's analysis of the mediation of British folk songs, which provides an indication of how these three meanings of mediation (intermediary action, transmission and social relationships) are brought together. Setting out to examine how written manuscripts, printed pamphlets and books were used to 'manufacture' a particular musical canon from the eighteenth century, Harker has written:

> By mediation I understand not simply the fact that particular people passed on songs they had taken from other sources, in the form of manuscript or print, but that in the very process of so doing their own assumptions, attitudes, likes and dislikes may well have significantly determined what they looked for, accepted and rejected. Not only that, but these people's access to sources of songs, the fact that they had the time, opportunity, motive and facilities for collecting, and a whole range of other material factors will have come into play ... while we cannot 'read off' what a person did with songs from, say, their class position, it is still the case that their social origins, education, occupation (or lack of it) and so on were obviously connected with how they felt, thought and acted, in relation to songs ... (Harker, 1985: xiii)

Harker's approach is that of a 'classical Marxist' who is concerned with the way that various bourgeois song collectors systematically neglected the music of working-class people and constructed and then managed to institutionalize a genteel, pastoral, ideologically biased 'tradition' of what he calls 'fakesong'. Later in this chapter I will be discussing how similar processes led to middle-class preferences in music programming playing an important part during the development of radio broadcasting in the British Broadcasting Corporation (BBC).

While social class is an important influence on the mediation of cultural forms in any class-divided society, there are further ways in which the social relations of race, gender, sexuality and ethnicity mediate the creation and reception of popular music. It is due to such factors that no music will ever simply 'reflect' a society but instead be caught within, arise out of and refer to a web of unequal social relations and power struggles. On this point, I am presenting the concept of mediation as a way of starting to think about the range of processes, movements, relationships and power struggles that occur *between* and *across* the production and consumption of popular music.

One of the points I should make clear here is that I am not introducing the concept of mediation as a solution to the dichotomy between production and consumption that I set up earlier. By itself the concept of mediation does not provide any straightforward answers – indeed, it can frequently lead to confusion, particularly when used in a narrow way to refer simply to the communications 'media'. Here, I am using the idea of mediation as a way of directing attention towards the movements in between and dynamics that connect together various people and processes involved in producing musical meaning.

In this part of the book I am going to concentrate most of my discussion on the mediations between popular music and radio broadcasting, followed by a consideration of the relations between sound and image in music video. I shall be framing this discussion by referring to the printed word and telecommunications, but these sections will be much briefer and less detailed. Many of the themes that I will be raising about mediation in relation to radio and video are intended as more general theoretical issues that should hopefully be of direct relevance to debates about the relations between popular music and other transmission technologies.

One of my reasons for focusing much of this chapter on radio is that it is a technology that has played an important part in the distribution of recorded popular music. It stands at a pivotal point between the slower spread of musical knowledge via print technologies and the more rapid transmission of digital sound and video images via cable and satellite. In outlining some of the mediations between popular music and media technologies, I shall be emphasizing the increasing mediation of musical knowledge and performance across space and time. I will also be highlighting how communication technologies have been accommodated to various social relations of popular music distribution in which particular class and commercial interests have had a significant influence on the reordering of musical repertoires. Hence, I shall be highlighting these three interrelated processes of mediation throughout this chapter. Before discussing this in relation to radio, I will step back very briefly to refer to the influence of the print media.

Popular music and the printed word

Before the mediation of music through radio broadcasting, it was communicated, distributed and exchanged in three distinct ways; orally through word of mouth – spoken and sung; via written then printed words and musical notation on a page; and on a phonographic cylinder and disc. Although such distinctions might suggest a historical periodization, these should not be taken to imply that one mode of distribution simply replaced the other in a developmental fashion. Not only has the spread of these different forms of musical mediation occurred at different paces and in a variety of ways across the world, the introduction of each did not simply replace the preceding mode but instead introduced new relationships between them. You should bear this in mind when reading the following section, in which I will only be giving the merest hint of such possible relationships and presenting a very brief history of a long period during which print was a key mediator of popular music.

The impact of modern printing on popular music started with the introduction of the printing press in Europe in the middle of the fifteenth century. This was closely connected to the growth of capitalist industrial production and migrations of people from the country to the expanding cities, factors which helped provide the conditions for a particular way of encoding and circulating musical knowledge. The printing press was very soon used to produce street songs or broadside ballads, which began appearing in the expanding cities of Western Europe from early in the sixteenth century. These were made up of song lyrics often accompanied by a woodcut image, printed on one side of a sheet of paper.

Much historical scholarship has been devoted to this period, and the impact of the printed word has often been viewed as symptomatic of a broader process of social change whereby collective, rural community life was replaced by a more atomized, individualistic approach, which became a characteristic of the cities. It has sometimes been suggested that the immediacy of the oral ballad was fractured by a new type of literacy that was introduced by printing.

Against such laments about a golden age of more immediate community expression, David Vincent (1989) has suggested that print had a far more complex and contradictory impact on popular forms of musical expression. He has made two points that are worth bearing in mind when thinking about the impact of new communication technologies. First, he has argued that print did not simply replace oral forms of expression. Instead, there was a very long period of transition and interaction between printed, hand-written and oral techniques of mediating songs. Second, he has pointed out that the past was not quite so pure, immediate and spontaneous as is often assumed.

While print did enable entrepreneurs to profit from this new media and although it contributed to the formal separation of musical creation and reception, Vincent has argued that the printed word also provided ways of retaining, preserving and passing on songs. Before the introduction of printing there had not simply been an oral tradition, as many popular ballads had been circulated in a hand-written form for many years (Pickering and Green, 1987). What printing did was to provide a more widespread way of *combining* oral forms with the uses of literacy. It was, after all, only the words of the song that were sold on the broadside ballad. Unlike the emerging classical music tradition of notation, the ballads rarely contained printed music. A song sheet might have occasionally included a note which suggested an appropriate melody and many were set to the same well-known tune. But, the success of most songs was very dependent on the skill of the hawker or shouter who sold and sang the ballads in public. Hence, orality was not simply replaced by the literacy of the printed word but was retained as an integral part of a song's distribution. As Vincent has argued: 'The sound of the human voice was magnified rather than quelled by the mass production and distribution of prose and verse. The simple relationship between the faceless publisher and the soundless reader was disrupted by men and women reciting, singing, shouting, chanting, declaiming and narrating' (Vincent, 1989: 201).

In this way, the printed word was adopted and used to draw

upon and elaborate existing practices of popular entertainment. In addition, the oral tradition had not been quite as anonymous, collective and immediate as has often been portrayed. There was often a distinct division of labour between song composers and performers. During the Middle Ages, professional singers had frequently sold their services, particularly to the nobility and clergy (Booth, 1981). Hence, the oral tradition had not simply entailed a fusing of creation and reception in a pastoral communitarian world. Instead, there were many notable individual performers, whether the aristocratic and trained bards or the jongleurs and travelling minstrels (Shepard, 1962).

The broadside ballad, facilitated by the printing press but drawing on oral traditions of performance and music circulation, was distributed by sellers who drew crowds of people onto street corners and into town squares and performed their songs. These ballads covered a rich variety of subjects. There were songs about war news, labour songs, love songs and joke songs about human relationships. There were songs about death and murders, gallows songs and tales of criminals and royalty. There were songs about sport and prominent figures and campaigning songs that addressed political or social issues. Combining together what would now probably be identified as news, commentary and entertainment, these ballads often achieved higher sales than the newspapers of the time. This has prompted some writers to suggest that the ballads were a precursor to what became the 'tabloid' newspaper: in these times the populace 'sang their journalism' (Booth, 1981: 109).

Gradually over time the relationship between the producers and consumers of these ballads became more organized and singers and shouters were replaced by more specialized reciters. Towards the end of the eighteenth century the broadsides were increasingly adopted by professional performers and began to be produced with a more theatrical quality as the street performances interacted with and became part of the music-hall tradition of entertainment. These changes were accompanied by municipal attempts to regulate public behaviour on the streets of cities. Laws were enacted that restricted public shouting and singing and which led to a sharp decline in the trade of the street performers. Eventually the street ballads were superseded by the formal production, distribution and plugging methods that were adopted to distribute songs by the sheet music industry. Yet, the practices of the song peddlers and ballad hawkers were retained in many of the practices of the boomers and pluggers who utilized public singing when promoting songs in music halls and vaudeville theatres (Laing, 1969).

The popularity of sheet music peaked at the end of the nineteenth century, but the song sheet and many of the techniques of ballad production (such as producing songs quickly in response to topical events) were adapted to the Tin Pan Alley tradition of 'song factory' production (Shepard, 1962). As Vincent has noted, the result of this long process of interaction between orality and literacy was that 'performance survived but it was taken off the streets and increasingly confined to reproduction rather than re-creation' (1989: 211).

Sheet music songs were popularized by professional singers and touring music shows and became well known initially through the spread of the piano but later through the phonograph, which itself did not simply replace printed representations of music (whether song sheets or notation) but set up another series of relationships between different modes of technologically mediating music (Booth, 1981). In more recent times the printed word has mediated music most prominently through the reports, reviews and articles about musicians and star performers that have regularly appeared in newspapers and magazines. But orality has not simply disappeared: contemporary popular music is often experienced as a form of 'secondary orality' (Ong, 1971) – the electronically mediated voice that we hear speaking and singing to us from the radio.

Radio mediations: the development of transmission technology

The history of radio can be traced back to the use of telegraphy at the end of the eighteenth century. Initially introduced in France to conduct point-to-point communication during military conflicts, electrical telegraphy was later used to help coordinate the expanding railway networks of Europe and North America. A turning point came in 1896 when Guglielmo Marconi first demonstrated wireless telegraphy (hence the phrase the 'wireless'). Unlike previous point-to-point communication, this device enabled 'broadcasts' to be transmitted simultaneously to numerous geographically dispersed people (Crisell, 1994; Lewis and Booth, 1989).

Like any new technology, radio did not just suddenly appear. Telegraphy had been developed from similar technological experiments that had also produced the phonograph and which would eventually lead to television (Williams, 1990). As was the case with these communication technologies, radio did not spontaneously emerge and then have an impact *on* social activity and musical practices. Instead, radio was adapted and adopted for public broadcasting following a series of struggles and disputes about patents, technological modifications and the use of different transmission frequencies.

Seeking a stake in the way that radio broadcasting would be developed were entrepreneurial scientist-inventors, governments eager to use this equipment for military purposes and civil communication, and companies who recognized its commercial possibilities. As a result of such struggles, radio developed in different ways across the world. In Europe radio broadcasting was more state regulated and organized according to notions of 'public service'. In North America radio systems were market oriented from the beginning, with content influenced more by the interests of commercial sponsors than ideas about 'serving the nation' (Scannell and Cardiff, 1991; Lewis and Booth, 1989). I shall be referring to the contrasts between different radio systems in more detail a little later. Before this I want to discuss some of the characteristics of radio as a social technology of musical transmission.

From group to individual listening

When radio broadcasting started in the 1920s the initial reception of broadcast signals was very poor and the first crystal radio sets required individual enthusiasts to listen with headphones. This soon changed and by the middle of the 1920s radio sets with valve-driven amplification and loudspeakers began to replace the crystal sets. These were heavy, cumbersome and expensive pieces of equipment that required a large aerial. Because of this they were not widely distributed and as a consequence people often listened to broadcasts in groups in the privacy of the home or in pubs, clubs and cafes.

This context of reception had an important influence on the way that radio broadcasters thought of their potential audience. It led to an initial approach to music programming which sought to avoid extremes and accommodate a range of preferences. It also led to a distinct style of addressing listeners as groups which was bold and declamatory, often like an 'informative' proclamation (Crisell, 1994; Frith, 1988a).

During the 1950s the cumbersome valves began to be replaced by small transistorized electronic components that required less electrical power. On account of this, receivers could operate from batteries and as a result radio sets became smaller, lighter and mobile. Individuals could take their transistor radios with them, whether into the privacy of the teenage bedroom or down to the beach. At the same time, radios also became an integral feature of the automobile. The listeners were no longer thought of as a stationary group listening in the home or crowded public place but as mobile individuals who may be on the move from place to place or listening alone in private. Further improvements in transmission techniques and modifications to the quality of microphone technology enabled broadcasters to introduce a style of address that was more intimate and which spoke to the individual as sole listener in a more 'personal' way.

Hence, the technical changes in radio technology enabled broadcasters to present programmes and address listeners in different ways. To pursue this issue further I will discuss the introduction of music programming in Britain as just one example of how the form, content and practices involved in using communication technologies are actively shaped by processes involving mediations *between* the technology of transmission, particular occupational groups and a wider series of social relationships.

Music radio programming: connecting artists with audiences

From its earliest days, music was an important element of radio programming. In Britain, the British Broadcasting Corporation (BBC) began transmitting events as they happened. This included broadcasts of sacred music from religious services, opera, variety entertainment from music hall, dance music and music from concert halls and cafes (Scannell and Cardiff, 1991). For listeners, this immediately provided 'access' to the sound of events that were happening in distant locations. People dispersed across the country heard sounds and voices that they would have previously had to travel great distances to hear. In the years that followed its introduction, radio gave many people across the world access to music of which they had no previous knowledge – whether white teenagers in the USA who heard recordings by black rhythm and blues artists for the first time (Chapple and Garofalo, 1977) or young people in Japan who tuned in to the rock-'n'-roll being transmitted by the US army's Far East Network (IASPM-Japan, 1991).

While listeners were gaining access to sounds from distant locations and experiencing the 'shrinking' of space (Berland, 1993a), for musicians and their publishers radio provided an outlet for recordings and seemed to have the effect of 'extending' space. In one broadcast a band or singer could potentially be heard by the listeners that they would have previously reached only via weeks of intensive touring and numerous performances across the country.

As these two dynamics came together, as radio became a *mediator* between the world of the listener and the activity of the musicians, publishers and recording companies, so radio broadcasting began to have an important impact on the distribution of musical knowledge, styles and preferences.

The ordering of repertoires

Before the introduction of radio, different types of music were very unevenly distributed across Britain. There were variations between metropolitan cities, provincial towns and rural areas and contrasts between the north and the south. Different types of music were listened to and the musical repertoire performed varied from region to region. There was not simply one easily identifiable type of 'British' music but a range of particular musics being practised in specific localities. This variety included the music of choral societies and brass bands, concert music, cafe and restaurant music, bar music, music hall, concert party, musical reviews, opera and operetta and various types of jazz-influenced dance music.

In addition to the range of music that was being performed and listened to across Britain, the 'logic' of musical change varied. New styles became popular in some parts of the country often months before they were taken up elsewhere. Paddy Scannell and David Cardiff have referred to the observations of the bandleader Henry Hall, who toured Britain during the early years of the dance band era, from about the year 1919, and who made judgements about the musical activity occurring in the regions he visited. He thought that Edinburgh and Liverpool tended to be 'selective and conservative', whereas Turnberry was 'two months behind' and Manchester and Glasgow were 'well up to date'. However, Gleneagles, a place that attracted a large number of US visitors who came to play golf, was 'totally up to the minute' (Scannell and Cardiff, 1991: 183). Hence, the temporality of musical change varied from region to region and was judged according to how quickly the new sounds, in this case from the United States, moved across the country.

Radio had two distinct impacts on this musical activity. First, it led to the construction of a national musical repertoire profile that was distinct from any regional variations. Second, it increased the speed with which new musical trends moved around the country. I shall give details about each in turn.

The new cultural intermediaries of radio became 'patrons' of musical performances before they became the programmers of recordings (Scannell and Cardiff, 1991). In doing so they selected from the diversity of musical styles available and classified music into categories that could be combined together and which would be suitable for broadcasting in the schedules they were developing. In the process, radio programmers 'uprooted all these musics from their particular social and economic settings and brought them together in a strange new abstract unity' (Scannell and Cardiff, 1991: 182). Different types of music making were lifted out of their social, cultural and immediate existential context and placed alongside each other on the radio.

In attempting to position different types of music side by side in the schedules, the programmers at the BBC adopted two approaches. The first involved providing a space for classical modern music in order to try and encourage the cultivation of serious tastes among the audience. At the same time – and against the wishes of many of its more elitist employees – the corporation programmed dance music, but presented it in a quite specific way as a form of diversion, relaxation and entertainment. In an attempt to offer both types of music, the BBC tended to steer a cautious course down the middle, and throughout the 1930s the category of 'light music' became a 'buffer zone . . . between dance music and serious music' (Scannell and Cardiff, 1991: 211). A type of music programming was introduced and then institutionalized that was firmly based around the middle-brow taste of the middle class (Frith, 1988a).

In addition to this construction of a safe middle-brow musical repertoire, radio broadcasting began accelerating the pace of musical change. It made the turnover time of popular songs much faster. Previously, when song pluggers and sheet music sellers had to travel around the country, the creation of a hit song could take months as it was promoted through different regions. However, radio accelerated the turnover time of hits and made plugging more immediate. This was occurring not simply in Britain, but throughout the parts of the world where radio was being introduced. As a study conducted in the USA in 1941 reported: 'before radio a best-selling song was popular for as long as eighteen months; now, however, the life of a hit is rarely more than four months' (MacDougald Jr, 1941: 71).

Although the duration of a song's commercial popularity had been shortened, the number of listeners that could be reached had been greatly increased. As a consequence, recording companies and publishers realized that radio allowed them to communicate simultaneously with far more people than had previously been reached through the process of plugging songs at performances around the country or by placing recordings in early versions of the juke box.

As radio began to broadcast music performances during the 1920s and 1930s, publishers adopted a number of legal and illegal methods to try and influence what was programmed. The most basic tactic involved offering cash inducements to bandleaders for agreeing to play certain pieces. Another technique was to promote vocal numbers rather than instrumental pieces, in part because many radio stations would not announce the title, and also because the title of a song was usually part of a refrain, and thus was more likely to be recalled by the listener. This continued a practice, which had been adopted by song publishers and ballad hawkers, of emphasizing a song's 'hook' – the distinctive and repetitive element that would be remembered by the listener and perhaps persuade them to make a purchase.

Since these early legal and illegal attempts by publishers and record companies to get their music played on the radio, there have been many cases of music promoters attempting to induce, persuade or simply pay broadcasters to play recordings on the radio. Such activities have often resulted in state investigations and the dismissal and prosecution of both radio station personnel and record company employees (Sklar, 1984; Dannen, 1990). At the same time, there have been many disputes about whether and how much broadcasters should pay for the 'right' to transmit recordings, conflicts that have been resolved in different ways around the world. Hence, although the relationship between radio and the record industry has often been described as one of mutually 'symbiotic' interdependence (Hirsch, 1972), it has often been far more tense. Broadcasters have been wary of and resistant to attempts to influence what they programme, but musical entrepreneurs have been continually frustrated by the way that radio has limited the opportunities available for their songs and performers.

Radio then provides various possibilities for but constraints on the distribution of popular music, and I want to pursue this issue a little further by outlining some of the different ways that radio stations operate. In doing this I shall return to a distinction I made in passing earlier, that between state-regulated and free market approaches to broadcasting.

Radio as public service or commercial commodity

As performed and recorded music began to be reorganized for and by radio programmers from the 1920s, two distinct styles of broadcasting were adopted. One was the state bureaucratization of media and cultural institutions to serve the interests of the nation, whether the 'paternalism' of the BBC in Britain or the authoritarianism of the music policy introduced under the Nazi party's dictatorship in Germany. The other tendency was the reorganization of music for radio to suit the requirements of commercial markets, where the pursuit of profit guided the rationalization of music catalogues.

Whether in the interests of serving the nation or pursuing profit, music was rationally reorganized and catalogues structured in terms of very particular selection criteria. I have already mentioned how the BBC attempted to represent the nation by steering a course down the middle in the hope that a middle-brow programming policy would not put off too many listeners. In the United States, radio was introduced in a quite different way.

In the USA radio developed as a system that could deliver the most concentrated, well-defined demographic audience to advertisers. Radio stations differentiated themselves by adopting a specific taste-genre format and targeting the specific listeners who would tune into this type of music. The first radio format that was introduced in this way was the country music station. Unlike with the British national system, the listener could tune in to such a station with the reassuring knowledge that the radio programmers were not going to attempt to entertain them with a jazz band or try and enlighten them by broadcasting the music of 'serious' composers. The advertisers and station sponsors, whose economic influence was decisive, knew that they had a very particular type of audience that could then be targeted for the promotion of specific products (hence their advertising money would go to this station rather than a rival).

This way of organizing music radio subsequently expanded until the entire radio audience in the United States had been rationalized for the presentation of specifically well defined formatted audience categories to advertisers. Rather than any one station serving the nation, radio was developed to serve specific market segments, whether metropolitan-based black rhythm and blues fans or those who listened to alternative rock on a college campus.

This commercial system of advertising-oriented programming has subsequently become widespread throughout the world. In many countries formatted commercial radio stations are increasingly competing for a share of the advertising revenue and sponsorship money of transnational corporations. Such competition induces them to target ever more specific, carefully market-researched audience groups who are then profiled and presented to the companies who may wish to influence their consumption habits. The radio stations then accommodate their music programming to match the market-researched preferences of this demographic group.

Simon Frith has argued that this type of competition between commercial stations leads to continual attempts to 'freeze the audience into a series of market tastes' (1978: 208) – static categories which do not correspond to the complex ways in which music fits into people's lives. Reebee Garofalo has made a similar point, maintaining that such segmenting strategies operate to limit 'the range of musical styles available to a given segment of the consumer market' (1986: 81). In this way, formatted radio stations contribute to the social divisions that music has the potential continually to move across. In addition, these static categories tend to inhibit musical change and present a formidable barrier to many new artists whose music does not fit neatly into such frozen musical taste formats.

Like this type of commercial model, the state-supported

approach to public service broadcasting that I referred to earlier has been duplicated in various ways around the world. However, since the middle of the 1980s this has also been influenced by the growth of commercial stations. In a media environment where more and more stations have been granted licences and started chasing listeners, the public service broadcasters have attempted to respond. In the process the ideals of public service broadcasting have begun to shift, from being based on the idea of maintaining a middle ground and serving an undivided public, to a concern with recognizing diversity and catering for a plurality of viewpoints (Morley and Robins, 1995). As this has happened a major issue of debate has concerned how such differing interests might be reconciled.

Writers advocating some form of public service broadcasting (for both television and radio) have had to grapple with three prominent questions: which 'public' is being referred to (who is being 'served')? How is the service to be funded, by a universal fee or subscription charged only to those who use it? To whom is it accountable, and does the public have the right to 'speak' or any form of access? Such questions are straightforward in the commercial model: the public is the market and it is funded by advertising revenue generated from public purchases in the market. The public has the choice to listen or not, so if a station is not effective then it will not generate enough revenue to sustain itself. The public, as and through a market, will decide whether it wants the radio commodity.

However, against the fragmented nature of commercial radio, the advocates of public service broadcasting argue that it can provide more diversity. Because it is not driven by commercial criteria, public service broadcasting can respond more sensitively to the complexity of social life by doing more than simply dividing people by commercial taste.

But the issue is far from resolved and a key question remains: can public service broadcasting provide an arena where a plurality of musics can coexist and where newer sounds can get some form of exposure? One potential problem here is that such an approach may lead to yet more attempts to educate and cultivate the tastes of the public. After all, if the markets should not decide, then who is going to judge what should and should not be played? In addition, there is considerable evidence (Barnard, 1989; Negus, 1992) to suggest that, when put under pressure from both record companies and other commercial stations, public service stations have tended to devote a large part of their programming to the most successful chart-based music and have segmented their schedules for particular publics. Ultimately, they have offered little more than the commercial stations. So, perhaps we should look elsewhere for greater possibilities.

Community and pirate: alternative variations on a theme

Both commercial radio networks and public service broadcasters have frequently made gestures towards specific communities, whether the BBC's Asian Network, which is transmitted in Leicester, or Greater London Radio's attempt to reach particular members of a locality as a niche market. In terms of radio broadcasting, a 'community' can refer to a physical locality (a neighbourhood or place) or to a 'community of interests' that might be stretched across a particular region ('gay community', for example).

Although sharing some of the characteristics that have already been mentioned, community radio tends to be driven by a very specific set of ideological principles. Often adopting radical democratic or cooperative working practices, community radio usually has the aim of being more participatory and accessible – to talk *with* people rather than *at* them (Girard, 1992; Hollander and Stappers, 1992; Lewis and Booth, 1989).

Community radio has often been set up with the object of creating an alternative radio space that is independent from the pressures of both commercial markets and state legislators. The participants in such ventures are often explicitly opposed to broadcasting the hits of commercial popular music, and often overtly against transmitting Anglo-American pop and rock music (Wallis and Malm, 1984, 1992). When music is played it is frequently part of a programme of supporting local or indigenous forms of cultural expression or allied to campaigns for political and cultural change (Girard, 1992).

Not so prominent in the large music markets of the world, community radio has tended to receive less attention than the commercial and public service stations. Might this mean that community radio is only of peripheral interest for understanding the mediation of popular music around the world? Or have its possibilities simply been neglected in favour of the radio systems preferred by the music industry?

Advocates of community radio argue that it provides the possibilities for a more accountable and participatory musical practice, one which connects and includes (rather than segments and excludes) the experiences of different musicians and audiences around the world. Community radio offers the possibility of an alternative musical space, independent from market-seeking entrepreneurs and nation-building states.

However, such possibilities have to be pursued in relation to a number of constraints. One of the main problems that community broadcasters confront is a continual shortage of resources. Run by enthusiasts and cultural activists, community radio has been supported by a range of interests including churches, governments, private investment, charitable donations, educational institutions and trade unions. In addition, money has been raised through subscriptions and fund raising and by relying on volunteers.

Despite these revenue sources, many community radio stations are continually short of cash and have responded by taking advertising and accepting the products of the music industry for transmission. The corporate control argument (Chapter 2) is not very far away from such a scenario, as critics have suggested that this will inevitably lead to compromise and cooption by the major entertainment companies.

A further obstacle for those who want to set up a community radio station is the practical and political necessity of obtaining a licence from state legislators. This is a particular problem if the state is not keen on alternative voices being heard within its borders. Here again, community radio may have to compromise with the strictures of state regulators. One alternative might be to broadcast without a licence and become a 'pirate', transmitting 'illegally' in contravention of the legislative regulations of the state.

Music pirates have ranged from those who have started transmitting for beliefs similar to those that have motivated community broadcasters to stations established by entrepreneurs merely to gain exposure for their own artists (Chapman, 1992). Pirates have broadcast from a variety of locations, including rural locations next to the borders with adjoining states, from ships at sea and from rooms high up in tower blocks in urban areas.

Pirate radio has often provided a forum for music that has been neglected and has in turn influenced the styles of programming and content of both commercial and public service radio (Barnard, 1989; Chapman, 1992). Pirate stations have also provided opportunities for connecting music with various political activities. For example, in March 1983 Radio Contemporain set up equipment and broadcast a performance of political rock music on a crowded Tokyo street in protest against the arrival of a nuclear powered US aircraft (Kogawa, 1993). Such activities were soon halted by the authorities, however, and this is one of the main problems that pirates confront – the raid from the forces of the state. Pirates have had their equipment destroyed and confiscated and been fined for transmitting. Less frequently, members of their audience have been fined for listening (Hind and Mosco, 1985). Despite such constraints, new pirates continue to begin broadcasting.

Pirate stations are usually run by enthusiasts and listened to by people who must actively seek out their transmissions. For this reason they can provide record companies with an indication of new trends and an important target group for specific types of music. Despite their illegal status many pirates have frequently received covert financial payments and promotional recordings from record companies (Chapman, 1992; Hind and Mosco, 1985). This has led to the accusation that pirates are also being coopted into the commercial system and hence are operating as little more than commercial entrepreneurs: behind the aura of illegality they have been targeting and segmenting markets just as carefully as their legal counterparts. Here again the situation is not as clear cut as such an argument might suggest, for, despite attracting commercial opportunists who wish to avoid the costs incurred by their legal counterparts, pirate radio remains an option as a 'rebel radio' for those who wish to challenge the commercial systems of musical property rights and the nation state's control of the airwaves.

The musical mediations of radio: brief summary

In the section above I have presented a fairly wide-ranging account of radio to give an indication of the three interacting and overlapping processes of mediation that I identified at the beginning of this chapter. First, I have referred to how the *technologies of transmission* have enabled musical experience and knowledge to be distributed across space and time. Second, I have indicated the *intermediary activity* of specific occupational groups who have attempted and been able to direct the development of radio practices and organize musical schedules in quite specific ways. Third, I have given an indication of the broader *social relationships* within which radio and music interact and raised a number of questions about the virtues of public service, commercial, community and pirate radio. I have also put forward these questions as part of my implicit argument that there has been no inevitability in the way in which music radio has developed so far, and also to indicate that there are a number of possible directions that radio broadcasting might take in the future. I now want to move on to a media technology that has often been viewed as a direct competitor to radio, music video.

Music video: the mediations of sound and moving image

Ever since sound was added to film in the cinema and the world's first talking picture, *The Jazz Singer*, was screened in 1927, the electronic mediation of music with moving images has been integral to the way that a large amount of recorded popular music has been experienced around the world. Music as a soundtrack and as performed by stars appearing in films and on television has contributed to the popularity of various types of music from jazz through the samba, rock-'n'-roll, soul and rap. In India, the most popular music has for many years been that of film soundtracks.

Like my account of radio above, a similar story could be told about how the mediations of the moving image have contributed a further dimension to the redistribution of musical experience and knowledge across space and time and also had an additional impact on the musical cataloguing systems of the recording industry. However, I do not want to repeat some of the ideas of my argument above with illustrations from another media form and a different historical period. Instead, I want to consider how the televisual media have contributed a further series of mediations – those *between* the recorded sounds and images of popular music. I want to pursue what has been a central question in much of the literature on this subject: what is the relationship between sound and image in video?

The domination of the image?

As video became part of the day-to-day production and promotion of popular music during the 1980s, the initial response of many performers, fans and commentators was to argue that it was trivializing music; the construction of an image had become more important than the production of sound and the ability of the listener to imagine their own images had been colonized and replaced by the promotional mechanisms of the industry.

Many writers were quick to take issue with such an argument by pointing out that for centuries music has been associated with performance and spectacle. Sean Cubitt (1991) and Jody Berland (1993b) both argued that the sounds and visuals of musical performance had actually become temporarily separated with the introduction of the technologies of the gramophone, radio, photography and silent film. But even then the visual had not disappeared completely. As Andrew Goodwin (1992) has pointed out, the 'image' was signified in the surrounding texts of popular music, such as album sleeves, newspaper and magazine articles, publicity photographs and descriptions of performers given on radio and even by the stereo 'positioning' of instruments. All contributed to how audiences were encouraged to 'imagine' the music. Video had not suddenly and simply added images to music, argued Goodwin, but built on visual codes that were already in circulation.

Goodwin made this point in an argument against the work of E. Ann Kaplan (1987), who had produced one of the first detailed pieces of analysis of music video on MTV. Kaplan had indeed presumed that the image dominated the music – an assumption that was apparent in the way that her analysis was based on film theory and conceptions of cinema spectatorship, and the manner in which she allocated videos into a typology of five categories based on visual narratives alone (romantic, socially conscious, nihilist, classical and postmodernist).

Kaplan interpreted music videos as elaborate advertisements that were programmed into an almost seamless collage by MTV and which at the same time were continually 'constructing positions' for the spectator. Her subsequent 'readings' of how specific videos 'positioned' the viewer then had almost nothing to say about how the audience were listening. The image dominated the music in

Kaplan's analysis not only because of her theoretical orientation but because she simply ignored the actual songs.

Sound and vision: semiotic connections

Goodwin took issue with Kaplan's analysis and, rather than treating them as mini-movies, approached videos in terms of the narratives of the pop song. Employing the concept of *synaesthesia* – the process whereby sensory impressions are 'carried' from one sense to another, in this case the visualization of musical sound – Goodwin argued that the images of music video were frequently connected to the music as a series of sonorial connotations, impressions and extra-musical significations.

For Goodwin, video images had not simply been imposed on a musical song but had been drawn out of the music due to the way that the music itself carried certain meanings and signified in various ways. Goodwin suggested that the sound–image relationship could be approached via the distinctions between icon, index and symbol. These terms are drawn from semiotics (the study of signs) and refer to the relationship between a signifier (what is received by our senses – word, image or sound) and what is signified (mental concept or idea):

Icons have a physical resemblance to what they signify. The most obvious icon is the image of the face which resembles the person to which it refers. The lyrics of songs can also be iconic: snarled words that resemble and signify anger, or intimate, breathy groans that attempt to communicate sexual activity, for example. Musically, synthesizers have been used iconically to signify police sirens or machinery and snare drums have been used iconically to resemble pistol shots.

An *index* connects the sign in a causal way with the object. So, for example, smoke is a visual index of fire. Here Goodwin gives the example of 'scratching', which is an index of a DJ manipulating a turntable. He also mentions various indexical signs that are used to 'place' the music, such as feedback and crowd sounds which signify a concert event and the '1, 2, 3, 4' count-in which is an index of an ensemble performance.

A *symbol* is a sign that is connected to an object as a matter of convention within a specific cultural context. An example here might be an electric guitar powerchord, which could be a symbol of macho prowess, which in turn can be reinforced by the way the image of the guitar might be used visually as a phallic symbol and also in the harsh, husky male vocals that might be sung to its accompaniment.

These three concepts can be used to indicate how musical sounds alone can signify a specific mental image. Such musical significations can then be combined with video images in various ways. In discussing this, Goodwin has introduced three further concepts to indicate how the relations between sound and image are mediated and combined in quite specific ways – illustration, amplification and disjuncture.

Goodwin uses the term *illustration* to refer to one of the most predictable ways in which sound and image are connected, whereby the visual narrative tells the story of the song lyric or the lyrics exhort listeners to 'feel' a particular way (sexy or like dancing) and the visual tries to illustrate the mood of the song. The visual may also illustrate the music by cutting on the beat or by emphasizing syncopations. *Amplification* occurs when the video adds new meanings that do not conflict with the lyrics but which are not necessarily apparent in the words, or when visual pulses and moving patterns are introduced in such a way as to elaborate on the narrative of the song. Finally, Goodwin points to videos in which there is a *disjuncture* between the lyrics and visual images, where the latter are not apparently signified by the words of the song. More generally, this is a type of video in which the visual does not seem to 'fit' the mood of the music.

Hence, Goodwin proposes a series of categories (icon, index, symbol) that may be applied to images, lyrics and music. He then proposes a way of identifying how such combinations might work together (illustration, amplification and disjuncture). This is just one way of approaching the sound–image relations in music video and may be a very useful method for developing an in-depth analysis of how particular videos are put together and signify meaning. Despite Goodwin's attention to the music in his analysis, however, the distinctions that he introduces between illustration, amplification and disjuncture are only really developed in his own study in relation to the image and lyrics. Such an approach might lead to the assumption that the listener will catch all of the lyrics of a song, which is something that frequently occurs only after several listenings.

With this point in mind, I want to introduce some concepts from Claudia Gorbman's (1987) analysis of sound in the cinema as a way of charting more general connections between sound and image in music video. As a way of making broader distinctions prior to going into depth and attempting to untangle the iconic, indexical and symbolic threads of illustration, amplification and disjuncture that bind lyrical, musical and visual meanings together, I shall refer to the concepts of *diagetic* and *non-diagetic* and *parallelism* and *counterpoint*.

Diagetic is a term for the music that seems to issue from a source within the narrative of a film (such as a radio, singer or trumpet player). In contrast, *non-diagetic* is the term for the music that accompanies the action in the film (the source of the sound is not visible). Although a number of music videos have contained dramatic non-diagetic sequences, most rely heavily on a diagetic approach; the sources of the sounds are usually quite explicitly signified. One of the most persistent *hooks* in videos is the use of the face of the singer. This tends to serve a similar function to that of the voice in a recording by directly addressing the viewer and listener (Cubitt, 1991; Goodwin, 1992). Faces tend to coincide with the vocal address in the song, with perhaps several faces appearing for the many voices of the chorus.

Parallelism refers to how music directly follows the action in a very predictable way. In movies a whole series of conventions and clichés have grown up in an attempt to do this, such as the high-pitched sustained strings that parallel the mounting suspense in a thriller, or the fast moving staccato bass, guitar and drums that may accompany someone running down a street. Parallelism has been most apparent in music video when the images have been merely following and 'illustrating' the lyrics of a song, or when the visuals have paralleled the rhythm, timbre or melody of the music. In contrast, and as the term implies, *counterpoint* attempts to add to or interact with the visual narrative in some way. Rather than just thinking about amplification and disjuncture – an elaboration or mismatch – between lyrics and visuals, the concept of counterpoint enables us to consider the interactions between musical sounds and visuals in a more general way.

An example of counterpoint can be found in David Bowie's video for *Let's Dance* (1982). In this video the soft polished funk and the singer's declamatory request to 'put on your red shoes and dance the blues' is not issued in a nightclub, as might perhaps be expected, but in a down-beat neighbourhood bar. The romantic lyrics and the bright brassy major chords of the song are then contrasted with the visual struggles of Aborigines against poverty and exploitation in housing and menial employment (with Bowie, the singer of the song, appearing in the visual narrative as a critical factory inspector who is contributing to this oppression). Bowie's tanned features, almost white blonde hair and all-white shirt, trousers and gloves are in stark contrast to the T-shirts, jeans and working clothes of dancers in the bar and the darker skin and hair of the Aborigines.

The contrast is emphasized as the hook of the singer's vocal address appears inserted as a visual bubble within a narrative that follows a young Aboriginal man and woman through the desert, forest and city. The video makes use of numerous diagetic sequences as Bowie sings while strumming a guitar and plays an electric guitar solo in the desert while the sun is setting. Counterpoint is used as a deliberate technique in a number of places: at one point the male Aborigine drags a heavy piece of machinery through traffic and the woman attempts to clean the tarmac on the road as a chorus sings 'let's dance'. At another point, a group of Aborigines trample on the red shoes that have been sung about, and then with a touch of romantic irony a loving Aboriginal couple buy jewellery with an American Express card.

This video, which demands a more detailed analysis than this brief sketch, provides some interesting examples of the interplay between lyrics, visuals and music. It contains a complex yet quite deliberately put together pattern of musical, visual and lyrical elements that work as icons, indexes and symbols, for example: red shoes – in the lyrics and image; the major seventh vocal harmony that introduces the song – one of *the* pop clichés; the use of various lyrical clichés – 'my love for you' would break 'my heart in two'; images of the desert, forests and people walking barefoot to the accompanying overproduced bassy funk driven 'urban' sound.

I mention this video here as just one example of the way that the meanings signified by the visuals and music can interact and provide a counterpoint to one another. But I also mention it because of the explicit way in which the musical, lyrical and visual elements refer to other songs, musical conventions, social relationships and political circumstances that are outside of the immediate world of this promotional video. Whether Bowie's video was a sympathe-tic political statement or merely involved the aesthetic com-modification of poverty and suffering is open to debate. But I would argue, at least from the discussions about this song in which I have participated, that the visual and musical hooks in this video have been arranged in such a way as actually to *raise* this as a question.

On this latter issue, I return to Goodwin's critique of Kaplan in which he opposes her idea that videos construct a 'position' for viewers: his point is that audiences cannot simply be *placed*. Instead, Goodwin argues that videos have been put together with an aware-ness that they will be viewed and heard by audiences who have acquired considerable knowledge of the codes and conventions of popular music, television and advertising. However, unlike the active audience theorists discussed in Chapter 1, Goodwin is scep-tical about the idea that videos are then open to numerous possible interpretations. Instead, he contends that music videos work in a relatively coherent way to 'frame audiences' responses to songs' (Goodwin, 1992: 89).

One of the implications of Goodwin's argument is that music videos may direct audiences to certain meanings and not others. Hence, we could perhaps think of music videos as producing a particular audio-visual agenda for the audiences of a song. As re-search on the combination of sounds and images in instructional films and videos (Seidman, 1981) and studies of music in film (Gorbman, 1987; Kalinak, 1992) have shown, music and images tend to work together to direct attention to certain themes and issues and not others.

Assuming, as Goodwin suggests, that the audience to whom *Let's Dance* is addressed were (and are) very knowledgeable about the codes and conventions of popular culture, then this video cannot simply be interpreted in numerous ways. Instead, the video 'frames' a particular agenda from which we can then make a limited number of interpretations (rather than simply providing the possi-bilities for multiple meanings). Like much popular art that attempts social commentary, however, this video raises issues about class, race and inequality in Australia, but it provides no clues as to how to resolve them.

This video song is also illustrative of Goodwin's point that videos combine a complexity of musical, visual and lyrical meanings in a *coherent* way. The reasons for such coherence can be pursued further by considering the more commercially oriented mediations of music video.

Repetition and the aesthetics of music video

Like listening to recorded popular music, one of the characteristics of video consumption is that it involves an engagement with a cultural form that is usually purchased or recorded from broadcasts and then subject to active reviewing a number of times. As Philip Hayward (1990) has pointed out, this is an aspect of which directors and performers are very well aware, quoting David Byrne's belief that it is because of this that music videos have to be 'multi-layered.'

Hence, quite regardless of whether a music video might start life as an 'advert' for a song, like a music recording it will gradually be understood and appreciated over time and through repeated viewing and listening. An awareness of this has led video directors to develop an increasingly 'decorative' aesthetic (Hayward, 1990) in which meanings can be generated by various combinations and juxtapositions of visuals, lyrics and music. In pursuing this point, I want to argue that this decorative aesthetic has been adopted by the music industry as the basis of a new type of audio-visual hook. Knowledge of how music video is experienced and used has come to inform the work of the intermediaries who are involved in the production and distribution of videos.

Semiotic particles: the multiple hooks of music video

Despite the numerous useful suggestions he provides for approaching videos, Goodwin's detailed analysis of music video tends to assume an *ideal* viewing and listening situation. Significantly neglected are the additional mediations produced by the *context* of reception and the *activities* that accompany video consumption. These additional mediations are significant because, unlike cinema, where the audience is seated in the dark with visual images projected on to a screen and with little else to look at, video can be received in a variety of contexts. While attendance at a cinema and the public activities that accompany cinema-going have been increasingly regulated (eating popcorn but no smoking), the activities that accompany the sounds and images of television are numerous.

As Cubitt (1991) has pointed out, the television image is smaller than film and watched in the light rather than the dark. Hence its 'messages' (whether in dramas, films or news) are in competition with other surrounding meanings. As a number of researchers have found, television is actively 'used' in a variety of contexts and is not simply 'watched' (Morley, 1992; Silverstone, 1994).

With this in mind I want to suggest that music video can become an element of audio-visual furniture. In a domestic environment it can be used as a mute moving picture or as a soundtrack to accompany other activities (eating and drinking, talking, reading, making love). The domestic experience of music video will also vary depending on how the television is watched within the family environment: whether collectively in the working-class home with one television set or more individually in the bourgeois suburban home with a television in each room. Outside of the domestic sphere, music videos can be experienced in a variety of places – in shops or showrooms, in nightclubs and bars – places of work for some and sites of consumption for others. Videos, on screens of varying sizes, can be encountered in malls, in train and bus stations and on many streets and in other public places.

Bearing these contexts and accompanying activities in mind, I want to extend Goodwin's analysis of video as composed of a number of musical, lyrical and visual signifiers that are put together in a coherent way. Instead of thinking about lyrics as poetry, visuals as narratives, and music in terms of melodic structures or rhythmic patterns, I want to argue that music video can be approached as being composed of a series of *repeated semiotic particles*. Such particles combine music, image and words in particular ways that mediate music in a manner that *allows* for various contexts and accompanying activities. In suggesting this, I am not denying that lyrics can be poetry, that melodies and rhythms have distinctive sequential and cyclical patterns and that visuals have a narrative. What I want to emphasize is that as audiences we do not often receive them in this way. What we get in many circumstances are bits and pieces that have been put together in a deliberately decorative and multi-layered way.

Just as songwriters and publishers responded to radio by emphasizing refrains, keywords and song titles, so music video directors and recording companies have developed ways of producing and employing identifiable hooks that *combine* visual, lyrical and musical elements. These hooks are created as repetitive semiotic particles that continually recur throughout a video. It is these which, even if we are only giving a video our partial attention in a bar or while waiting to cross a street, can hook us and make us remember important elements of the song and the singer.

By making this point I am arguing against the idea that the 'commercial' element of a video aesthetic is present as the subordination of the popular song to the conventions of advertising and promotional propaganda. It is far more subtle. The commercial that is 'within' the creative practice of video can be located in the way that hooks are developed which can both attract us as distracted consumers giving videos our partial attention but also give pleasure over repeated concentrated viewings and listenings.

To approach music video as a coherent and ordered series of semiotic particles that can be accessed at any moment of their duration while engaging in other activities would place the contexts of mediation and consumption more firmly in the frame of reference. From this starting point, connections could then be made to the practices of the intermediaries who are in a position to put together and programme videos (whether at MTV, Viva or Sky). In addition, an analysis of how individuals appreciate and build up interpretations and understandings of videos over time might help explain how music videos sustain themselves, give pleasure and generate new meanings over repeated listenings and in the process become much more than advertisements. However, the research programme that I am implying here will take us back to the audience, and, as I concluded in Chapter 1, there is much to be learned about music audiences.

Conclusion: mediations as distribution struggles

In this chapter I have provided various examples to illustrate the idea that popular music is mediated by particular transmission technologies, the work of specific occupational groups and in relation to a wider series of social relationships. One of the issues that has been implicit in this chapter is that of *distribution*, the processes whereby music comes to be allocated among different audiences. Although this is often viewed as an element of production – as the networks of warehouses, trucks and routines through which sub-contractors relay the industry's recordings for purchase – I would like to advocate a broader approach to the concept of distribution and suggest that it is thought of as an aspect of mediation. We could regard the mediators I have referred to in this chapter as intervening in the communication of music, but we can also conceive of them as involved in the distribution of music. So, historically, ballad peddlers, radio broadcasters and video programmers have all been playing a part in the way that musical knowledge and experiences come to be distributed among particular audiences. I am thinking of distribution as an important *dynamic* and *consequence* of processes of mediation. Hence, significant struggles over musical meaning are not just occurring during production or among audiences but among those moments in between. To illustrate this conclusion in a concrete way I will briefly refer to the increasingly important role of retailers and telecommunications companies.

Since the beginning of the 1980s the large entertainment megastores (such as Tower, HMV, FNAC, Virgin) have expanded the size of their premises, increased the number of their stores and broadened the geographical scope of their operations. Taking an ever-increasing share of the recorded music retail market and forcing out of business many of the small specialist record shops, the megastores have developed increasingly sophisticated ways of gathering information about consumer activity. Making particular use of computers, they have been able to use their 'knowledge of the consumer' to exert a significant influence on the production of music and on the way recordings are purchased (du Gay and Negus, 1994).

Megastore retailers have influenced record company catalogues by restricting space for newer and less easily classifiable music (sounds that a retail buyer assumes will sit on the shelf for long periods before being purchased). Together with the formatting strategies of radio stations, this has contributed to a reduction in the risks record companies are prepared to take with new and unusual artists. In addition, retailers have been exerting an influence on the packaging and designs that are used in promotional material and on album covers. Artists whose profile is not compatible with the corporate identity of the store are often unlikely to receive prominent retail promotion.

Retailers have also been exerting an influence on consumers by providing very specific purchasing environments (divided up very much like the radio station format categories) by allocating music to different locations within the stores. Routes are then signposted through a store in a quite calculated attempt to lead the prospective purchaser to certain types of music and to encourage more than one purchase per visit. Retailers have been researching consumer behaviour and then acting on this in a quite deliberate attempt to direct purchasing activity towards certain products and not others. Hence, retailers are important mediators who are bringing together production and consumption in quite specific ways and exerting a direct impact on how music comes to be distributed (for an extended discussion of this, see du Gay and Negus, 1994).

According to some commentators, however, we do not need to worry about the power of retailers, because the record shop is shortly to disappear. As music is digitalized, so it is argued that electronic delivery (or digital audio broadcasting) will enable the transmission of compact disc-quality sound directly into the home. The claim here is that music will no longer be disseminated by the traditional process of manufacturing cassette tapes and discs, and then distributing these in bulky parcels over land, sea and air to be finally placed onto the racks in record shops. Instead, electronic delivery will transmit compact disc-quality sound via satellite and along fibre optic cables directly into the home.

Consumers will no longer need to visit a recorded music shop. Instead, those of us who can afford the technology will simply study a catalogue of music via a computer screen, make a selection and then wait for the sound, lyrics, graphics and moving images to be delivered directly into the home. This will then be charged when the telephone bill arrives at the end of the month. As more and more recordings are converted into digital information, the entire back catalogue of recordings (in principle all sound recordings that have ever been made) could be held in a databank. The electronic recorded sound store of the future could be an electronic cultural warehouse that will be directly accessed from the home or work place. However, when considering such possibilities it is worth bearing in mind one of the points I made earlier, that new forms of mediation and distribution do not simply replace existing practices but set up new (often completely unforeseen) musical relationships and activities.

This means of distributing music is being taken very seriously by the International Federation of the Phonographic Industry (IFPI). This is the recording industry body that attempts to monitor and control who is producing, distributing and listening to music. One of IFPI's primary concerns is with the production and distribution of illegal 'pirate' recordings. It is a lot harder to spot the electronic movement of music across continents, however, than it is to follow and intercept a lorry full of unofficial pirate tape recordings or discs (itself an operation requiring considerable investment in surveillance and detective work, etc.) (Fox, 1993; IFPI, 1993).

It is not only music industry organizations that are interested in such developments. Telecommunications companies have also recognized the potentials of using existing fax and phone networks and their fibre optic cable and satellite systems for the distribution of music. In 1993, music video retailer Blockbuster negotiated a deal with IBM that enabled them to download electronically delivered sound in-store and manufacture their own CDs. This infuriated Al Teller, the chairman of MCA, who angrily declared that record companies were already in the 'distribution business' and that they did not want to see somebody else taking over the music industry's distribution networks (Goodman, 1993).

The increasing involvement of computer companies and telecommunications corporations in the distribution of sounds and images (Miller, 1994) will mean that, perhaps more than in the past, studying the recording industry will also involve studying a communication industry: British Telecom and AT&T may become as important as Polygram, Sony or Time-Warner. As the major record labels and their parent companies complete ever more deals with telecommunications corporations, I will conclude by reminding you of one the themes of this chapter: communication processes and media technologies have been central to the production and consumption of popular music for centuries, and these have been introduced within and shaped by very specific social circumstances and political and economic relationships. There are many mediating links that connect the 'control' of the industry with the 'creativity' of the audience.

CHAPTER FOUR
IDENTITIES

The issue of identity – the characteristic qualities attributed to and maintained by individuals and groups of people – has been the subject of increasing political argument and theoretical debate throughout the 1980s and 1990s. The 'crisis of identity', in Kobena Mercer's (1994) words, has concerned the fact that something which was once taken for granted and assumed to be 'fixed, coherent and stable' has been called into doubt and become loaded with uncertainties. A central question has concerned the individual subject: do we have a core personality or 'nature' that remains unchanged over time or do we take on, acquire or simply make up and adopt new characteristics throughout our life? A further question has been raised about the way in which groups of people are labelled and socially categorized. Do terms such as man, woman, English, Asian, lesbian, Latin and working class capture the qualities and shared experiences that bind people to a common identity, or are these merely arbitrary imposed labels based on the most superficial of indices (physical features, place of birth, sexual preference or social location) which obscure a diversity of activities and values? If this sounds complicated, yet another question has been asked about how individuals live their lives across such categories: do we possess multiple identities which are manifested in various ways at different moments? Are identities to become increasingly hyphenated (white-working-class-heterosexual-male)? With such apparently fragmented identities, is political solidarity and a shared social world to be lived through the recognition of difference and diversity rather than through old conceptions of community, class, ethnicity, gender and nation?

While there is no clear-cut answer to such questions, they have placed on the cultural and political agenda important issues which are of direct relevance to the study of popular music. In its own way, the study of music has something to contribute to current debates about these issues. For many years music has been discussed through the use of a number of identity labels which have implied certain correspondences between the characteristics of individuals or groups and musical styles – notable here are terms such as Irish music, Latin jazz, working-class music, Brazilian music, gay disco. Yet, as the stability and coherence of social identities has been called into question, so the idea that there may be any fixed link between a social group and particular musical sounds has also become an issue of contention. In this chapter I shall outline and illustrate recent debates about this matter in three broad areas. First I shall discuss how music has been racialized through the label of black music. I shall then consider how salsa music has been understood as a specifically Latin and working-class cultural form. In the final section I shall focus on some of the ways that different genres of popular music have been sexed and gendered.

A general theoretical idea will weave throughout this discussion, one that draws upon the broader debates about identity to which I have already referred. This concerns a shift from *essentialist* ideas about cultural identity – the notion that individuals of a particular social type possess certain essential characteristics and that these are found *expressed* in particular cultural practices – towards the idea that cultural identities are not fixed in any essential way but are actively created through particular communication processes, social practices and 'articulations' within specific circumstances. The meaning of and uses to which essentialist ideas can be put should hopefully become clear through this chapter. The concept of articulation will be used more implicitly and alluded to in places before being outlined more fully at the end of the chapter.

Black and white music

The term black music signifies a connection between a particular people and a specific type of music. In *Sound Effects* (1983) Simon Frith drew on Marshall Stearns's definitions from studies of jazz to identify a number of characteristics of black music. He argued that

black music is performance music rather than composition music . . . [it]
is based on the immediate effects of melody and rhythm rather than on
the linear development of theme and harmony . . . it is improvised –
spontaneously composed . . . the value of black music derives from its
emotional impact . . . black music is immediate and democratic – a performance is unique and listeners of that performance become part of
it . . . – the qualities that are valued in spontaneous music making are
emotional rather than technical . . . (1983: 16–17)

In stressing performance, immediacy, improvisation and emotionality, Frith argued that 'the essence of black music is the expression
of the performer's feelings . . . black music is essentially "body music" ' (1983: 17–20). I want to emphasize the way that Frith identifies
an 'essence' to black music here because I shall shortly be moving
on to a critique of such an argument.

Frith suggested that it was this 'spontaneous basis of black music'
that 'initially limited its pop possibilities' (1983: 17). But it was also
this spontaneous quality that attracted hip white musicians and
critics. Drawing on the corporate control position (Chapter 2), Frith
maintained that 'white popular music has been invigorated by
styles and values drawn from black culture – styles and values that
lose their original force and meaning as they pass through the bland
wringer of mass music but are rediscovered by each new generation
of hip musicians and audiences' (1983: 16).

Frith suggested that there had been a continual, cyclical
cooptation of black musical forms by the white industry and audiences. But, more than this, he presented a scenario in which black
music has a dual impact – 'white popular music' had become a
bland mass-mediated version of more immediate original black
styles, while black styles and values had provided inspiration to the
more hip white musicians.

Although offering a comprehensive definition of black music,
Frith did not provide such a detailed characterization of what
'white popular music' might be. As Richard Dyer (1988) has written,
when considering this issue in the cinema, the characteristics of
whiteness are often more elusive; there are far more definitions of
what is black. In addition, Dyer argued that white representation
always seems to refer to something more (a class position and
geographical place, for example). Such tendencies can also be found
in discussions of music in which the 'something more' is often
signified in the terms 'Western' or 'European classical'.

When identifying some of the characteristics of white music,
Frith contrasted the 'collective' dialogic call-and-response that black

music establishes between performer and audience to the way in which 'white pop' addresses listeners in terms of a private conversation (1983: 18). Frith also set up a contrast between 'western dance forms' and black music, arguing that, 'whereas western dance forms control body movements and sexuality itself with formal rhythms and innocuous tunes, black music expresses the body, hence sexuality with a direct physical beat and an intense emotional sound – sound and beat are *felt* rather than interpreted via a set of conventions' (1983: 21).

According to this argument, black music is music of the body, and the body – on this definition – means uninhibited and 'natural' expressions of sexuality. Black music is spontaneous, it is improvised and felt rather than thought about, and it is not played according to conventions. In contrast 'western dance' (by implication, white popular music) is restrained, composed and played according to a series of learnt conventions.

The dichotomy that Frith employed to characterize black music in this way combined two 'essentialisms', one socio-biological and the other musicological. First, it was based on the idea that black people are more 'natural', physical and spontaneous than white people, who in turn are more constrained by social conventions. Such an approach located black music in what Paul Gilroy has referred to as the 'place prepared for black cultural expression in the hierarchy of creativity generated by the pernicious metaphysical dualism that identifies blacks with the body and whites with the mind' (1993a: 97). Second, and connected to this idea of bodily spontaneity, black music was characterized as having certain intrinsic musical features – improvised and spontaneously created rather than composed. In the following sections I will outline arguments that challenge such assumptions, and which suggest that the category black music should be employed with a critical awareness of the ways in which it has been and can be used in a racially essentialist way.

Unpacking the category of black music

An argument for adopting a more critical approach to the category of black music has been put by Philip Tagg (1989) in an article in which he also raised questions about the characteristics identified with European and African-American music. Tagg's starting point was with basic dictionary definitions, on which he drew to argue that there can be no music that is in some essential way black. Black is a colour: music a particular way of organizing sound. It may seem like an obvious point, but Tagg sought to make it clear from the outset that the blackness is not *in* the music but has been identified with certain stylistic traits that can be *found* in the music made by *people* who are described as black. The issue is therefore social rather than musical. Tagg also noted that the term black music was not usually used in a universalistic way to refer to all 'black people' but more often adopted as a synonym for African-American. With these issues highlighted, Tagg then moved on to his main socio-musicological discussion.

Tagg has claimed that there are no essential characteristics to black music, European music or African-American music and illustrated this argument with a discussion of blue notes, call-and-response (antiphony), syncopation and improvisation – all have been identified as key characteristics of African-American or black music. Although acknowledging that these stylistic traits *can* be found in much music created by black people, Tagg's point is that they have no *necessary* or essential belonging to black music and can be detected in the music created by different peoples at various times across the world.

In more detail, what are called 'blue notes' are the bluesy slides between notes that are characteristic of much popular music. They are often interpreted as 'felt' rather than played according to conventions because they cannot be easily written down in European musical notation. Frith drew on such assumptions when contrasting black and Western forms of expression, comparing melismatic 'blues vocal techniques . . . with the perfect pitch and enunciation of a classical singer' (1983: 18).

Whether or not you understand musical notation, if you listen to a lot of music then you would probably recognize blue notes, particularly when singers seem to slide their voice up or down across an instrumental backing. Tagg has neatly compared blue notes to 'singing between the cracks on the piano' (1989: 288), and points out that these can be found in numerous vocal styles throughout the world and in many white European folk traditions, particularly in Ireland and Scandinavia.

Tagg noted the appearance of blue notes in Europe in order to take issue with those who characterize European music as formal, rigid and innocuous. According to Tagg, what is often referred to as 'European music' is frequently a highly selective stereotype that contains 'the most reactionary, elitist, bourgeois, conservative and non-dynamic view of European music imaginable' (1989: 292). For Tagg this is not straightforwardly European music but a highly selective caricature that ignores hundreds of European musical traditions (particularly rural folk and urban working-class music) and which is ignorant of the 'classical' music which contains blue notes, syncopation and improvisation. One of the reasons why black people have often been portrayed as improvisers rather than composers is that racism has rendered their compositions invisible and inaudible. Early in the twentieth century Scott Joplin wrote an opera, but could not get it staged by white entrepreneurs and spent his time performing ragtime. Similarly, despite his ability, jazz pianist Art Tatum could not gain employment as a performer of classical music. In addition, when black jazz musicians were improvising they were not simply feeling their way through music in a spontaneous way, but attempting to create quite specific aesthetic and social effects. As Frank Kofsky has pointed out, in the 1940s Charlie Parker, Dizzy Gillespie and Thelonious Monk were attempting to substitute a 'paradigm, bebop, based on harmonic improvisation with the metrical unit an eighth note, for one based on melodic improvisation with the metrical unit a quarter note' (Kofsky, 1970: 157).

Tagg's further point was about call-and-response, the dialogic exchange between singer and other members of an ensemble or between vocalist and audience. This has often been identified as a characteristic peculiar to black or African-American music. Frith, for example, contrasted the way black singers combined individual and collective expression through call-and-response with the way 'white pop' singers directed their messages to individuals as private conversations (1983: 18). Likewise, Gregory Stephens, when analysing rap music, has made a similar contrast between 'Eurocentric discourse' as unidirectional and speaker oriented and 'Afrocentric discourse' as interactive and audience oriented (Stephens, 1991: 75).

Tagg has acknowledged that call-and-response is a prominent part of certain Christian churches in Africa, the United States and the Caribbean, but argues that this style of dialogic cultural communication is not unique to black people or Africa. Call-and-response patterns can be found in music produced throughout the world over the past two thousand years. It is not call-and-response *per se* that is a characteristic of African-American music, but particular types of call-and-response pattern. Hence, any claims about the essentially more democratic character of black music would need to demonstrate how this was more democratic than other patterns of call-and-response found in white music.

Tagg's general point is that there are no intrinsic musical styles that are essential to black music or African-American or European music. This does not imply that we can not identify particular characteristics in the music performed by black and white people, but it does suggest that these need to be approached far more carefully and in relation to specific social circumstances and cultural factors. In particular we should be wary of simple binary stereotypes that have been used to separate black and white musics and European and African culture. Black music made by African-American people is not necessarily any more spontaneous than white music made in Europe, and as much thought has gone into the development of the 'spontaneous' techniques of bebop as into the 'improvisations' of Bach.

A non-essentialist approach to black music

One possible response to Tagg's critique might be to conclude, as David Hatch and Stephen Millward (1987) do, that the term black music is a 'counter-productive' category and hence to be avoided in serious scholarship. However, we cannot escape the issue so easily, and neither Hatch and Millward nor Tagg provide much guidance for seeking an alternative. This poses a particular dilemma in light of the fact that so many people use the term, notably black artists and audiences who are struggling with the legacy of being *defined* in racial terms in the first place. For this reason, and for indicating the way in which musical practices have continually to negotiate racial classifications, Paul Gilroy has maintained that the terminology should be retained but used in a non-essentialist manner. In his writing about the historical and contemporary forms of black expression, Gilroy (1993a, 1993b) has argued against two theoretical tendencies.

First there is an 'exceptionalist' claim that relies on a model of an essential, unchanging, racial self – a type of 'ethnic absolutism'. When associated with white writers this might be construed as a romanticization of the apparently 'natural' spontaneous, expressive and emotional traits of a stereotype 'other' judged against the convention-riddled world of middle-class restraint. When proffered from black writers, this is often associated with black 'nationalism' and calls for self-determination, separatism or self-supporting communities. Guiding this approach is often the belief that all black people are essentially African or that there is a 'black thing' that those who are not black cannot understand. From this perspective the diversity of black populations is unproblematic; there is an underlying racial self, a source of identity that produces the characteristics of a particular aesthetic and corporeal sensibility.

In contrast to this is what Gilroy has characterized as a 'constructivist' or pluralist position. For Gilroy such an approach abandons any notion of similarities or a shared identity between black people. Instead, racial identities are seen as being signified and constructed through various codes and everyday practices so that what it means to be black will vary across space and time. In contrast to the cultural insiderism of 'it's a black thing', such a pluralist position is signified in the popular vernacular phrase 'different strokes for different folks'. Gilroy argues that the problem with this position is that, while it challenges any essential nature to blackness and hence *does* critique the essentialist position, it then ignores the appeal of the first position as a popular affirmation of black culture.

Gilroy has attempted to steer a course between these positions while retaining the racial category, reasoning that, for the large numbers of people who have to comprehend their life through the practices of racial subordination, the terminology of race and blackness cannot simply be removed from the analytical vocabulary or reduced to an activity of social construction. In seeking to avoid any notion of a black or African essence and to emphasize the variations in black expressive styles, Gilroy has argued that black music should be understood in relation to two key theoretical concepts: that of the diaspora of the black Atlantic world and the idea of a changing same. I shall give a brief outline of each concept.

Historically, the black people of the Atlantic world – a space connecting Africa, the USA, the Caribbean and Europe – are living with the legacy of being forcibly removed from Africa and shipped to the 'new world' as slaves (Gilroy, 1987). The *roots* of the contemporary black experience can therefore be traced back to Africa and the sudden brutal disruption introduced by slavery. Yet, the subsequent *routes* that black people have taken and the cultural forms that have been created cannot be understood simply in terms of common origins in Africa. Against forms of ahistorical 'ethnic absolutism' (an unchanging Africanness) Gilroy suggests that the cultural and political connections that bind black people together have been continually *created* through identities and practices that have been generated during processes of movement and mediation (1987, 1993a). Gilroy's concept of a 'black Atlantic' is an attempt to move away from essentialist, bounded and nationalist perspectives and towards a diasporic concept of black identity.

Gilroy has also drawn on LeRoi Jones's (1965) account of how African slaves *became* American and in the process created a cultural 'blues continuum' to suggest that black cultural forms – particularly music – can be understood in terms of the concept of a *changing same*. Gilroy acknowledges that this is a difficult task, but urges that black cultural forms should not be understood as an expression of the continual transmission of fixed essences through time. Instead, black music should be approached as part of a more discontinuous process in which cultural traditions are continually remade and new 'hybrid' identities are created. In the following section I want briefly to illustrate how Gilroy's concepts are useful by considering some of the characteristics of reggae and rap.

Reggae and rap: musics of the black Atlantic

Reggae began gaining widespread distribution during the early 1970s and became particularly influential just before Bob Marley's untimely death in 1981. Since this time the reggae rhythm has continued to be produced and enjoyed across the world and Marley's recordings have repeatedly featured in the lists of international best-selling albums. An essentialist analysis of this music might view reggae as an inherently black form of expression, the reaffirmation of African roots being expressed by ex-slaves in Jamaica. However, reggae was a 'hybrid' music that took on slightly different forms depending on when and where it was being created.

Dick Hebdige (1977) has described reggae as polymorphous, a musical mosaic in which no one element dominates. Originally developed in Jamaica, it combined the smooth sounds of soul and rhythm and blues that were being produced in the United States (and heard via recordings and radio broadcasts transmitted to the Caribbean), and overlaid these with syncopated rhythms derived from Africa. Reggae employed the call-and-response patterns typical of the Pentecostal Church, but connected these with the scans and patois of Jamaican street talk. The musical mosaic was integrated with lyrics whose reference to an experience of slavery was signified in the use of creole language that was a particular mutation of seventeenth-century English. To this was added a specific form of redemptive Christian imagery and metaphor based on an interpretation of the Bible that had again developed under slavery and which led to the belief in Rastafari and the concern with a spiritual reunification with Africa (Hebdige, 1977, 1987).

But reggae was not used just to signify the historical legacies of a black experience in the Caribbean. When brought across the Atlantic 'it ceased, in Britain, to signify an exclusively ethnic, Jamaican style' (Gilroy, 1993a: 82). In London reggae was used as a musical form to express the experience of emigration across the Atlantic and the attempt to find a place and a voice as a first- and second-generation immigrant within Britain. Struggling with poor living conditions and facing police harassment and racism, many black artists recorded songs that made a direct comment on their experiences in 1970s Britain. Notable here was the reggae poet Linton Kwesi Johnson, who combined political critique and poetic cultural commentary with the flowing bass and staccato brass-driven reggae of the Dennis Bovell Dub Band.

But, if reggae was developed initially as a way of signifying a particular experience of being black, it was soon used by white musicians to construct a sense of their own 'ethnicity' and their relationship to blackness. Linton Kwesi Johnson was at one point a support act for The Clash, a white punk band who explicitly acknowledged their affection for reggae and their sense of identification with its overtly socio-political use by black people. The Clash mixed up reggae and rock, frequently employing the distinctive syncopated reggae off-beat guitar and more fluid bass lines but retaining the conventional rock bass drum and snare pattern. Hebdige has referred to such cultural forms that emerged during this period as a 'white translation of black ethnicity' – an often confused and occasionally contradictory result of the interaction of young black and white people in London and a particular white response to black music. By the end of the 1970s, the reggae rhythm had become a 'global' beat, partly through the popularity of Bob

Marley and also as new bands began basing their full repertoire on reggae rhythms (The Police and UB40 being two of the most commercially successful) or employing reggae rhythms on specific tracks (as did ABBA, Elton John and Bob Dylan, for example).

Like reggae, rap is a music that was originally connected to the particular experiences of black people but which has also become a global beat. When approaching rap, however, it is even harder to maintain an essentialist position. As Tricia Rose (1994) has pointed out, the music so clearly brings together a variety of elements that any continuities with the narratives of the blues or emotionality of southern soul have to be heard as only one of the many threads that are woven together in this music.

Rap is one element of a broader hip-hop culture that was being created throughout the 1970s by predominantly black and Latino dancers, musicians and graffiti artists in New York. As a musical form rap began to appear on recordings from the late 1970s and drew on the Caribbean vocalizing associated with Jamaican sound systems, African rhythmic patterns, rhythm and blues and soul styles. These were connected to fragments of Euro-disco music and particularly to the synthesized electronic sounds of Kraftwerk, a German band who had themselves taken basic rhythm and blues patterns and mutated them into an often ironic electronic synthesizer-based style. This was then reused when imported back across the Atlantic.

Rap was created out of a series of musical exchanges across the Atlantic, forged together with the techniques of scratching and mixing, using turntables, mixers and drum machines. It was formed initially out of specific conditions within the Bronx area of New York City. Unlike British reggae artists, who were responding to the experience of *immigration*, rap in the USA was formed out of the experience of urban *segregation*. Following blues, jazz and rhythm and blues (Kofsky, 1970), the ghetto was central to the emergence of rap, and the music's 'cultural potency' was fostered in the racially segregated conditions under which it was created (Rose, 1994).

Although rap emerged as a 'black music', it was not exclusively black musicians who created it nor was it just black audiences who danced and listened to it. Latin and white musicians were involved in its creation, and it has enjoyed wide appeal among different audiences. Unlike Hatch and Millward (1987), who proposed that the involvement of white musicians in the creation of black music is a reason for not using the term, Rose has suggested that rap music *prioritizes* black culture and articulates the problems of black urban life, but it does not deny participation in this to others.

On this point, Rose argues that rap has emerged as a 'bifocal' form of black expression – one that seeks to communicate to white people while creating a sense of solidarity and shared knowledge among black people. Like Gilroy, Rose proposes a conception of 'black music' as a cultural form that is created out of the specific historical conditions and experiences of black people (not through any implied essential characteristics) and *in relation* to the surrounding cultural context in which black people are living. Such a formulation implicitly introduces a further issue, that of the relations between musics of the black diaspora and this surrounding context. In particular, it raises arguments about the theft, diluting and exploitation of black styles and musical practices by white artists and the white-dominated industries.

The appropriation, exploitation and recuperation of black music

In his discussion of black music, Frith drew on the corporate control position to argue that, when the music industry became involved, 'commercial mediation replaced direct emotional experience'; black music's emotional vocal qualities were 'subordinated to the star system' and the soul (feel and spontaneity) was 'marketed as a gimmick' (Frith, 1983: 18). A similar argument has been made by Nelson George about how the white-dominated industry has instituted the conglomerate control of black music and how the pressure to 'crossover' (produce music that moves between different categories, but specifically from the rhythm and blues/urban charts into the top 40) has forced performers to modify their music to become more acceptable to white audiences. George suggests that, as a consequence, audiences have been presented with 'alarmingly un-black' performers (1988: 174).

Variations on this type of argument can be found in a number of places in popular music scholarship and informed Adorno's theories about jazz in the 1930s. In an article first published in 1936, Adorno wrote about the jazz that was becoming commercially successful across Europe and argued that 'the extent to which it has anything at all to do with genuine black music is questionable'

(1989: 52). The fact that jazz was often performed by black people and that a category of 'black jazz' was popular with the public when Adorno was writing was not to be taken as an indication of any authentic relationship to cultural forms developed by black people. Adorno drew a parallel between the relationship of jazz to black people and that of salon music to the wandering gypsy fiddle players of Europe. Although both groups and their music seemed to have triumphantly entered the cities of Europe and the United States, this was far from the case. Adorno maintained that they had merely been 'hired' by 'the European-American entertainment business . . . to appear as their flunkies and as figures in advertisements, and their triumph is merely a confusing parody of colonial imperialism' (1989: 53). Adorno thus placed the production of black music firmly within the context of racial exploitation and imperialist domination – two dynamics without which reggae and rap would not have taken on their distinctive characteristics.

There is considerable evidence that the appropriation and use of styles developed by black musicians has resulted in economic exploitation – from the non-crediting of composers and non-payment of royalties to the privileged promotion accorded to white performers singing 'covers' of songs originally written or recorded by black musicians. Despite enjoying immense popularity and cultural influence, many black jazz, blues, soul and rap musicians have been economically exploited and lived and died poor. It has often been their white counterparts (whether Dave Brubeck, Eric Clapton or the Rolling Stones) or, more frequently, the entertainment corporations who have made most of the money. Historically in the USA during most of the twentieth century it has been white people who have owned the companies, the distribution systems, the radio and television networks and, ultimately, the rights to the songs and recordings of black performers (Chapple and Garofalo, 1977; Kofsky, 1970).

However, as Kofsky and Rose have argued, it is important that an acknowledgement of these types of exploitation does not leave us with an image of poor black victims. Such a conclusion would overlook the continuing attempts at resistance and endeavours at recuperation (Kofsky, 1970; Rose, 1994). Although black artists have often lacked the economic power to be able to control or benefit fully from what happens to their compositions, many have offered cultural challenges to white capitalist exploitation, two examples being Thelonious Monk's attempt to develop a style of playing which white artists and entrepreneurs would not be able to imitate and commercially package (Kofsky, 1970) and Public Enemy's attempts to 'reclaim a definition of blackness and aesthetic control over black cultural forms' (Rose, 1994: 6).

It is out of such struggles, arising from unequal relations of economic and cultural power, that black music has been made. Black music has become an important category because of conditions of oppression, segregation and ghettoization and due to the way that a particular population has had to live and make meaning within and across such 'racialized boundaries' (Anthias and Yuval-Davis, 1992). While there is racism, social segregation and economic inequality, the term 'black music' will continue to have a resonance as a signifier of a culture created out of these experiences.

Going global: black music outside the Atlantic

In the above section I have drawn on Gilroy's work to argue that black music is an important category that refers to forms of cultural practice produced in changing circumstances within a 'black diaspora'. I have referred to reggae and rap to illustrate how the 'changing same' of black cultural expression is created from specific social experiences rather than as a result of any essential characteristics.

However, despite Gilroy's attempt to find a position between essentialism and constructivism, the concept of diaspora is open to the charge that it still privileges a moment of origins and a common kinship in Africa (Helmreich, 1992). In a similar way, the notion of the 'changing same' can imply, despite the widely differing experiences of black people, that there is still a unity – what Gilroy, writing of Britain, calls an 'intricate web of cultural and political connections that bind blacks here to blacks elsewhere' (1987: 156).

For Kobena Mercer the differences between black people are such that this unity can be misleading. As black people take ever more routes and as forms of expression undergo further mediation, then new hybrids emerge through the *meeting* of various diasporas. Taking a different view of the situation in Britain, Mercer argues that black forms are not created 'inside' a self-contained black diaspora but at a 'site of many, overlapping diasporas, including the Indian, Pakistani, Bangladeshi and broader South Asian diasporas' (1994:

251). In this context it seems to become even harder to retain a sense of the 'prioritizing' of black cultural forms as suggested by Rose.

Gilroy himself has recognized this problem and has raised the question of how to deal with 'black cultural forms' that are 'originated but no longer the exclusive property of blacks dispersed within the black Atlantic world' (1993a: 3). In many respects Gilroy has self-reflexively posed the question with which I would like to end this section. He has written that 'the globalization of vernacular forms means that our understanding of antiphony will have to change. The calls and responses no longer converge in the tidy pattern of secret, ethnically encoded dialogue. The original call is becoming harder to locate' (Gilroy, 1993a: 110).

If the original call is becoming harder to locate and the subsequent forms of 'black music' are not the property of black people, but at the same time are not simply being commercially exploited – but created by rappers seeking a political voice in China, Poland, Mexico or Singapore – then how do we start thinking about 'black music' that has left the black Atlantic? Should the term finally be abandoned? Or should it be retained to indicate further routes across a 'black planet'? Similar issues to these arise when considering another musical hybrid, salsa – a label that has usually signified 'Latin music'.

Salsa: Latin identity and popular music

The Spanish word salsa means 'sauce' or 'spice' and was originally used, as far back as the 1920s, in a similar way to the exhortations to make music 'swing' or 'funky'. For many musicians and commentators, salsa is a euphemism for Cuban music. As John Storm Roberts (1979) notes in a historical survey of the impact of Latin-American music on the United States, the word salsa was used by Cuban musicians for many years before it became widely employed in New York during the late 1960s. For Sue Steward, writing in a guide to 'world music', 'salsa is essentially Cuban music' (1994: 485).

The claims for a Cuban essence to salsa are based on two related arguments. One is musicological: that the main musical elements on which salsa is based – the son and the clave – are derived from essentially Cuban styles (Roberts, 1992). The second argument is political: that following the 1959 revolution in Cuba and the economic blockade by the United States, salsa was introduced as a neutral label for the benefit of commercial marketing by a music industry which sought to conceal the music's origins (Perez, 1986; Manuel, 1986).

However, as Peter Manuel (1986) has pointed out, and as both Roberts and Steward have acknowledged, the problem with attempting to locate salsa in such a way is that the music 'is produced outside of Cuba', mainly by Cubans and Puerto Ricans living in Puerto Rico and New York City, but also by musicians in other countries of Latin America with a Caribbean coast, such as Colombia, Mexico, Panama and Venezuela.

The involvement of other Latin peoples in salsa's musical development has led to counter-claims that, far from being essentially Cuban, salsa is the music of Puerto Ricans based in New York City and on the Caribbean island. Jorge Duany (1984) has adopted this position and argued that salsa is a 'hybrid genre' in which the Cuban elements are less significant than the contribution made by Puerto Ricans. For Duany, when salsa emerged it had an inherent link to a specific population; it was created as a means of expression for working-class Puerto Ricans. Thus, Duany (writing in the early 1980s) claimed that salsa expressed 'the unmistakable voice of the Puerto Rican barrio. It reflects the sorrows and the dreams of the rapidly growing urban proletariat of the last four decades' (1984: 198).

Felix Padilla (1989; 1990) also acknowledged that salsa has Cuban elements but has maintained that these were actively changed as the music was initially created as an 'ethnic-specific' Puerto Rican style. However, Padilla argues that as the music subsequently changed stylistically there was a corresponding shift in its relationship to Latin groups; from initially being closely associated with the lives of Puerto Ricans, salsa became an expression of a wider 'bond of Latino identification and unity . . . a cultural expression of Latino consciousness' (Padilla, 1989: 28–9).

Hence, three distinct 'identity claims' have been made on behalf of salsa music. First, that it is Cuban in origin and essence. Second, that it is a music that expresses the lives and dreams of working-class Puerto Ricans. Third, that it is a music that expresses a broader pan-Latino consciousness. In the following pages I will consider the evidence upon which each of these claims is based in more detail, and in doing so highlight how the methods adopted and arguments made are relevant to other claims about the links between musical style and cultural identity.

The musical mixture: Cuban essences in the salsa sauce

Any attempt to claim salsa as essentially Cuban has immediately to confront the complexity of rhythms, melodies and lyrical patterns that make up a music that has often been called a 'mixture of mixtures'. In light of this, the argument that salsa is Cuban relies on identifying certain key ingredients of this musical sauce and establishing an implicit hierarchy which privileges these as essential elements found in Cuban music before the salsa label was added in the 1960s.

This claim is supported by a political argument that the presence of Cuban elements has been deliberately obscured for commercial marketing by US entertainment corporations which sought to conceal the music's geographical origins during the Cold War – a practice helped by the Cuban state, which favoured protest song and initially provoked salsa musicians to go elsewhere to create music (Boggs, 1992).

Those who argue that salsa is basically Cuban point to the distinctive character of its musical qualities. As Roberts writes: 'Cuban music presents a more equal balance of African and Spanish ingredients than that of any other Latin country except Brazilian' (1992: 7). Roberts notes that the practice of Spanish folklore and the endurance of an illicit slave trade during the nineteenth century created circumstances in which 'western African melody and drumming – and even the Yoruba language – were brought cheek by jowl with country music based on Spanish ten-line decimal verse and Southern Spanish melody. The coexistence of European and African rhythmic, melodic, and harmonic procedures lead, of course, to their blending, and that blending took place at the most profound level' (1992: 7–8). This blending resulted in two distinct musical elements that came to characterize Cuban music and then salsa: the clave and the son.

The clave is a staccato rhythmic 3–2 (occasionally 2–3) pattern (usually played on wooden claves) which combines European measure patterns with West African rhythms and leads to what musicologist Emilio Grenet has referred to as a 'discrepancy between melody and rhythm' (cited in Roberts, 1992: 8). In a similar way, the son – described as 'the essence of Cuban music' (Robbins, 1990: 182) – was a way of arranging music which formed the basis of the rumba in the 1930s. Starting as a regional performance genre, the son developed into a 'cluster of specific musical elements' based around the idea of a rhythmic *matrix* rather than the type of rhythmic *beat* that is found in North American pop music (Robbins, 1990: 188).

The son matrix combines polyrhythms and melodic phrases in such a way that the melody appears to have no rhythmic connection to the underlying percussion. In addition, the movement of the 'anticipated bass' (Manuel, 1985; Roberts, 1992) seems to swing across the melodies and rhythms – rather than providing a persistent anchor to both rhythm and melody as in rock, rap or soul.

However, prominent as these Cuban elements might be in salsa, when listened to and danced with, the music does not suggest a musical hierarchy in which specific elements dominate. Instead, salsa is a flexible and variable sauce that manages to blend many stylistic components that have found their way to the Latin Caribbean and New York City and which have been reblended and given slightly different flavours in differing locations (Quintero Rivera and Manuel Alvarez, 1990; Boggs, 1992). In moving on to arguments against the Cuban essence to salsa, it is worth considering this geographical context in slightly more detail.

Salsa and the Latin Caribbean

Cuba is one island in the Caribbean region. On both islands and mainland, the Caribbean has a varied and complex musical culture in which many similarities can be detected but also in which a rich range of contrasts can be found. A consideration of the culture of the Caribbean makes even more dubious the dichotomies between European and African music which were critiqued earlier. In a survey of the Caribbean as a 'musical region', Kenneth Bilby (1985) has argued that its musics are characterized by 'simultaneous newness and oldness' and are a complex 'syncretic' or 'creolized' mixture of African and European (folk and art) elements. The forms of music found in the region have their 'feet planted in both musical worlds yet belong to neither' (Bilby, 1985: 194).

Bilby observes that European influences (mainly French, Spanish and British) can be found in the melodic patterns and diatonic harmonies of the social dance music that has been regularly played for many years; a number of islands have ensembles performing waltzes, mazurkas, polkas and quadrilles, with their European in-strumentation of violins, guitars, flutes and concertinas. Alongside this are many rhythmic elements which are derived from West, Central and East Africa, particularly syncopated polyrhythms using rattles, scrapers, sticks and bells, and drumming based on interlock-ing leading and supporting parts. These elements can be found across the Caribbean in a variety of combinations and to varying degrees of synthesis and separation, from 'purely European-derived' to 'neo-African'. Bilby has described the Caribbean as a 'polymusical' region, stressing that it is not a patchwork containing a series of fragments, but a distinctive musical region containing styles formed by the meeting of slaves from Africa, indigenous populations and European colonizers. This has created what Bilby has called an 'African-European musical spectrum' (1985: 184), a continuum across which musicians, dancers and listeners are frequently moving.

It is from out of such a musical spectrum (and a corresponding complex web of social, economic and political relationships) that salsa emerged as a music associated with the movement of Cuban and Puerto Rican musicians to meet the modern recording process and urban life of New York City. Despite the claim that salsa is organized around the basic pattern of the Cuban son and clave, numerous other features have been detected in the music, including Puerto Rican 'folkloric' forms such as the bomba and aguinaldo, big-band jazz, soul, call-and-response patterns from work songs and Afro-Protestant religion, and even funk and rock elements (Bilby, 1985; Boggs, 1992; Calvo Ospina, 1995).

Such a mixture means that any claims about salsa's relationship to a Latin community cannot be based on the musical elements alone (as in the argument that black music is essentially African). Instead it must involve other methodological strategies.

The words: salsa as an expression of ethnicity and class

With salsa being quite clearly a complex mixture of musical ele-ments, it is difficult to sustain any claim for a unique or essential Cubanness or Latinness from the music alone. Hence, those writers who have identified salsa as an expression of Latin cultural identity have tended to ignore this musical complexity in favour of establishing an intrinsic connection between the social context of its production-reception and the song lyrics. This is particularly so in the arguments of Duany and Padilla.

Duany, in an anthropological study of the historical development of salsa, acknowledges both its complex musical mixture and its prevalence of identifiably Cuban musical elements. However, he contends that such elements bear a close resemblance to musical styles that have developed in parallel in Puerto Rico. Duany argues that the Cuban influence has therefore not been so important. Instead salsa has been produced as an expression of Puerto Rican national identity for working-class migrants forced into a process of continual movement and constituting a 'semi-nomadic population, perpetually in transit between its homeland and exile' (Duany, 1984: 197).

In order to support this argument, Duany suggests that, despite salsa being a form of dance music, its lyrics are more significant than its musical and rhythmic elements. Hence, he sets out to explain the dynamics of identification between Puerto Ricans and salsa through 'an analysis of song texts . . . as a means of exploring the psychological processes of the people to whom this music is directed' (1984: 201). In doing this, Duany focuses specifically on three songs written and performed by Rubén Blades: *Pedro Navaja* (from one of the most commercially successful salsa albums, *Siembra*, first released in 1978), a song about the exploits of the bully in the Puerto Rican barrios of New York; *Juan Pachanga*, a song about the fashionable playboy dandy who is concerned only with appearances; and *Pablo Pueblo*, a narrative about 'Paul People', a humble working man whose life is a series of missed opportunities and broken dreams.

Duany argues that the lyrical narratives of these songs refer directly to the lives of urban lower-class Latin communities in the United States by making use of a colloquial streetwise language and employing images familiar to working-class urban people. These narratives are presented in a folkloric and picaresque style of story telling that has a special meaning for working-class Latin communities.

Duany notes that Blades's songs, particularly *Pedro Navaja*, are performed and listened to on numerous occasions when Puerto Ricans meet to celebrate and socialize. Observing the enduring popularity of such a song, Duany argues that 'the only satisfying way to explain the song's continuing popularity seems to be to posit a deep connection between the writer, the lyrics of his song, and the people for whom he writes. In short, Blades's lyrics reflect the prevailing concerns of his reference group, Puerto Ricans in New York' (1984: 201).

In Blades's lyrics, and particularly in the choruses to his songs, Duany detects the 'unmistakable voice of the barrio' and concludes that Blades 'reflects' the experiences, 'the sorrows and dreams' of a particular class and ethnic group. Despite all of the musical mixture to which people are dancing while socializing and celebrating, Duany implies that the dynamic of identification occurs mainly on account of the lyrical content of the song.

Such an analysis is not uncommon in popular music theorizing: a performer or band of musicians are often observed to 'express' or 'reflect' the feelings, lives, desires and sorrows of an audience. This may be generational (John Lennon as the voice of the 1960s counter-culture), class based (Bruce Springsteen as the expression of blue-collar working-class life in the USA) or racial (Bob Marley as the international voice of black people). The assumption in such theorizing is that the singer-songwriter-performer in some way shares in and then expresses the experience of the listeners, that there is an essential link between the life of the artist creating the music and the world of the audience.

Duany argues that this is indeed the case and supports his claim by observing that Rubén Blades is from a lower-class background, of a Panamanian father and a Cuban mother. He migrated to New York City, where he lived in the barrios with other Latins, predominantly Puerto Ricans, from whom he learnt about musical techniques and performance and where he experienced the social life he sings about at first hand.

Before raising some questions about this argument I want to mention a similar approach that has been adopted by Padilla, who, like Duany, uses a content analysis of song lyrics (again Rubén Blades features prominently) to explain how salsa has both represented the 'ethnic-specific' experience of Puerto Ricans in New York City and subsequently come to 'embody' aspects of a wider 'Latino consciousness'.

Padilla points to a slightly more complex and mediated relationship between social experience and musical form than Duany's suggestion that Blades is able to 'reflect' the experience of his reference group. Instead, Padilla (1989, 1990) argues that salsa has been created out of a tension between the 'hegemonic determinations' of the music industry and the 'cultural creative responses' of individual Puerto Rican musicians. While the music industry has sought to manufacture and distribute a sound that could be sold to the Puerto Rican community of New York, and then expand this into a music that could be distributed more widely in Latin America, the musicians have been resisting this and attempting to use the possibilities opened by the music industry as 'vehicles for community political and cultural expressions' (Padilla, 1990: 93).

Against the commercial pressures to construct audiences as markets, Padilla argues that salsa musicians attempted to develop a music 'through which the different Latin life circumstances could be spoken to' (1990: 100) – a music that would 'speak direct to' the working-class barrio experience and then to a broader Latino consciousness.

Padilla examines the 'correspondence between salsa music and Latino consciousness' through the lyrics of songs produced by artists such as Rubén Blades, Celia Cruz, Raphy Leavitt and Willie Colón. Identifying themes of attachment to a Latin-American homeland, survival against injustice and ideas of Latin unity, Padilla argues that these songs directly 'speak to' the experience of Latin people. Indeed, Padilla suggests that the influence of music in the processes of social identification and community formation is particularly significant, claiming that 'salsa music is a leading force in the rise and spread of the Latino bond in the United States' (1989: 43).

Padilla suggests a more mediated relationship between social grouping and musical expression, indicating that salsa was assuming a prominent social position at a time when Latins in the United States were struggling for community control and self-determination against a backdrop of urban unrest and inequality, injustice and exploitation. At the same time, the music was being created and commercially distributed. However, he ultimately still bases his claim for salsa as an expression of Puerto Rican life and pan-Latin consciousness on the song lyrics of those who are 'speaking to' the Latin people. He has little to say about who is being spoken to – about the actual dynamics of the interrelationship between Rubén Blades, for example, and his Puerto Rican audience.

After all, while Rubén Blades *is* Latin American and does sing about Latin Americans, he is *not* Puerto Rican. He may have *come* from a 'lower-class background' but he has *become* a wealthy pop star and actor who has sold millions of albums, and who appears in movies, in magazines and on television shows, like so many other performers and songwriters. He is also a qualified lawyer with a degree from Harvard University and in 1994 was a candidate for high political office in Panama. While Rubén Blades's song lyrics, pronouncements in interviews and political activities make clear his commitment to Latin unity and concern with the plight of working-class Latins in the US barrios, what is less clear is *how* his music and lyrics might 'express', 'reflect' or 'speak to' the actual experience of working-class Latin life. How, for example, might we account for the way salsa music is listened to and enjoyed by vast numbers of people who do not share in or who have little experience of the Latin barrio? How do people with a limited knowledge of Spanish, hence who will miss the significance of the lyrics, still 'identify' with the *music*? Here we come across a similar problem that theorists of diaspora have encountered: once in circulation, music and other cultural forms cannot remain bounded 'in' any one group and inter-preted simply as an expression that speaks to or reflects the lives of that exclusive group of people.

In addition, the idea that music can in some way express the unity of a particular group of people must continually confront the apparent disunities and differences that can be found in the world. Like the concept of a shared culture of the black diaspora, the idea that salsa is an expression of Latin unity tends to ignore significant ideological, political and class differences among different Latin populations. Manuel has made such a point when noting the 'ex-treme polarization of the salsa listening audience, from the radical proletarians in New York, San Juan and Caracas to extreme right-wing Cuban-Americans based in Florida' (1986: 169). As Manuel notes, many Cuban-Americans boycotted Rubén Blades for his support of the Sandinista government in Nicaragua.

Such issues lead me to a wider question of how a black rapper, white rock singer or Latino salsero might relate to the class from which they come or to which they speak. Is it possible to think about this issue without resorting to ideas about music as a 'reflection' – as a mirror – of social life, or without simply presenting an artist who occupies a quite different social location as a 'representative' of a particular community, group or class? After all, it does seem that there is a relationship between what Panamanian lawyer-actor-musician Rubén Blades sings about and the lives of working class Latins.

A more convincing suggestion, from my perspective, has come from Ruth Glasser, who has argued that there is no simple correspondence between an ethnic group and a mode of cultural expression. Musicians and their songs cannot simply express, reflect or represent a particular group of people. Instead, Glasser maintains that musical and lyrical elements have to be actively 'converted into a potent symbol of ethnicity' by a range of people, including 'audiences, musicians, promoters, club owners and record company executives' (Glasser, 1990: 71).

Roberta L. Singer has made a similar argument, suggesting that 'music performance may become part of a political process in which ethnicity is an organizing principle' (1988: 148). Singer has argued that Puerto Rican music in New York has continually made use of 'displays of ethnicity', particularly when confronted with the 'pressures of immigration, urbanization and acculturation that call identity into question' (1988: 149). Hence, the processes of identification and identity formation here and the cultural forms associated with them are far from spontaneous; the cultural correspondences are established through particular social practices and political activities.

Drawing on Glasser's and Singer's points here, I want to suggest that the terms of debate might be shifted slightly. Instead of searching for authentic forms of spontaneous and unmeditated black, working-class or ethnic expression, and rather than seeking the cultural mirrors that might reflect social identity, we could ask a more specific question: under what conditions and at which moments do particular musical codes, signs and symbols become used and claimed as expressions of particular social and cultural identities? This is a question that suggests that a far more actively political *process* is entailed. It also implies that music and cultural forms are just as much a part of the making of cultural identities – the process is not simply one way, whereby some fixed identity leads to (or is 'reflected' in) a particular type of music.

While Duany and Padilla have provided important insights into the content of salsa and the lives of the Latin communities to whom the music refers, it is perhaps not the lyrics of the songs that give us the most useful information about how music creates a sense of identity and connects with the lives and experiences of particular groups of people. Rather I would argue that it is the social interactions, relations and mediations that occur around and across the music as it is created. This is a theme I now wish to pursue a little further in relation to music and sexuality.

Gender, sexuality and musical identity

For many years discussions of sexuality were informed by a distinction between 'sex' and 'gender' whereby the sex of a person was judged to be 'biologically determined' and their gender to be 'culturally and socially constructed' (Abercrombie, Hill and Turner, 1988: 103). According to this type of reasoning, gender distinctions arose from the way that 'biological differences' were used to classify and attribute certain characteristics to people and to establish a series of behavioural codes and conventions. These were sometimes referred to as 'gender roles' and frequently based around the idea that women are expected to be more passive and emotional and men more assertive and rational.

However, such a definition and such distinctions have come to be viewed as profoundly misleading. As Judith Butler has pointed out, the 'biological' or 'natural' cannot be separated from the social in such an easy way; bodies exist with a variety of characteristics and possibilities *prior* to their categorization as 'male' and 'female'. Sex is not simply a neutral biological category nor a straightforward natural activity. Sex is an idea that is used to explain, categorize and understand our bodies; as such '"sex" is as culturally constructed as gender' (Butler, 1990: 7). This does not imply that biology is not significant, but it does mean that the capacity of the body is given meaning only in specific social relationships. As Jeffrey Weeks has argued, biology merely provides 'a set of potentialities that are transformed and given meaning in social relationships' (1986: 25).

One of the reasons why gender has perhaps often been considered to be more 'social', and 'sex' in turn more natural, is that gender is usually more visible as a series of conventions about dress codes, expected public bodily behaviour, work place organization, manner of speech and so on. Sex, however, is closely connected to 'sexuality', the quality of *being* sexual, which has often been informed by beliefs that this should be a more 'private' affair (it is then, of course, frequently attributed and the subject of gossip and media 'exposures'). The distinction between sex and gender is thus both ideological (based on a very specific set of values) and misleading. Here I follow the approach of Weeks, who has argued that gender is the 'social condition of being male or female, and sexuality, the cultural way of living out our bodily pleasures and desires' (1986: 45).

Like previous sections of this chapter, debates about sexuality also come with essentialist and anti-essentialist approaches to identity and music. The first type of essentialism that can be found in this area is the idea that men and women 'express' some essential masculine or feminine forms of sexuality. The second type is that this is in turn can be found manifested in the content of particular cultural products and practices. Such an argument has informed the idea that rock is a 'male form' of musical expression, and it is with this issue that I start this section. A discussion of rock and sexuality will lead me to raise questions about the conventions that have resulted in the 'sexing of genres' (for example, the idea that disco is more gay than jazz). I shall then pursue this issue by considering country music in relation to displays of lesbian sexuality and the identity of the performer k.d.lang. Threading through this section is the same tension that has been present throughout this chapter, that between essentialism and anti-essentialism.

Rock as a male form of sexuality

One of the earliest attempts to start theorizing the relationship between rock music and sexuality can be found in an essay written by Simon Frith and Angela McRobbie (1978), in which they argued that rock operated as a form of sexual *expression* and as a form of sexual *control*. Observing that production was controlled by men, who exerted a decisive control over the 'presentation and marketing of masculine styles' and systematically limited the number of options available to women, Frith and McRobbie declared that, in terms of 'control and production, rock is a male form' (1978: 5). As Jenny Taylor and Dave Laing (1979) were quick to point out, this distinction (expression/control) was based on an assumption that it was the corporations who were exerting the control and audiences who were finding means of expression. As such, Frith and McRobbie were reproducing the dichotomy between active audiences and manipulative corporations in their discussion of sexuality.

This argument was illustrated with reference to a further dichotomy between two types of music: cock rock and teenybop. Cock rock is a term that was coined by feminists during the early 1970s to refer to male performers such as Mick Jagger, Roger Daltrey and Robert Plant, who were 'aggressive, dominating and boastful', always seeking to remind the audience of their prowess and control (Frith and McRobbie, 1978). Cock rock musicians symbolically used the electric guitar as a phallus or gun, and women were often portrayed as subordinate in their songs and represented as sex objects on LP covers. The music was 'loud, rhythmically insistent, built around techniques of arousal and climax, the lyrics are assertive and arrogant . . . cock rockers' musical skills become synonymous with their sexual skills' (Frith and McRobbie, 1978: 7). Frith and McRobbie compared this with teenybop, which was judged to be consumed almost exclusively by girls, who found a contrasting representation of male sexuality based on softer ballad styles and evocations of self-pity and vulnerability which encouraged female fantasies about being the partner of a singer.

Although Frith and McRobbie raised a number of questions in passing about the range of expression that might be found between these two poles, their central argument was based on a narrow series of essentialist assumptions which privileged heterosexual behaviour. It was constituted within what Butler (1990) has called a 'heterosexual matrix' of assumptions, values and beliefs about sexual and social activity. As Weeks (1986) has argued, male and female sexuality is far more varied and differentiated.

Frith and McRobbie partly acknowledged, but in general evaded, the wide variety of male and female cultural forms, sexual activities and social practices and how these have been given a range of different meanings in musical performances and compositions. In fact, Frith (1990) provided his own critique of the essentialism that had informed this essay in a series of 'afterthoughts' in which he conceded that they had taken sexuality and ideas about male aggressiveness and female passivity as a 'given' rather than something that is constructed. As Frith acknowledged in later writing, 'sexuality is not a single phenomenon that is either expressed or repressed . . . but a range of ways in which people make sense of themselves as sexed subjects' (1983: 238).

Rock and the performance of identity: forging masculinity

Against Frith and McRobbie's argument that rock is male because it is controlled by men and therefore expresses a male sexuality, Robert Walser (1993) has proposed a more dynamic and historical approach by claiming that rock has been actively *made* as male. Focusing on a specific subgenre, heavy metal, he notes that heavy rock is not enjoyed entirely by a male audience and neither does it communicate one type of masculinity. Walser contends that heavy metal musicians do not simply express some essential maleness but instead are involved in what he calls 'forging masculinity'. This is not a type of unmediated cultural 'expression' but a conscious and deliberate 'strategy'. Walser argues that for most of its early history heavy metal was actively made as male through a series of quite particular practices, strategies and tactics. Walser identified four such strategies that he found articulated in song lyrics, through the use of musical codes and in music videos. These he has identified as 1) exscription, which means no girls are allowed and involves the straightforward exclusion of women from the world of male bonding; 2) misogyny, an anti-women strategy which results in women appearing in songs and videos as mysterious or dangerous and as a threat to male control; 3) romance, a cultural strategy whereby love, escape and fantasy provide a means of transcending everyday problems; 4) androgyny, which, as Walser observed, is an ambiguous and contradictory strategy. While using elements of conventionally feminine clothing (lace, stockings and make-up), many hard rock musicians seek to assert their heterosexuality and are anxious that their androgyny should not lead to their sexuality being wrongly attributed as gay by fans, other musicians or journalists.

Unlike Frith and McRobbie, Walser has proposed that hard rock musicians and fans do not in any simple way *express* their sexuality, but are involved in what he calls 'identity work' (1993: 134); musicians and audiences actively work at creating an identity. Through this approach, Walser has suggested that a great variety of gender constructions and strategies of sexuality are possible. Heavy metal may have been made in a very heterosexist manner, but it still might provide a number of possibilities for the making of an anti-sexist rock.

The Riot Grrrl challenge to male rock

The idea that rock may provide the possibilities for anti-sexist forms of popular music is a theme that has been taken up by Joanne Gottlieb and Gayle Wald (1994) in an article on Riot Grrrl. In general terms they wish to challenge the essentialism that links bodies to cultural forms, and to oppose the idea that the 'expression' of specific sexualities is tied to particular instruments. More specifically, Gottlieb and Wald have argued that rock cannot simply be referred to as a male form because the music has no essential characteristics. Like Walser, they suggested that the music and its relationship to sexuality is actively constructed, negotiated and contested. The appearance of Riot Grrrl was employed as a case study to pursue such issues.

Riot Grrrl emerged in the United States in 1991 as a self-defined rock 'underground'. Gottlieb and Wald argue that, through the use of fanzines, meetings and women-only shows, it was created as a movement of young feminist women through which female rock musicians sought to expand 'the possibilities for women's public expression'. Gottlieb and Wald highlighted a number of specific strategies and tactics that were adopted. For example, women musicians challenged the use of the guitar as a symbol of male power; the female voice was employed to challenge the macho assertiveness of rock – in particular through screaming and the adoption of a variety of vocal sounds that were used to 'evoke rage, terror, pleasure and/ or primal self assertion' (Gottlieb and Wald, 1994: 261). Visually, an attempt was made to turn being looked at into an aggressive act. As performers, women neither tried to become one of the boys nor played up to the traditional feminine image by seeking the heterosexual male gaze. Lyrically the songs dealt with 'taboo' or 'private' issues such as menstruation, incest, abuse, birth, motherhood and lesbian sex.

Drawing on Hebdige's (1979) theory of subcultures (Chapter 1), and indicating how Riot Grrrl drew inspiration from the 'radical appropriations' of punk, Gottlieb and Wald used the example of Riot Grrrl to argue that rock can provide a means by which women can actively create distinctive female subcultures. Hence, their conclusion was that rock is not simply a male form but can be used to challenge previously established gender codes and sexual conventions. However, Gottlieb and Wald tempered their optimism with the observation that, despite the advances made by a few female performers, the 'ongoing tradition of rock is still deeply masculinist' (1994: 252). After all, where are the female rock musicians who might challenge the success of Guns 'n' Roses, U2 or REM?

The conclusion that might be drawn from this writing on rock and sexuality is that rock is a genre that has been sexed in a very particular way, and as such its generic codes and conventions can present a formidable barrier to musicians who want to challenge and change them. But, it is not just rock that has been generically 'sexed', as the following sections that move through disco, jazz and country should make clear.

Sexuality and genre: is disco more gay than jazz?

When writing about rock, Frith and McRobbie had argued that disco expressed a sexuality which was 'cool, restrained and under-stated' (1978: 19). Basing many of their observations on the disco movie *Saturday Night Fever*, they wrote of the social relations of disco as 'traditional' – girls dreaming of 'disco romance' and boys dreaming of quick and easy sex (1978: 19). Yet disco music, far from being associated simply with traditional heterosexual conventions, is a genre that has frequently been linked with gay male sexuality.

In an article entitled *In Defence of Disco*, first published in 1979, Richard Dyer (1990) set out to challenge the many rock fans who were dismissive of disco music. In his article Dyer was careful to suggest that, although disco is a musical form that is produced as a result of capitalist systems of production and circulation, it does not necessarily encode or reproduce a specifically 'capitalist ideology'. Adopting a similar reasoning to the active audience theorists discussed in Chapter 1, he argued that 'disco has been taken up by gays in ways that may well not have been intended by its producers . . . capitalism throws up commodities than an oppressed group can take up and use to cobble together its own culture' (Dyer, 1990: 413).

However, Dyer then employed a form of sexual essentialism to counterpose rock and disco music. In a similar way to Frith and McRobbie, he seemed to deny the possibilities that rock might provide for female musicians by arguing that 'rock's eroticism is thrusting, grinding – it is not whole body, but phallic . . . no matter how progressive the lyrics and even when performed by women, rock remains indelibly phallo-centric music'. In contrast, Dyer suggested that disco produces 'an open-ended succession of repetitions . . . it restores eroticism to the whole of the body for both sexes, not just confining it to the penis' (Dyer, 1990: 414–15).

Not only does this deny the possibility for women to use rock for producing a music that is not 'phallo-centric', it also ignores the way that the consistent 4/4 bass drum of disco can provide an impetus for a highly distinctive style of 'thrusting' and 'phallic' dancing. While Dyer's article was a defence of disco against the sneers of rock fans, his argument still posited a form of genre essentialism (suggesting that, even if women play rock, it is still, somehow, a male form).

The apparent gayness of disco has been questioned by John Gill (1995), who has been critical of many of the assumptions that have been made about gay preferences in music (e.g., who says that gay men prefer opera, show tunes and disco?). Gill is particularly critical of the way that gay disco music has become something of a sexual stereotype among both gay and non-gay music fans. In discussing this he has made some interesting observations on the sexing of musical genres and in particular about the 'sexing of jazz'.

Gill has noted how the lesbian, gay and bisexual aspects to the lives and music of many prominent composers and musicians have often been excluded from jazz biographies. He has illustrated the point further by referring to the experiences of the gay jazz musician Gary Burton, whose experience has led him to conclude that 'jazz's public image does not fit well with being a gay person' (1995: 75). This is an interesting observation because for many of its devotees jazz is thought not to have an 'image' (unlike the excesses of rock performance and video, for example). Yet, as Burton observes from touring and performing: 'Many people still persist in wanting jazz to be played by fucked-up addicts and alcoholics, in cramped smoky clubs, while wearing garish clothes and silly hats and sunglasses and talking jive talk. I get complaints all the time about not looking the part' (Gill, 1995: 75).

However, Gary Burton has not only been frustrated by the expectations of general jazz audiences, he has also found attitudes in the gay community that have been constraining. One gay bookshop that he approached was not interested in stocking jazz recordings, and for similar reasons a national gay newspaper did not want to write a profile of his band because they made a judgement that their readers would not be interested in jazz. As Gill has observed, there are assumptions being made here that genres and styles of music are sexed which are based on beliefs that certain forms of music are 'more gay' than others. In many ways such assumptions probably correspond more to the segmentation of people for commercial marketing purposes than they do to the actual distribution of musical preferences at any one time (an issue I also raised in Chapter 1 in relation to taste publics and subcultural categories). To pursue the issue of sexuality and genre in slightly more detail I shall now discuss this in relation to country music and k.d.lang.

Country, k.d.lang and lesbian style

Country music has often been portrayed as a 'conservative form carrying a conservative message' (Frith, 1983: 24–5). There has been much evidence to support such an assumption, not only in song lyrics and performers' attitudes but within the infrastructures of production, broadcasting and promotion that have been established in the country music capital of Nashville. However, like the characterization of rock as a male form, the portrayal of country as conservative ignores many of the radical influences that have come from white working-class traditions, cultural populism and evangelic Protestantism and which have had an impact on the formation of distinct country styles. In noting these elements, George Lipsitz (1990) has argued that country contains both progressive and conservative possibilities. Such contrasting possibilities were visible and audible during the 1980s as country became associated with a distinct lesbian subculture and the eventual coming out of k.d.lang.

Much could be, and indeed has been, written about the music, image and lyricism of k.d.lang and how she has confronted a particular set of problems that lesbian artists encounter within the music industry. What I want briefly to highlight here is how the k.d.lang story provides an indication of a dynamic of identification between artist and audience. By focusing on k.d.lang I want to highlight how the audience became a central part of the public articulation and formation of her sexual identity. I also want to illustrate how a particular musical genre can take on different meanings in different places, and actually mean different things for artist and audience at the same time.

When k.d.lang was seeking a record deal during the early 1980s, she initially had problems obtaining a contract. She was considered to be too country for the rock/pop market and too unusual for the country market. However, she eventually signed to Sire (part of Warner Brothers) and produced two albums that had a distinct country style. Her third album, *Absolute Torch and Twang*, was actively promoted as a country album in the United States. Yet, the country radio stations were reluctant to give it airplay, and when they did broadcast music from it the disc jockeys would often frame her recordings with comments about k.d.'s appearance and short hair cut. During 1989 she clashed with many people in Nashville who liked neither her androgynous and 'unfeminine' appearance nor her independent manner. The music industry establishment felt that she was too impatient and not prepared to play the waiting game by knowing her place as a newcomer and 'paying her dues'. The situation was made worse by her public stand against beef production and active promotion of vegetarianism (in a part of the USA where beef farmers had a significant influence in the community).

Frustrated at how she was being treated by the musical community in Nashville and being blatantly ignored by country music radio stations, k.d. angrily declared: 'I don't eat meat, I'm not a Christian and I don't have big fluffy hair, which basically stands against a lot of the fundamentalist values on which country music is based' (Starr, 1994: 157). For k.d. audiences had a slightly 'romantic view' of country, yet she had seen the reality, and it was 'rednecks, injustice and religious intolerance' (Starr, 1994: 180).

k.d.'s outburst would seem to confirm the conservatism of country music. Yet, at this very moment there was a growing lesbian country and western music scene developing in clubs in both Britain and North America, in which k.d.lang's iconography and music were central; k.d.lang had become an idol for lesbians. Louise Allen (1994), from her research in the UK, argued that lesbian audiences were creating particular meanings through the consumption of k.d.lang products and that country and western style was being appropriated and adopted as a visible signal of lesbian identity at a number of women-only clubs. Such an activity was subverting the codes and conventions of the genre, as 'the lesbian cowboy' became an ironic parody of masculinity. The codes and conventions of country and western music – the twanging guitars, the walking bass, the sentimental whine of the pedal steel guitar, the jeans, work shirts and distinctive style of dancing with partners – were appropriated and redefined to challenge gender codes and the particular way that this genre had been sexed (Allen, 1994; Ainley and Cooper, 1994).

At the same time that k.d.lang was becoming frustrated with the constraints being imposed in Nashville, country and western was being appropriated by the audience as something quite different. While k.d. moaned about the stifling atmosphere created by rednecks and reactionaries, her audience had become a visible phenomenon that was being commented upon by many critics. Journalists began remarking on the 'fanatical cult following' of 'k.d. heads' who were travelling hundreds of miles to her concerts, imitating her hair style and swapping videos of her performances (Starr, 1994). Large groups of women were surrounding the theatres where she was performing, portrayed by one journalist as a rather stereotypical population of 'gigantic women in plaid shirts and Stetsons jostling with punks in leotards and spike heels . . . manicured women in pinstripes embracing motorcyclists in chains' (cited in Starr, 1994: 202). The point is not the accuracy of such a report, but the fact that this journalist was giving voice to considerable media gossip and listening in on the talk among k.d. fans.

Her fans had appropriated and interpreted k.d. in ways that contributed to the production of a whole series of public meanings around the artist. These meanings were certainly not actively promoted by the record company (biographies and press accounts suggest that her record company did not want her to come out in public), yet such meanings were signified all the same. In addition, k.d. often played on this aspect in performance, making comments such as 'I guess you've all heard the rumours, its true I'm a L l l l-awrence Welk fan' (Starr, 1994). k.d.lang's sexuality had become an issue partly as a result of the way that her lesbian fans had recognized and then interpreted the signs that she had been communicating. In doing this her fans played an important part in creating an environment in which she could come out, as k.d. eventually did in a very public manner. As Sonya Andermahr wrote, 'with her cropped hair, sharp baggy suits, masculine stance and pinkie ring, all signifiers of lesbian butch, lang was out even before she was out' (1994: 36). And, as k.d. herself remarked, acknowledging the importance of such processes of identification, one of the most positive aspects of the experience of coming out had been 'the intimacy between me and the audience' (quoted in Bennahum, 1993: 43).

It is perhaps ironic and significant that k.d.lang has subsequently recorded very little country music. After coming out she went on to produce the more polished, jazz-inflected and new-agey style of music that can be found on *Ingénue*. It is significant because, as Victoria Starr (k.d.'s biographer) found, there are many lesbians and gay men who are reluctant to come out in Nashville for fear of the constraints and limitations that will be imposed upon them by the conservative country establishment.

However, while much country music may well convey a message that might be heard as conservative, the music and style can be articulated to different meanings and experiences which cannot be dictated by those exerting control over its production. In this example of k.d.lang, the audience presented a public display of sexuality that was completely in contrast to the constraints experienced by and behaviour expected of the performer in Nashville. But, then, as subsequent country performers such as Garth Brooks, Mary Chapin Carpenter and Lyle Lovett have demonstrated, country music is by no means inherently conservative and can be connected to different meanings and identities.

Conclusion: music and the articulation of identities

In this chapter I have focused mainly on issues of race, ethnicity and sexuality to illustrate some of the ways that the meaning of popular music is mediated by cultural identity. In doing this I have indicated how theoretical assumptions about identity have shifted from ideas about identities as essential, given and fixed to a more dynamic perspective which approaches identities as constructed, actively made and open to further change. The specific point I have tried to emphasize with regard to the study of popular music is that there is no straightforward or intrinsic link between the lives of fans, the meaning of musical texts and the identity of a particular artist. Songs and musical styles do not simply 'reflect', 'speak to' or 'express' the lives of audience members or musicians. A sense of identity is created out of and across the processes whereby people are connected together through and with music.

Implicitly throughout this chapter, I have been adopting the concept of articulation as a tool for thinking about some of the connections that are established in the making of musical identities – as another concept that enables us to ask questions about the relations *between* production and consumption. The concept of articulation has a long history, and here I am adopting a particular use of the term that draws on Stuart Hall's (1974) reading of *Grundrisse*, in which Karl Marx (1973) had written of the complex overlapping and interacting relationships between production and consumption and referred to an 'intermediary movement' that occurs between the two (you may recall that a similar idea informed my discussion of production in Chapter 2 and mediation in Chapter 3).

In discussing how production and consumption were interrelated, Marx had evoked the idea that a 'product receives its last finishing touches in consumption' and suggested that a railroad on which no one rides is only 'a potential railroad' (Marx, 1973). Following this approach, I would argue that, for a song to be fully realized, for it to have any social meaning, then its production has to be *connected* to consumption, to an audience for the song. In this way artist and audience can be said to 'articulate', in the sense that articulation involves a process whereby elements are connected that do not necessarily have to belong together (Hall, 1994).

In proposing the concept of 'articulation' as a way of thinking about the connections that link production and consumption, I follow Hall (1986), who has pointed out that this has two senses. First, we articulate to communicate. We always express ourselves by articulating to some person or group (using language, but also employing other cultural codes such as non-linguistic expressions, bodily gestures and so on). Our articulations are directed towards others; we do not simply articulate in a vacuum. The concept can be applied to popular music, to indicate that an artist is always articulating, via various intermediaries, to audiences who are always part of the process of 'articulating' cultural meaning.

The second aspect of articulation derives from the general definition of the term as involving the linking together of two elements. For example, an articulated lorry is made up of two separate sections: a tractor and a trailer connected by a pivoted bar. The act of articulation involves a process of bringing these together. Hence, articulation involves 'the practice of linking together elements which have no necessary relation to each other' (Grossberg, 1992: 397).

Both Richard Middleton (1990) and Lawrence Grossberg (1992) have adopted this concept, in a similar way, to argue that studying popular music should not simply involve attempts to follow the linear communication of musical messages from producers to consumers. Instead, it should entail examining processes of 'articulation' in which particular sounds have to seek out, be sought by and connect with particular audiences. In this way, processes of production and consumption can be approached less as discrete, fixed and bounded moments and more as a web of mediated connections. During such a complex social process, the meaning of music and its relationship to cultural identity and any social effects that it may generate arise out of a process in which performer, industry and audience 'articulate' with each other and with the surrounding culture and social-political system.

By adopting this concept of articulation along with a non-essentialist approach to identity, critical questions can be raised about the way that particular cultural forms become connected to specific political agendas and social identities without assuming a necessary link between someone's social labels (black, Latin, lesbian or working class) and a particular type of music.

CHAPTER FIVE
HISTORIES

In this chapter I want to raise some questions about the writing of popular music history by considering what has been referred to as 'the rock era'. This is a particular history that can be found narrated in numerous books, magazines and journals and which has frequently set agendas for academic curriculums, particularly in Britain and the United States. It is a period that starts with the emergence of rock-'n'-roll in the middle of the 1950s and which then 'progresses' through various significant moments or stages until it ends with punk rock in the 1970s.

In focusing on this period, I want to raise two general questions. Although specific to this discussion of rock, I hope that these and the further issues that they generate might be useful when considering other popular music histories. The questions I want to address and which will thread throughout this chapter are 1) why did this epoch start at a particular moment and how was it different to what was happening before the rock era? and 2) what came after the rock era? This last point will lead me to consider the idea that rock is 'dead'.

Because the particulars of this history can be found in many books (e.g., Gillett, 1983; Chambers, 1985; Miller, 1980; Wicke, 1987), I shall not be focusing on the details in this chapter, but raising some critical theoretical questions about this history. In general I shall be suggesting that, while pinpointing historical tendencies and understanding social change is important, we should be wary of attempts to draw neat boundaries around musical eras. I am arguing for a critical questioning of the history of musical sounds as narratives with distinct breaks involving beginnings and endings or births and deaths. As music making occurs through multiple ongoing historical processes and human relationships, so the writing of music history should be approached with an awareness that this involves a process of re-presentation. As such, there may be other ways of telling the story.

The importance of historical knowledge

Before moving on to some of the details of my argument, I want to preface this discussion with a few words about the importance of history. Writing on this very point, John Tosh has observed that a sense of history plays an important part in social life. History can, he argues, serve as 'collective memory, the storehouse of experience through which people develop a sense of their social identity and future prospects' (Tosh, 1984: 1). History is important for an individual and group sense of identity; it provides knowledge and ideas from which 'we' decide who 'we' are, where 'we' came from and where 'we' are going. Many of the struggles over identity to which I referred in the last chapter depended upon a consciousness of a shared experience of the past. History is frequently drawn on in this way to provide a sense of continuity and has often been written in an attempt to supply an orientation towards the future.

Thus the writing of history is important and has implications for how we understand and identify with contemporary forms of popular music. For example, the participants in various activities associated with Riot Grrrl which I discussed in the last chapter were claiming their music as part of a long tradition of women's involvement in rock music. This was explicitly presented against the writings of many male journalists who were describing Riot Grrrl as a fashion fad or media hype (Gottlieb and Wald, 1994). Many gay and lesbian writers have also been writing history as part of a project which aims to make visible and audible those audiences and musicians who have been hidden from various music histories, showing how gay and lesbian people have played an important part in the history of popular music (Gill, 1995).

Hence, my first point in this chapter is that historical knowledge is directly related to how different people develop a sense of identity as an active process – as coming from somewhere and going towards something else. Musical identities are created out of knowledge and experience of the past. As George Lipsitz has put it, popular music is the 'product of an ongoing historical conversation in which no one has the first or last word' (1990: 99). The performance and reception of popular music, he argues, involves a 'constant dialogue with the past'. Bands, audiences and performers are continually referring back to something that was occurring before.

Yet, such multiple dialogues and the numerous possible 'pasts' have been made in quite specific ways. As Karl Marx observed in the nineteenth century, people 'make their own history, but they do not make it just as they please; they do not make it under circumstances chosen by themselves, but under circumstances directly encountered, given and transmitted from the past' (Marx, 1954: 10). New music and new cultural dialogues are made within the context of the possibilities provided by existing social relations (the industry organization, the political arrangements, the entire patterns of mediation and methods of social distribution), technological means (studio and instruments of music making, methods of storage and distribution) and aesthetic conventions (the complex of performance practices, bodily techniques and discriminations to select chords, sounds, notes, words and imagery, and then combine them in a specific way).

Such musical history making cannot be known in any innocent sense. Arranging a vast number of sounds, words and images into musical 'eras' is not a neutral activity. It involves a process of imposing patterns and order onto the many events taking place across space and through time. History is *produced* (Tosh, 1984). Certain noises, words and images are selected as significant and other events, people and places are neglected. Hence, while 'everyone enters a dialogue that is already in progress' (Lipsitz, 1990: 99) they also confront writings and beliefs about history in which specific barriers have been erected and boundaries drawn. Some dialogues are presented with specific beginnings and endings and seem to dominate particular periods of time; other dialogues seem strangely absent from history.

In this chapter I will argue that the idea of the 'rock era' involves a particular way of disrupting the dialogues with the past. It entails placing specific boundaries across ongoing musical activities. In pursuing this theme, I shall draw on Lipsitz's conversational approach to history as a humanistic dialogue and Marx's general conception of history as actively made through human struggles within quite specific circumstances. This I will contrast to approaching musical genres as if they were living bodies which are born, grow and decay – for example, the often narrated idea of the rock era as 'born around 1956 with Elvis Presley, peaking around 1967 with Sgt Pepper, dying around 1976 with The Sex Pistols' (Frith, 1988a: 1). Not only does this type of approach present rock as a unified 'body', it also privileges those who were there at the moment of birth and raises a number of problems about what might be living on after the death. In the case of rock, I would suggest that rumours of its death have been greatly exaggerated and that many people have been communing with the spirit of rock since 1976. The idea of a 'rock era' is based on a particular experience of rock (biographical, geographical, generational and social) which fails to allow for how musical forms are transformed and move on in different ways across the planet, acquiring new significance in different situations and as part of other dialogues.

In this chapter I shall also be questioning the idea that rock was an affect of or a response to social conditions or market demand (Peterson, 1990). Drawing on Lipsitz's approach to history as a dialogue, I want to suggest that rock (as a particular way of *making music*) was created from many years of musical activity; rock is a label for a musical activity that was produced through and brought into various dialogues without any clear beginnings or endings. As such, the endings and beginnings have been produced as particular rock stories have been constructed and narrated.

In the final part of this chapter I shall consider The Beatles' *Sergeant Pepper* album, and in focusing on this work ('the peak' of the rock era) I will ask a question that is often evaded: what is rock? I shall then point to a tendency towards what I call rock imperialism – an attempt to ignore differences between musical sounds and to define rock very loosely so that numerous musics can be accommodated and *claimed as* rock. My point here is that rock needs to be understood as *one* genre and style that can be adopted and adapted in various ways and used to engage in multiple historical dialogues. As active audience theorists have argued, no one can have the last say in the history of any musical form. On that point, then, this chapter is intended as another contribution to the ongoing dialogues about rock and music history.

The revolutionary moment

'1956 is the year when it begins', wrote Iain Chambers. The appearance of rock-'n'-roll had made it 'possible to refer to a new and distinctive pop music' (Chambers, 1985: 18). This is a view that is shared by many commentators. According to David Hatch and Stephen Millward, 'that rock-'n'-roll involved a revolution within the music world is an assessment few people would quarrel with' (1987: 68). The issue of debate, for these writers, is about the dating and nature of this 'revolution'. In this section I want to quarrel with this assessment by arguing that, while this moment was quite exciting for some people, it is misleading to view rock-'n'-roll as 'revolutionary'.

My claim here is not particularly new. Back in the late 1960s Dave Laing wrote that rock-'n'-roll was far from a radical break with preceding musical traditions. Laing noted the very 'restricted sense in which rock-'n'-roll as music can be described as new or revolutionary' and gave examples of how 'many singers in the mid-fifties were able to ride high on the rock wave with only minimal changes in their customary style' (Laing, 1969: 65). This is a point that has also been made by Dave Harker (1980), who has referred to rock-'n'-roll as musically a 'caricatured version' of elements from the rhythm and blues and country traditions. Nelson George has also observed such continuities by highlighting how the term rock-'n'-roll was introduced as a marketing concept often with the intended aim of concealing the music's black origins, a tactic which made the 'young white consumers of Cold War America feel more comfortable' (George, 1988: 67).

If the music was not that unique then why has rock-'n'-roll so often been written of as revolutionary? Why should the history of an era start here, with this music? There are a number of interrelated answers that have been offered in response to such questions. Most are associated with different aspects of the *meta-context* within which the music was interpreted and understood and the industrial processes through which the music was produced and distributed. Many observers have sought to explain the appearance of rock-'n'-roll as an *effect* of changing industry arrangements or because of the way this music met the needs of a particular audience (see Longhurst, 1995; Peterson, 1990).

As far as the audience argument goes, rock-'n'-roll emerged in the USA at a time of conservatism, Cold War paranoia and increasing affluence for some people. When it was received elsewhere around the world (whether in Britain, Japan, Mexico, Australia or Germany, for example) it was also experienced by young people as a challenge to conservative attitudes (Bradley, 1992; Wicke, 1987; IASPM-Japan, 1991; Palacios, 1995). The identification of rock-'n'-roll with the working-class young male style of teddy boy, in Britain initially but then in various countries around the world, connected it to the conspicuous consumption of the newly labelled 'teenager'.

Rock-'n'-roll, as a new category of music for sale, was facilitated by demographic changes related to the increased disposable income among a new post-war 'baby boom' generation within the North American and Western European economies. This shift in patterns of music consumption has been referred to as a 'realignment underwritten by the industry for sound economic reasons' (Laing, 1969: 77). The music business reorganized some of its production and distribution practices so as to cater explicitly for this new 'teenage' rock-'n'-roll consumer (Gillett, 1983).

In doing this the industry made use of a number of important new methods of distribution. During the mid-1950s three technologies helped the industry reorganize for the distribution of rock-'n'-roll music. First, there was the introduction of the small seven-inch single record which turned at 45 rpm and which was less fragile and provided better sound quality than the old 78 rpm record. Second, the transistor radio, first manufactured by Sony in 1955, enabled many people to take music with them on the move (whether carried personally or in an automobile). Third, the adoption of television as a domestic entertainment medium meant that the images of performers could be transmitted simultaneously into many homes. This did not occur just in the United States; these three technologies of distribution provided the conditions for rock-'n'-roll to be rapidly circulated around the world (Wicke, 1987).

It was within these circumstances that rock-'n'-roll became a label for the music of particular artists. As Harker has noted, the music industry in the United States drew on a variety of local amalgams of styles and distributed these with the label rock-'n'-roll as a 'nationally recognizable style' (Harker, 1980).

Two aspects of rock-'n'-roll performance practice were considered to be particularly new (even 'revolutionary'). First, rock-'n'-roll explicitly foregrounded the meeting of black and white performance techniques which had often been kept separate (at least as far as many white audiences were concerned, particularly between the 1920s and the 1940s, when the recordings of black performers had to be sought on so-called race records). Black performers adapted various white show-business styles of songwriting and delivery and white performers drew on mannerisms that had been developed by black performers, particularly vocal gospel styles (Chapple and Garofalo, 1977; George, 1988). The meeting can perhaps be heard in the recordings of The Coasters, whose songwriters Jerry Leiber and Mike Stoller created 'an aesthetic in which Tin Pan Alley tunesmithing was as important a part of rhythm and blues as black skin' (George, 1988: 64). George has argued that these two young Jewish men who had grown up in black neighbourhoods produced songs in which they displayed an 'uncanny ability to write convincingly from the viewpoint of blacks' (1988: 64). Songs like *Riot in Cell Block No. 9* (released in 1954 when the band was called The Robins) is a blues with a similar interaction between guitars and voices that can be heard on Chuck Berry's *No Money Down* or Elvis Presley's similarly themed *Jailhouse Rock*. Songs such as *Young Blood* and *Yackety Yak* were delivered in an ironic manner that fused elements from blues and Tin Pan Alley songwriting with some of the vocal mannerisms of cartoon characters (Hardy and Laing, 1990). The latter songs also addressed the teenage consumer (clean up your room and 'don't talk back') in a similar way to Eddie Cochran's *Summer Time Blues* and Chuck Berry's *School Days*.

The meeting of elements from black and white music traditions (and indeed the incorporation of Chicano and Jewish musical elements) was important for many young people growing up at a time when the Civil Rights Movement was gaining momentum. But, the meeting of various black and white distinct styles was not particularly new and had occurred on numerous occasions during the making of jazz, blues, ragtime and spirituals. Moral guardians and religious leaders may have been perturbed by the way Elvis Presley adopted the 'iconic image of the white Negro' (George, 1988: 64) – but such a practice was not *that* revolutionary.

Rock-'n'-roll was also associated with the display of a particularly visual, explicit male sexuality. This was observed to be personified in Elvis Presley. Part of Elvis's appeal was due to the way he was attractive to men and women in different ways. While heterosexual male writers identified with Elvis as a macho folk rebel, Sue Wise (1990) and John Gill (1995) have noted how gays and lesbians adopted a variety of different responses to his sexuality.

This is an important point, because for many years the mediations of male rock journalists played an important part in contributing to rock discourses about Elvis. Elvis's sexuality was 'written into a heterosexual missionary position' and female responses were decoded by men who ignored much of the homoerotic subtext (Gill, 1995: 87). Again, while many young male rock writers saw Elvis as the epitome of youthful rebellion and male heterosexuality, ignoring his more tender ballads and blues songs, for many journalists and commentators he became an all-American hero, a saint-like figure that continues to stare out at the world from portraits in hotel lobbies and from postage stamps (Marcus, 1992).

All of the above explanations (new teenage consumption, black–white meetings, new modes of distribution, more explicit public displays of male heterosexuality) have been offered as attempts to explain why rock-'n'-roll happened or was revolutionary at the time (see Bradley, 1992; Longhurst, 1995). Hence, what caused many writers to conclude that rock-'n'-roll required the label 'revolutionary' was not *in* the music. Instead, it was to do with the way a particular form of music articulated with social, economic and cultural changes. Rock seemed to matter and was experienced as central to the social changes with which a new generation of young people (particularly in Western Europe and North America) were growing up (Grossberg, 1992).

Yet, as rock was being constituted as a commodified form of entertainment across the mediations between production and consumption, it produced different meanings for audiences, industry and musicians. For the industry it provided the impetus for a significant expansion in scale and scope of operations (Chapple and Garofalo, 1977). For the audience, the new 'baby boomers', it was the start of a revolt of the body that would lead to a 'revolution in the head' during the 1960s (MacDonald, 1994). As for the music, as I have already noted, it was not that new. As Peter Van Der Merwe has written, 'the teenage rock-'n'-roll fans of the 1950s may have been exerting their newly acquired spending power. They may have been expressing rebellious attitudes to their parents' bourgeois cultural values. But they were also expressing a liking for twelve-bar tunes, for blue notes, for certain types of syncopations, for certain melodic contours' (Van Der Merwe, 1989: 214).

If the music itself was not that new, then where do such musical sounds and rhythms go back to? How far back can we pursue the roots of rock-'n'-roll music? Many writers who have addressed this issue have sought the 'roots' of rock in the weaving together of elements from distinct US styles: rhythm and blues, country, folk, gospel and blues (Frith, 1983; Gillett, 1983; Longhurst, 1985). Van Der Merwe (1989), however, goes much further. His argument provides an example of the problems that can arise when searching for the origins of musical roots.

Van Der Merwe traces back a number of the 'antecedents' of twentieth century US music in his search for the 'origins of popular style'. Here I shall briefly refer to what he says about two characteristics associated with rock music: nasal delivery and the (irregular, continually modified) 12-bar blues pattern. A nasal vocal delivery is characteristic of much rock music. It can be found in many blues recordings, rock-'n'-roll performances and the vocal delivery of artists such as REM, Neil Young and Bob Dylan. Van Der Merwe traces nasal delivery to an 'Afro-Arab culture' in North-Western Africa around the year 1700 (Christian calendar). Against those who wish to trace 'American instruments and instrumental styles back to Africa', he argues that this should be seen as 'Arab-influenced Africa'. Thus he has explicitly sought to question the claims about the 'African' origins of rock (1989: 28–30).

Van Der Merwe also searches for the origins of the blues – which he treats as a three-chord, I, IV, V pattern, for example, C, F, G or E, A, B – the staple chord pattern on which so many blues and rock songs are based. Via various geographical routes he follows the blues back to early sixteenth-century Italian and French dance music. More specifically, Van Der Merwe argues that the rock-'n'-roll hits *Long Tall Sally* and *Good Golly Miss Molly*, although 'Africanized', are 'ultimately of British origin', and he manages to follow the basic theme and music of Chuck Berry's *Reelin' and Rockin'* back to an Irish ballad published in 1796 and then back to a comedy from 1640 (1989: 82).

Fascinating as this musical time travel is, the method is rather formalistic. Van Der Merwe tracks down musical, lyrical and rhythmic elements without any sense of their actual sound qualities or contexts of production and reception (without any notion that the music elements might be significantly different when played on electric guitars compared with how they must have sounded in the sixteenth century). This approach is also ahistorical in that it ignores the active participation of people in the processes of mediating musical traditions over time. It is as if musical sounds are transmitted unchanged through 'long-range pipelines to a distant past' (Pickering, 1987: 44).

Van Der Merwe has produced a history in a quite specific way. To trace back the 12-bar blues to Europe in the sixteenth century is clearly different to following it back to Africa in the eighteenth century. The quest for beginnings, and the decision to stop at a particular moment of 'origins', has clear political implications for how identities are understood in the present. As Robert Walser has pointed out, to 'describe the songs of Little Richard as "ultimately of British origin"', to attribute blues harmonies to the sixteenth-century passamezzo moderno, is fundamentally to misrepresent the nature of African-American music making, trivialising it by defining as derivative or peripheral the activities of many of this century's most creative musicians' (Walser, 1992: 130).

I share Walser's concern, and in advocating a 'dialogic' approach to history I do not mean to suggest that we should search for a moment when the conversation might have started. Van Der Merwe's attempt to locate the origins of musical style leads to a type of musicological formalism which merely engages in a game of finding connections between musical and lyrical features across history. Presumably the historical quest must end when no more evidence can be located (it's interesting to note that Van Der Merwe's origins go back to around about the time when printed records become available in Europe, and the origins of these 'popular styles' are conveniently located in this continent).

So, while I am suggesting that it is important to think across apparently 'revolutionary' boundaries, I am not advocating the adoption of a quest for *births* of new cultural forms and *origins* of styles. Instead I am arguing for an approach that can identify the continuities and the dialogues through which – in this specific case – a 'blues continuum' (Jones, 1965) interacted with and became part of a rock continuum. I have already referred to Laing's argument that many artists 'adapted' to rock-'n'-roll, as musicians are always doing in a variety of settings. I would extend this by suggesting that at any one moment a variety of distinct musical practices are being performed. As a way of thinking about this I want to characterize three types of musical dialogue that may be going on at any one time (even at apparently revolutionary 'moments'). As a way of starting to think about this I want to introduce the idea that popular musicians can be identified as genericists, pastichists and synthesists.

By *genericists* I mean those performers who accommodate their musical practice and performance to a specific genre style at a particular time and stay within this. These artists have a repertoire in which all musical pieces fit the particular codes, conventions and 'rules' of a genre (Fabbri, 1982) and precisely play everything in such a way. They compose and perform *within* the codified conventions of a generic style. In the period under discussion here this would refer to the generic rock-'n'-roll acts who either changed their style when they realized that a bandwagon was rolling or got together because they wanted to play only this type of music.

By the term *pastichists* I refer to those artists and performers who recognize that a new style has appeared or has become popular and so include this in their set as yet another style to be performed as *part* of a varied repertoire – a practice that involves the combing of stylistic heterogeneity with little coherence or logic other than the fact that some songs are popular with some people some of the time. Hence, during the 1950s many bands added a rock-'n'-roll number to their set, but continued simultaneously playing waltzes, polkas, jazz numbers, standards and show tunes. In making this point I also intend to indicate how music genres are adopted in a broad context and played among cabaret and club circuits around the world. New musical generic styles should not just be understood in the context of teenage consumption or the most commercially successful recordings of artists in the top 40.

By *synthesists* I mean those who draw on the elements of an emerging generic style but blend them in such a way so as to create a new distinct musical identity. These are not unique individual geniuses but synthesists working at the fuzzy boundaries where generic codes and stylistic conventions meet and create new musical patterns. Such 'creativity' involves a 'combinatorial activity . . . the bringing together of previously separate areas of knowledge and experience' (Koestler, 1978: 131). Koestler's observations on creativity are useful for thinking about those artists who do something more than the generic musicians and the peddlers of pastiche.

As Koestler (1964) notes, much creative activity involves working at producing new versions by combining existing elements in various ways. Dick Hebdige has made a very similar point in a critique of Albert Goldman's (1982) claim that Elvis Presley was simply a 'marvellous mimic'. What Elvis did, argues Hedbige, was to make 'his own style by blending all the other styles together' (Hebdige, 1987: 13). By borrowing different voices and styles, Elvis created his own style. While Goldman uses such evidence to imply that Presley was a 'commercial copycat', Hebdige suggests that this provides one of the keys to his greatness. Elvis was, in my terms, a synthesist who drew on existing styles and through these dialogues created his own recognizable style. While Goldman hears just imitated elements, Hebdige points to the way that existing elements are brought together to create new sound relationships. As Koestler also argued, new 'discoveries' in art and science do not necessarily come from moments of 'inspiration' but can be made from quite mundane hard work: 'it would be foolish to underestimate the achievements of which skilled routine is capable' (1978: 142). This is also an important point here, as much new popular music has appeared from an industry organized around day-to-day recording routines (as accounts of musical production at Atlantic, Sun and Motown have attested). It is often through the struggles of the synthesists (sometimes against the expectations of industry person-nel, journalists and audiences) that generic boundaries are broken and remade.

My point in identifying these schematic creative practices is to suggest that *different* dialogues were taking place at the revolutionary rock-'n'-roll moment. These were dialogues that involved different musical meanings depending on whether a band or performer's musical practice involved working within genre codes or stylish pastiche, or utilizing the ways in which a codified genre always provides possibilities for transformation (Fabbri, 1982).

The end of the era

The narratives written about the 'rock era' present an often re-counted story: following the 'formative' rock-'n'-roll moment (Chambers, 1985) the story leads through the beat boom of the 1960s and then by way of a variety of stages of rock development and decay such as progressive rock, folk-rock, acid rock, heavy metal or hard rock, and glam rock, to conclude with punk rock in 1976. As Harker (1994) has observed, referring to the way that this history was codified into a flow-chart diagram by Steve Chapple and Reebee Garofalo (1977), rock is often presented in terms of a 'Dar-winian progression' which involves a continual flowering of sepa-rate flora that have all grown from the rock-'n'-roll seed that was sown in the 1950s. According to this seemingly ineluctable process it is during the middle of the 1970s when the blooms start wilting, the body decays and rock starts dying.

Why should rock die at this moment? Again, the circumstances within which the music was interpreted and understood and the changing conditions of its musical production have been offered as explanations. If rock is often observed to have started when the industry was reorganizing to cater for young consumers, then rock ends when executives within the industry are beginning to realize that the business needs to reorganize to cater for older buying patterns. If rock is brought in with the single, the transistor radio and early television, then it is taken away by the compact disc, the music video, multi-channel cable and satellite television and the Walkman – technologies of distribution which were introduced from the end of the 1970s and which took off during the 1980s and helped the industry find older consumers and distribute a broader range of music-related commodities.

It is these technologies that enabled the industry to begin restructuring and to de-emphasize rock. It was this that led Simon Frith to argue that 'the rock era is over. People will go on playing and enjoying rock music . . . but the music business is no longer organised around rock – around the selling of records of a particular sort of musical event to young people' (1988a: 1). There is much visible and audible evidence to support Frith's argument. Such a change can be observed in the segmentation of music into ever more generic categories by record companies, in record shops, on radio stations and in the growth of life-style-specific music magazines.

However, the idea that the industry was 'organized' around rock is open to the criticism that this selectively ignores a vast amount of music that was being distributed at the time, privileging the musical listening habits and buying patterns of a particular generation of listeners and therefore only one audience group for whom the industry was organized. As Harker (1992) has pointed out, during the peak of the rock era, the top-selling albums included the film soundtrack *The Sound of Music*, classical recordings such as Carlos and Folkman's *Switched on Bach*, Van Cliburn's performance of Tchaikovsky's Piano Concerto No. 1 and the easy listening soul of *Johhny Mathis Greatest Hits*. While such examples say nothing about the cultural influence and actual social use of such recordings, they do indicate that for many people the defining sound of this era was not rock.

Rock music certainly made the industry money, but there was more than an industry organized around rock. There was also an audience who organized their experience around rock – and then wrote about it. The death of rock is therefore also related to changes to this experience. This is a further point made by Frith to support his claim that rock has 'died'. According to this argument, punk rock finally challenged, deconstructed and exposed the mythologies of rock at the very moment when the original teenagers and youth of the rock generation were growing old and beginning to hear things in a different way: songs of generational rebellion, sexual liberation and social concern were starting to be used to advertise wine coolers, executive cars and personal insurance (Frith, 1988b).

For Frith, the practices of rock were exposed as dependent upon a particular *ideology* of music making – a series of beliefs and value judgements that musicians and audiences used to legitimate rock against other forms of music. In discussing this, Frith (1983) has identified three distinct aspects of the ideology of rock. First, the notion of the rock 'career': this was an ideological construct that was based on assumptions of a craft mode of artistic learning and the belief that legitimate rock success required years of struggle and 'dues paying'. Second, rock was viewed both as a complex art form and as an expression of specific generational sentiments and feelings. Such beliefs were informed by ideas derived from a romantic aesthetic. Third, appreciation of rock music was informed by the belief in an integral link between performers and audiences and the idea of the 'rock community'.

An indication of how the ideology of rock influenced the way that music was listened to can be seen in the following extract written during the 'peak' of the rock era:

> Rock music is now much more than music for its devotees, it is a subculture in the strictest sense of the word – and the term 'pop' must be redefined radically . . . rock now must be seen as an art form like any other that arises from and talks to the people in direct, charged and organic ways . . . there is a less distinct line between the audience and the performer, where there is less and less a tangible effort on the part of a musical-taste elite to impose standards on its listeners . . . we seem to be back in the days of Chaucer – in a more verbal era when poetry and music are back in the hands of the people . . . rock music was born of revolt against the sham of Western culture; it was direct and gutsy and spoke to the senses. As such it was profoundly subversive, it still is. (Eisen, 1969: xii–xv)

It is easy to dismiss such a proclamation as rather quaint in hindsight, but what this quote indicates is how those who thought of themselves as part of a 'rock community' were attempting to articulate their own practices and sensibilities. Rock fans distinguished themselves from the vast majority of popular music listeners who, judged according to this ideology, liked 'pop music' in which there was no 'bond between the audience, singer and song' and whereby music merely brought people together as 'isolated customers united by their wish to consume' (Street, 1986: 214). Rock, in contrast, became a way of 'uniting' audiences, artists and songs through a common 'sense of community'.

For Frith, the rock community had always been an imaginary ideal and punk had finally managed to show that this could no longer be maintained by either artists, audience or critics. As post-punk writers began to celebrate rather than criticize the commodification of music, many began to argue that rock critics had mystified the whole process of music making. Dave Hill, for example, wrote that 'rock liked to think it was somehow more profound, non-conformist, self-directed and intelligent. Rock-think foolishly, innocently, imagined itself to be a bit above the manufacturing process. It refused to admit it was a commodity' (Hill, 1986: 8). At the same time, many post-punk bands (particularly in Britain) displayed their commodity status in a detached and cynical manner that was consonant with the free market beliefs that were evangelically being promoted by Margaret Thatcher and Ronald Reagan during the early 1980s. Indicative of this was the way that John Lydon left the Sex Pistols and formed the corporately named Public Image Limited and subsequently took up residence in the United States, where he started trading in real estate. In a similar way, the British Electric Foundation was formed from members of the Human League who then presented themselves on their album covers as suit-wearing executives attending corporate meetings. Both of these 'bands' signalled post-punk rock as a knowingly corporate activity. But, then, as many writers observed, it had been like this since the large process of restructuring during the 1960s (Chapple and Garofalo, 1977). Charlie Gillett had argued that in the 1960s many rock artists used what was often viewed as a more calculated 'pop method' but made a conscious effort to pretend that they hadn't (1983: 376). Likewise, many supergroups of the early 1970s were assembled with calculated deliberation 'cloaked in the guise of artistic experimentation' (Cable, 1977: 48).

The argument here is that the death of rock was not simply due to the way it had been coopted by the industry (Chapple and Garofalo, 1977). It was that the ageing rock audience were realizing that they had been deluded by the ideology of rock and a newer generation of musicians and consumers were embracing the commodified, contrived and free market pluralism of a reorganized music market. Within this context, a celebration of the plurality of 'postmodern pop' replaced a belief in the idea of the rock community for many Anglo-American music writers. Chambers (1985), for example, argued that punk rock had been a 'notorious instigator' that had contributed to a new diversity in the music market place. Punk had created a breach, and from this moment Chambers prophesied that the future would promise 'a proliferation of margins rather than a predictable return to a renewed "mainstream" and a subordinated "alternative"' (1985: 200).

If the advent of rock-'n'-roll is often portrayed as a revolutionary beginning, then punk often appears as an apocalyptic ending. For Chambers, the breach that was 'instigated' by punk had led to a profound change in which 'a sequential version of pop's history has been transgressed, violated. Causal explanations have been circumvented by a confusion of cultural margins' (1985: 200). Chambers argued that punk rock had been responsible for something more profound than simply the death of rock. It had broken the sequential history of pop. The future was to promise a proliferation of the margins, a carnival of styles, rather than a renewed linear narrative based around the concept of a mainstream and musical tributaries. Chambers narrated a sequential history of popular music from 1956 to the early 1980s and then concluded by declaring that writers who followed him would not be able to continue his narrative, because the sequential history of pop had ended.

In retrospect, such postmodern end-of-history prophesies seem as quaint as ideas about the rock community. Since Chambers's narrative was published in 1985, rock bands such as U2, Dire Straits, REM, Guns 'n' Roses and Oasis have featured prominently in the top 40 music sales charts and an alternative guitar rock scene has been counterposed as a direct contrast to the mainstream. In addition, major pop stars such as Madonna, Michael Jackson, Phil Collins and Prince have continued to engage in mainstream musical dialogues with the past.

The popularity of The Smiths during the 1980s and Nirvana and REM in the 1990s and movements such as Riot Grrrl indicate that rock has been alive and living, but within the musical dialogues of different generations. For many of these musicians and audiences rock has been experienced as part of a different history, one that doesn't necessarily 'begin' with a revolutionary moment during the middle of the 1950s.

Not only has rock been lived through different generational experiences since 1976, it has also grown up and left its Anglo-American home and gone out into the world. At the very moment when it was dying for some citizens of Britain and the United States, for other people rock was very much alive and being used to articulate dissent, whether in creating a 'sphere of dissidence' as a challenge to the dictatorship in Argentina (Vila, 1992) or being employed as 'an alternative means of communication' to register opposition in Uruguay (Martins, 1987). Rock was also becoming an important part of a repertoire of oppositional political practices in a number of the former Stalinist states of Eastern and Central Europe (Szemere, 1992; Ramet, 1994). In the German Democratic Republic (the former East Germany) during the 1980s, rock was articulated to social changes that seemed a lot more 'revolutionary' than what was going on in the United States during the middle of the 1950s. According to Peter Wicke, rock became part of the political struggles that led up to the dismantling of the Berlin Wall.

As Wicke has narrated when making this claim, in the GDR under the previous Stalinist regimes, music was heavily censored and regulated. In 1965 Erich Honecker, then Chief of National Security, had deemed that rock music was not compatible with the goals of a socialist society, hence as part of a general regime of cultural repression particular sounds were effectively banned. Rock could be performed only by state-approved bands and performers. As a result, the performance and transmission of unapproved rock music became a way of communicating opposition to the system. Wicke has highlighted how rock music was shared by musicians and audiences and used to communicate ideas of solidarity and contribute to building resistance. By improvising performances on trailers or trucks in public places and by distributing sonorial material within the state and across its borders into surrounding territories (via illegally produced recordings and broadcasts) rock became a central element in the organization of 'private', 'underground' and public events and in the process was integral to the articulation of opposition and generation of an affective sense of solidarity. Although not all rock music was used in such a way, and while many musicians were colluding with the regime that was sponsoring their activities

(Pekacz, 1994), rock musicians played an active part as 'cultural catalysts' who mediated cultural values that symbolically and materially challenged the system (Wicke, 1991, 1992a, 1992b).

I have included reference to Wicke's argument about rock in the GDR here to indicate how rock has been living as part of other musical dialogues: there has been more than the ghost of rock stalking the world (or being digitally repackaged) since 1976. Hence, there are other histories of rock and, rather than characterize punk rock as a decisive historical break, I would argue that this period can again be approached in terms of a number of specific musical dialogues. During the end of 1976 and the beginning of 1977 numerous *generic* punk bands were formed or adapted their styles to suit what very quickly became a standardized punk noise, vocalized sneer and specific sartorial conventions (Gendron, 1986; Laing, 1985). At the same time there were *pastichists* such as The Stranglers who added a mannered misogynistic punk pose to their blend of psychedelic progressive rock and pub band boogie, while television entertainers the Baron Knights added a comedy 'punk' number to their cabaret repertoire.

This was also a time of *synthesis*. The Clash created a briefly realized punky synthesis of rock, reggae and funk and the Talking Heads more self-consciously synthesized an art school aesthetic with punk and funk patterns. In addition to this, at the very moment when rock was apparently dying in Britain, David Bowie was living in Berlin, where he produced three albums, *Low*, *Heroes* and *Lodger*, that fused rock and soul elements with styles from more Central European experimental electronic sounds. In the process, Bowie was placing rock within a series of musical dialogues that connected electro bands such as Kraftwerk and Can to New Order and then to the later rap styles developed by artists such as Grandmaster Flash. Rock was not ending, and has not died; it was just going 'somewhere else' (Grossberg, 1994) and becoming a part of other musical dialogues.

The peak: *Sergeant Pepper*

For the final section of this chapter I want to break up the implicit historical chronology by returning to the mid-point of the rock era and The Beatles' album *Sergeant Pepper's Lonely Hearts Club Band*.

This has been called the 'peak' of the rock era (Frith, 1988a) and the 'quintessential rock album' (Denisoff, 1975). Yet, this album has been described in other quite contrasting ways. For some writers it was far more than simply a rock record, it was a major cultural artefact. According to Ian MacDonald:

> When *Sergeant Pepper* was released in June [1967] it was a major cultural event. Young and old alike were entranced. Attending a party with a group of rich older women, EMI boss Sir Joseph Lockwood found them so 'thrilled' by the album that they sat on the floor after dinner singing extracts from it. In America normal radio-play was virtually suspended for several days, only tracks from *Sergeant Pepper* being played. An almost religious awe surrounded the LP . . . The psychic shiver which *Sergeant Pepper* sent through the world was nothing less than a cinematic dissolve from one Zeitgeist to another. (MacDonald, 1994: 198)

MacDonald's reverence for this album and the significance he accords it is in keeping with the contemporary views of Kenneth Tynan, who when reviewing the album for *The Times* in London described the LP as 'a decisive moment in the history of western civilization'. For others, though, the album's aesthetic qualities and spiritual power were somewhat less profound. A reviewer for the *New York Times* called it 'a package of special effects, dazzling but ultimately fraudulent' (quoted in Wiener, 1985: 38). In his history of rhythm and blues, Gillett adopted a similar position, referring to it as 'a suite of songs in a specific order' that was put together 'as a convenient way of packaging twelve randomly collected tracks. Many of the songs were obscurely surreal . . . and seemed rather too casually put together to justify the intensely philosophical interpretations that were read into them' (1983: 267). Gillett's observations, first published three years after the album's release, were not that far removed from the views of the LP's producer, George Martin, who has recalled thinking that it was 'a funny collection of songs, not really related to one another, all disparate numbers' (1994: 150). Having finished the recording and mixing of tracks, The Beatles had left Martin to put the songs into a sequence, which he then did through trial and error (rather than conceptual thematization) until he came up with the eventual track order. Martin also worried at the time that both the band and producer were being rather 'pretentious' and trying to be too clever.

Such reservations were not countenanced by those who were embracing this LP as a harbinger of a new type of 'art'. *Sergeant*

Pepper was released at a time when the 'ideology of rock' was being codified by a new generation of writers who were legitimating 'their' music in terms of an aesthetic tradition into which they had been educated. Crucial to the mediation of *Sergeant Pepper* were the opinions of a new occupational group, the professional rock journalists. The 'turning point' with which this album coincided was less about a shift from one Zeitgeist to another or a dramatic change in Western civilization, but something a little more ordinary: the young educated middle classes of Europe and North America had discovered and then claimed rock music in their own terms.

As Chambers has noted, rock-'n'-roll had initially been associated with the leisure activities of working-class teenagers. However, in the years from the middle of the 1950s to the middle of the 1960s rock articulated with changing class dynamics and in the process various elements of rhythm and blues and rock-'n'-roll were 'appropriated' and 'rechristened rock or progressive music by its recently enfranchised grammar school, student and hip middle class audience' (Chambers, 1985: 84). Graham Vulliamy (1977) has made a similar point, noting how middle-class young rock fans adopted an aesthetic vocabulary derived from the appreciation of 'high' culture. Rock musicians, audiences and journalists sought to distinguish themselves by claiming that rock was not motivated by commercial considerations and that the rock performer was a sincere, creative artist producing something that was musically complex. Vulliamy's point is that the 'increased legitimation of rock music' through these particular ideological beliefs accompanied a 'shift in the social class composition of the audience and the performer' (1977: 193). The privately educated, grammar school and university graduate middle-class rock audience, and performers from a similar background who were making reference to poetic and literary themes, sought to present their music as more legitimate than that of a predominantly working-class young that was more concerned with sex, love, romance and everyday issues. A liking for rock music among the educated young from upper-status groups, and the ways this music was produced and used, was justified 'in the terms and criteria of excellence used by other members of their status group' (Vulliamy, 1977: 193). Such interpretations were codified and communicated by professional rock critics who promulgated this ideology in 'quality' newspapers and the 'underground' press (Frith, 1978, 1983).

If *Sergeant Pepper* was heard at the time of its release as a new type of high art by the educated middle class or dismissed as little more than a contrived glossy package by those who believed that popular music should be more direct and spontaneous, so subsequent interpretations have been equally contrasting. Both Hatch and Millward (1987) and Allan Moore (1993) agree that this album signals the emergence of 'progressive rock', but disagree about the consequences of this new 'maturity' in rock music making. For Moore it signals a point when musicians began to 'progress' beyond the limitations of the seven-inch single record and started to extend the possibilities of rhythm and blues 'through the infusion of a variety of foreign influences' (1993: 61). In contrast, Hatch and Millward (1987) considered that this album has directly contributed to the 'decline' of rock music by inspiring technical self-indulgence and displays of pointless virtuosity that in the years following its release led to an increasing separation of the experiences of audience members from the lives and compositional themes of the musicians.

Rather than pursue this issue here and argue about whether *Sergeant Pepper* signals a point of maturity or the moment of decline in rock music, my own retrospective contribution to the continual reassessments of the album is to argue that it should no longer be heard simply as a 'rock' album. Instead, it can be listened to as a work that both highlights and transcends the generic boundaries of rock through its flawed synthesis of a variety of generic codes. It is not that The Beatles incorporated 'foreign' elements *into* rock (as Moore suggests of progressive rock), but that the limits of rock are noticeable due to the way that this album draws upon and breaks *out* from the ways in which rock had become codified. In the context of my discussion here, the album is important due to the musical dialogues with which it intersects and for the way it breaks across the boundaries of historical 'eras' and genres.

As the album has been heard so many times and discussed in numerous places I will not give an extended description here, but refer to a few songs to highlight just some of the distinct elements of synthesis and boundary spanning that can be found on this recording. The first point to note is that The Beatles presented themselves as more than simply a rock band. The album's title track and the theme of the cover packaging work together to produce a musical and visual pun on the concept of both a rock band and a brass band. The expectant audience sounds with which the album starts are more in keeping with a carnival or circus than the frenzied screams that had been greeting the band over the previous five years. The rock beat and staccato rhythm guitar of the opening song is quite explicitly disrupted by the entry of an Edwardian-style brass band after first verse and chorus. This musical reference is reinforced by the use of crowd noises and laughter along with vaudeville and music-hall clichés, particularly as the track segues into the second song, *With a Little Help from my Friends* (Whiteley, 1992). This song again combines rhythm and blues patterns with music-hall elements, and sets the tone for much of an album on which references to nineteenth-century British music-hall styles have been identified in numerous places (Mellers, 1973).

As the album accumulates meanings and historical reference points with the addition of each track, so the much discussed track *Lucy in the Sky with Diamonds* appears as far more than a rock song. The lyrics to this song are a typical example of John Lennon's surrealistic and 'nonsense' style of word play and punning that appeared in many of his songs and particularly in his books (Lennon, 1964, 1965). Although this track has frequently been claimed as a song about the experience of LSD (Whiteley, 1992), a connection that Lennon continually denied while also admitting to numerous drug associations on other songs, it can be heard as a continuation of Lennon's preoccupation with the language use and word play of Edward Lear and Lewis Carroll. The sur-realism or ir-realism and cartoon-like quality of many of the lyrics are reinforced by the use of a Mickey Mouse type of voice that was deliberately produced by speeding up Lennon's vocal. Rather than the knowing expert guiding the novice through a drug trip, as Sheila Whiteley (1992) suggests, the dreamlike evocations of this song would seem to be more consonant with the references to childhood experiences and feelings that can be found evoked in other songs recorded at same time but not included on the album (e.g., *Strawberry Fields Forever* and *Penny Lane*). Indeed, songs about the experience of childhood or songs written with children as an integral part of an imagined audience were features of both Lennon and Paul McCartney's writing during the lifetime of The Beatles and in their solo work (*Yellow Submarine* is one of the most obvious examples; others include *Goodnight* – written as a children's lullaby – McCartney's *Mary Had a Little Lamb* and *We All Stand Together*, and various tracks on Lennon's *Double Fantasy* album, which contained songs alluding to his son Sean's childhood). *Lucy in the Sky with Diamonds*, with its dreamlike 3/4 waltz verse and rather clumsy walking-bass 4/4 rock-boogie chorus, is perhaps more innocent than many writers have often supposed.

My implicit point here is that there is perhaps a children's history of The Beatles at the same time as the world-wise counter-culture version (a history I perhaps notice because I was a child at the time). Children were and continue to make up a large part of The Beatles' audience, and *Being for the Benefit of Mr Kite*, although again often interpreted as a song about drugs, can also be heard far more obviously as a song about circuses. This interpretation was supported by Lennon himself, who produced a copy of the Victorian circus poster from which he had drawn inspiration when writing the lyrics. Directly quoting lyrical details from an advert for a nineteenth-century circus, Lennon together with producer Martin attempted to create a musical recording that could also evoke the sense of a circus. Martin recalled that Lennon wanted to try and approximate the sound of the children's television programme *The Magic Roundabout*, and this was attempted by using a harmonium, harmonicas and a tape of Victorian steam organs and calliopes (MacDonald, 1994; Martin, 1994).

Before the compact disc, side 2 of the original vinyl album started with *Within You Without You*, a George Harrison composition whose musical arrangement was performed by Indian musicians from the Asian Music Circle in London. This segued directly into *When I'm Sixty-Four*, a 'whimsical musical hall number' that was deliberately arranged with clarinets to make it sound slightly more tongue in cheek (Martin, 1994: 34). I have already mentioned that The Beatles' music appealed to children; it should also be remembered that The Beatles had and continue to have a great appeal for older people, as the quote from MacDonald about the president of EMI suggests. *When I'm Sixty-Four* is a track that both addresses the young who will get old and celebrates ageing musically and lyrically in a manner far removed from the paranoia of ageing exhibited by many of The Beatles' contemporaries (such as The Who or The Doors). This song is an example of one of The Beatles' many historical musical dialogues across generations and genres.

Moving on selectively to the last track on the album, *A Day in the Life* is yet another song that has been scrutinized for numerous drug references. It might, with hindsight and from a vantage point where the utopian dreams of the drug experience embraced by the counter-culture seem rather more naive and complacent, be possible to hear this track, as Wilfred Mellers (1973) does, as a more ordinary ballad of everyday life. It is a song that brings together snippets taken from everyday conversations, vernacular phrases and stories from newspapers (many of The Beatles' songs started in a very practical way as the composers searched for ideas in newspapers). Lennon's laconic and lethargic 'I read the news today, oh boy' is almost a modern version of the blues sigh 'I woke up this morning', wearily delivered by a member of a generation who had grown up surrounded by the modern mass media. Such a connection is quite explicitly signalled in the middle section, where McCartney does indeed sing about waking up and getting out of bed. Although the 'classical' elements that were added to this song's arrangement (particularly the dissonant rising pitch crescendo up to the final E major chord that concludes the album) have led some writers to highlight the use of heavenly signifiers from an eighteenth-century European system of musical signification (Mellers, 1973), the track is perhaps, like so many of The Beatles' greatest songs, more down to earth and rooted in vernacular language and the common everyday experience which it communicates.

One of my intentions in referring to these selective moments from *Sergeant Pepper* is to highlight the 'ordinariness' of this album in contrast to claims for it as high 'art'. But I am also arguing that this is far more than a simply a 'rock album'. In terms of its production and the musical elements employed, The Beatles used Indian instrumentation, brass bands, orchestras, circus sound effects, music-hall devices, romantic ballads and surrealistic sound collages and drew on a range of identifiable generic musical styles. As George Martin remembered (while worrying about how such a project might be 'pretentious') the album was a deliberate attempt to use new sounds and studio techniques and to combine a range of musical influences. As Martin noted, it drew from 'jazz, folk music, rock-'n'-roll, rhythm and blues, but it had a tremendous classical vein too' (1994: 150).

Not only was it not produced as a 'rock' album, it was not listened to just by rock fans but by numerous people of differing ages across the world. The history of the 'rock era' often presents the meaning of The Beatles' music only from the perspective of British or US 'rockology'. To refer to *Sergeant Pepper* as the peak of the rock era or the quintessential rock album is therefore selectively to privilege very particular musical elements on the album over others and the specific meanings that this music has for one audience over those of others.

My own argument here is that *Sergeant Pepper's Lonely Hearts Club Band* should be replaced and appreciated in a broader historical context as one contribution to dialogues whereby musicians break with what are conventionally perceived as European and African-American musical codes (see Chapter 4) and in doing so create a synthesis that cannot be neatly tied down to the boundaries of generic categories. The Beatles were participating in numerous dialogues and creating a synthesis that was more than rock, as many other artists have done during the 'rock era' – whether Kraftwerk's computerized European rhythm and blues, Stevie Wonder's blend of classically orchestrated funk or the African-American-Euro-Classical disco epics of Dan Hartman and Isaac Hayes. These are just some of the frequent moments of synthesis that disrupt the historical geographies of 'rock' in a similar way to how Duke Ellington's classical African-American-European music continually disrupted the neat and tidy historical geographies of jazz and binary categories of 'black' and 'white' music.

Conclusion – rock on and on

Through a critique of the idea of the 'rock era', I have been following an approach to history as an ongoing process during which music is actively made through 'dialogues with the past'. I have adopted this approach in contrast to studies that attempt to draw boundaries around musical eras and search for the births and deaths of particular musical styles, and against the idea that musical styles appear as an 'effect' of various social and economic factors. I have also been stressing the fact that there is not one rock history and indicated some of the ways in which songs intersect with and are understood in relation to a variety of experiences and social circumstances.

On this latter point, I have also emphasized that the meaning of rock is not simply conveyed by the music alone, but through the circumstances whereby that music and its meanings are mediated (a particular generation of journalists were important in constructing the notion of a 'rock era'). This is a theme which follows from much that I have covered in previous chapters. However, in making this point, I do not mean to imply that there are no common musical features that distinguish rock as a generic form. This is an issue I

wish to emphasize at the conclusion of this chapter to distance my
own argument here from those writers who have extended this line
of reasoning to the point where it seems that a very broad range of
musics can 'become' rock.

Such a position has been adopted by Lawrence Grossberg, who
has maintained that 'rock cannot be defined in musical terms' (1992:
131). Grossberg, who is concerned with the articulations of rock
with broader social and political processes in the United States,
employs a definition of rock whereby it seems possible to accommodate any sound to this musical label. He argues that 'there are, for
all practical purposes, no musical limits on what can or cannot be
rock . . . There is nothing that cannot become a rock song or, perhaps more accurately, there is no sound that cannot become part of
rock' (1992: 131).

Although a large part of this chapter has been concerned with the
context within which 'rock' is understood and its meanings contested, it seems important to remember that if rock is anything then
it is music as well as a component of social or subcultural forma-
tions. While rock is clearly a lot more than music, and although its
meaning depends on a complex process of circulation, mediation
and reception, Grossberg's claim that there 'is no sound that cannot
become part of rock' raises a number of issues for the social study of
popular music and its history. Not only does Grossberg's formulation seem in stark contrast to the way in which fans, musicians,
government administrators and industry personnel continually
make distinctions about which sounds are and are not rock, it also
places rock at the centre of a popular music universe.

A similar tendency can be found in Roy Shuker's writing
on popular music, which is only slightly more specific than
Grossberg's. Shuker uses the term rock 'as shorthand for the diverse
range of popular music genres produced in commodity form for a
mass, predominantly youth, market' (1994: 10). Such a formulation
begs the question of whether all the people who make up the youth
markets of the world might judge that they are listening to rock. I
suspect that many young fans use their genre labels with far more
precision and experiential reflection than these scholars. For many
music fans across the world, there are numerous sounds that cannot
be rock and there is much music being listened to by the 'youth
market' that would be described using a label other than rock,
such as rap, merengue, soul, reggae, cumbia, country, techno and
so on.

I have selectively picked on one aspect of the writings of Shuker and Grossberg here to highlight a common practice in much English-language popular music writing – what I would call rock imperialism. This is an approach to studying popular music that ignores the vast numbers of generic distinctions made by musicians and audiences across the world and which reduces popular music to the category of rock. Although often adopted as a pragmatic tactic by 'those wishing to institutionalize rock as a subject for serious study' (Bennett et al., 1993: 1), this can then result in a methodological strategy whereby other categories are included *as* rock (often rap or reggae) or simply excluded. Rock is then often studied (as popular music) and used to make many generalizations about diverse musical forms and practices across the world.

Many writings about popular music have often been overconcerned with rock and paid little attention to the dynamics of musical genre and style distinctions and differences. Throughout this chapter I have been using rock as a label to refer to a particular type of musical practice. In contrast to Grossberg and Shuker, I would suggest that rock is more specific and particular than is implied in their formulations. Yet, in contrast to Frith's concept of the rock era (1956–1976), I would suggest that rock is not that specific. Such sociological accounts of rock's universalism and particularism might benefit from an engagement with rock's musicological specificities and transformations.

As Moore has pointed out, rock can be distinguished from other types of music due to the 'degree of stylistic consistency which can be found within its musical rules and practices' (1993: 1). In his discussion of these characteristics, which he has identified and elaborated through extended discussion of particular types of instrumentation, syncopation and the use of the voice, Moore is concerned with rock as a 'stylistic practice'. A focus on the stylistic practices of rock and how these change and intersect with other styles might provide a way of studying how different participants in the mediations of music making become involved in organizing musical boundaries – how musicians, industry workers, journalists, audiences and academics are involved in drawing boundaries around what is and is not rock.

I have tried to indicate how the boundaries of eras are not so stable, and by characterizing musical practices as involving synthesis, pastiche and genericism I have highlighted how the dialogues of rock may be engaged with in different ways and can take on different characteristics simultaneously. The boundaries of musical genres and components of styles are often transformed as they intersect with other musics. On this point, it is worth emphasizing that, for many people, important years during the 'rock era' were filled with the sounds of reggae, folk, jazz, country, salsa, blues, funk-soul, disco, enka and film soundtracks. Musical genres do not fill eras, nor do they continue neatly along the path of progressive development – being born, maturing and then dying. They arise out of and are actively made through dialogic – or perhaps polylogical – movements through time but also in space. On this point, the routes of rock may be more important for future study than its historical roots. Rock, like the rap and salsa I discussed in Chapter 4, has not died but has become more geographically mobile.

CHAPTER SIX
GEOGRAPHIES

The geography of popular music, the routes of recorded musical sounds through social spaces and between particular places, will be discussed here through a focus on two interrelated issues. First, I will be considering theories that attempt to understand the dynamics and consequences of the geographical distribution of recorded popular music around the world. Second, I will focus on how particular musical sounds become associated with specific places. In considering these issues I shall take some space to provide general theoretical background material to arguments about cultural imperialism. I do this because in discussions of popular music the term has often been employed in a casual manner with little regard for its origins in debates about imperialism. As Reebee Garofalo has noted, 'cultural imperialism' has often been introduced into discussions of popular music in a vague manner which tends to 'conflate economic power and cultural effects' (1993: 18). One of my aims in this chapter is to make the idea of imperialism and cultural imperialism a little less vague. I shall argue that imperialism is a useful concept for understanding the world-wide movement of music, providing that it is employed without assuming that it refers to 'effects' (impacts *on* culture) but to the *processes* and struggles through which dominant power is exerted. My general aim in this chapter is to provide theoretical ideas that might be useful in analysing the geographical mediations of popular music, whether approached from a 'global' or international perspective or a 'local' or place-specific level.

Cultural domination: from Americanization to cultural imperialism

Fears about the detrimental influence of cultural forms produced in and distributed from the United States became widespread throughout the world from early in the twentieth century (particularly with the advent of film, radio broadcasting and the phonograph). In Europe, a broad range of interests on both left and right of the political spectrum seemed to agree that national folk traditions, authentic working-class cultural practices and European high art were threatened (and, indeed, being corrupted) by media forms and cultural products from the United States (Hebdige, 1981). Such anxieties about 'Americanization' informed state policy in the Stalinist regimes of Eastern Europe and the former Soviet Union from the 1930s to the 1980s and in Nazi Germany during the 1930s, and became a preoccupation of many European intellectuals and folk theorists between the 1930s and the 1950s. Arguments about Americanization also surfaced in Japan following the US occupation after the Second World War, and in Latin America (particularly in Chile) this issue was the subject of considerable debate during the 1970s. In the 1990s the notion of Americanization was again on the agenda in Europe, frequently informing discussions about the adoption of national and pan-European media policies (Morley and Robins, 1995).

Earlier in the twentieth century these arguments were frequently based on the anxieties of intellectuals who had come into contact with cultural products from the United States for the first time (radio, films, music recordings). But they were also based on empirical statistical evidence which indicated a predominantly one-way movement of entertainment products from the USA to the rest of the world. During the 1970s, this concern about 'Americanization' led to a more theoretically informed approach which sought to explain this situation and its implications in terms of a particular model of political domination, that of cultural imperialism. In this section I'm going to outline the argument about cultural imperialism by making a distinction between the theory of *imperialism*, the theory of *media imperialism* and the argument about *cultural imperialism*. These are important distinctions that, as already noted, are sometimes ignored in arguments that (con)fuse economic and cultural dynamics when explaining the movement and influence of musical commodities around the world.

Imperialism and capitalism

Ali Mohammadi has succinctly summarized one of the most basic forms of imperialism as 'the domination of one nation by another' (1995: 364). This domination may be exerted in a variety of ways. It might be direct and highly visible, or it may be indirect and exerted subtly. There may be troops and tanks on the streets. Alternatively, there may be covert intelligence units operating to undermine a democratically elected government which is implementing policies considered to be detrimental to the interests of the imperial power. In practice, imperialist domination has often been exerted via a combination of military force, political or economic forms of control and the manipulation of cultural symbols.

Throughout world history there have been many types of imperial relationships and there have been a number of imperial powers; for example, the Greek, Roman, Persian and Ottoman empires all subordinated and dominated other regions of the world (Mohammadi, 1995). However, contemporary debates have their starting point with a type of domination that resulted from a form of empire and a type of imperialism that developed during the late nineteenth century. This involved the formal conquest and occupation of a territory, followed by its annexation and then administration by an external imperial power. From the 1880s to the outbreak of the first World War in Europe (1914) large parts of the globe outside of Europe and North America were divided up into territories and formally ruled by one or more of just a few states, the main ones being Britain, France, Germany, Italy, the Netherlands, Belgium, the USA and Japan (Mohammadi, 1995).

In 1916 Lenin wrote a small book called *Imperialism: The Highest Stage of Capitalism*, which became important for both the analysis of and the struggle against imperialist domination during the twentieth century. Lenin had lived through the time of imperial activity to which I have just referred. In analysing the processes involved, he argued that imperialism was the inevitable consequence of the development of the type of industrial capitalism that had first emerged in North-Western Europe.

Lenin argued that capitalist enterprises inevitably develop into a series of big conglomerates, cartels and monopolies which swallow up the smaller entrepreneurial businesses. These cartels and monopolies then manage to exert such a firm control over their domestic economies that, in order to maintain their dominance and to expand, they start to move geographically outwards in search of new sources of profit.

Lenin maintained that as capitalism developed, it was inevitable that the leading capitalist nations would start supporting their own industries and economies by competing with other nations. This would then involve competition for the most profitable parts of the world and a drive to gain access to both markets and raw materials. As this happened, the interests of the corporations and the colonizing nation state coincided in a continual quest for new territories. As parts of the world were colonized, so nation-based companies could gain access to cheap sources of land, labour and raw materials and could operate in newly created markets in which capital was scarce.

Hence, one of Lenin's central arguments was that, in order to maintain their dominance in a home region, expanding corporations were forced to seek profits from overseas territories. This inevitably brought them into competition with one another. The contemporary relevance of this to the study of popular music and its associated media industries is readily apparent and can be found simply by looking through the annual reports of some of the major entertainment companies, as well as by reading trade magazines such as *Music Business International*, where there are continual discussions of the way that US-, Northern European- and Japanese-based corporations are seeking to expand their operations into numerous 'territories' around the world.

It is important to note that the particular theory of imperialism that was proposed by Lenin was not simply an argument about imposed forms of domination. It was a theory of imperialism as a *process* – a competitive struggle between the major capitalist nations and their companies which as a consequence will result in specific imperialist patterns of domination. This is not a monolithic or a homogenous process, and such struggles may lead to a variety of types of imperialism (which may involve pharmaceutical companies, petro-chemical corporations or agricultural businesses). By adopting this theoretical perspective it can be argued that different industries have adopted different imperialist strategies as they have moved out from their home bases and, usually supported by governments, have struggled against other companies to establish imperial relations in which the practices of indigenous people have often been changed with the imposition of new methods of producing and consuming. So, for example, methods of cultivating crops using machines and chemical fertilizers manufactured in Europe or the United States have replaced traditional methods of farming and the consumption of mass-produced drugs has often replaced local herbal remedies. In mentioning these here I do not mean to imply that one method has necessarily any more intrinsic value or quality than the other. The point I'm making is that a relationship of *dependency* can be established: people in one territory become dependent upon products and services from outside (Mohammadi, 1995; Reeves, 1993).

Music and modes of media imperialism

Within this context, media imperialism has been posited as a theory about a specific form of imperialism. A useful version of this has been developed by Oliver Boyd-Barrett, who defines media imperialism in national terms as 'the process whereby the ownership, structure, distribution or content of the media in any one country is subject to substantial external pressures from the media interests of any other country or countries – without proportionate reciprocation of influence by the country so affected' (Boyd-Barrett, 1977: 117).

Boyd-Barrett, acknowledging that imperialism is about competition – the processes that lead to domination rather than domination *per se*, stresses that more than one country may be operating as an imperialist force at any one time (even though a large part of the writing on media imperialism has been concerned with the activities of the USA).

At a very general level, the media imperialism argument is about the way that media forms, practices and arrangements around the world (whether news programmes, movies, soap operas, advertising billboards as well as recorded music) have come to exhibit basic characteristics that are derived from the United States, but also from Britain, France, Spain and Japan. Rather than give too many details of Boyd-Barrett's model, I want to use it here as a way of identifying some of the processes and practices involved in the distribution of popular music. In particular I will focus on Boyd-Barrett's argument that media imperialism involves more than the straightforward economic relationships posited by Lenin but entails 'structures of dominance' that are exerted through four 'modes of media imperialism'. These are 1) the shape of the communication vehicle; 2) a set of industrial arrangements; 3) a body of values; and 4) media content. I shall go through each in turn.

1) *The shape of the communication vehicle* By this Boyd-Barrett refers to the actual technology that is used for communication. The radio, television and phonograph were developed as means of distributing sounds and images initially in Britain, France, Germany and the United States and specifically as one-way communication media for domestic distribution. They were not, for example, developed as two-way interactive communications technologies, like the telephone (although such possibilities are now being pursued with the introduction of 'interactive' multimedia). These communication technologies were then distributed to countries which had played no part in their technological development. The phonograph, magnetic tape recording and radio broadcasting were not neutral technologies, but had been developed for the production and distribution of cultural forms and broadcasting of programmes in relation to quite specific social, cultural and political circumstances. The technologies of musical production, reproduction and distribution that have become standardized across the world were developed to suit the requirements of people and corporations within the industrial capitalist nations. Most of the poorest countries usually import rather than manufacture musical equipment. Hence, a relationship of dependency was established through the very development and distribution of the equipment for recorded music production, broadcasting and reception.

2) *A set of industrial relationships* These are the systems of ownership and organizational control that have been developed in specific regions and introduced with extensive European, North American and Japanese capital. Many media and entertainment systems (record companies, television stations, radio networks, magazine and book publishers) that appear to be national are actually owned by a few conglomerates based in Europe, the United States or Japan. These corporations can exert direct control over local media organizations by appointing particular staff, or by directly interven-

ing in day-to-day operations, or by withdrawing or supplying investment.

3) *A body of values* This refers to the professional codes and working arrangements, the everyday ways of doing things within media and entertainment organizations. These are sometimes explicitly set out as specific working practices, signified by the division of staff and allocation of particular tasks and job titles and formalized in copyright law and ideas about 'intellectual property'. Very often they entail the more subtle ideological beliefs and values that guide working practices. In the music industry these would include such everyday decisions about the acquisition, promotion and marketing of artists and the 'professional judgements' about what is a good song or suitable music video. Boyd-Barrett's point in proposing this mode is that such judgements and values have often been derived from European or North American models of how media organizations should operate and how media professionals should go about their daily work. Here I would add from my own research (Negus, 1992, 1993) that such professional judgements are not just geographical (national or continental) in origin but are cut through with culturally encoded assumptions about class, race and gender.

4) *Media content* Here Boyd-Barrett focuses attention on the content of the media products that are distributed around the world. In the case of music recordings, a number of writers have pointed out how music from a few prominent nations has tended to dominate international musical consumption and radio and television programming patterns. Following research in the 1970s, Larry Shore suggested that there was 'a strong indication of a predominantly one-way flow of music from the United States, and to a lesser extent Britain, to other parts of the world. There is more of a two-way flow between the US and Britain although the flow is greater from the US side' (Shore, 1983: 264).

My own research on the music industry in Europe during the early 1990s suggested that there were similar patterns, whereby British and Anglo-American recordings were being privileged over the music produced in many of the European nations (Negus, 1993). Other research has highlighted the movements of music between Latin-American countries and across to Spain and Portugal, and the significance of Chinese pop sung in Mandarin as a pan-regional genre moving between the nations of South-East Asia (Gorman, 1995; Scott, 1994; Shore, 1983). Hence, it is not simply Anglo-

American music that is on the move and causing concern about the possible consequences of such movements.

This point is particularly important in light of the claims made by those who reject the imperialism thesis and assert that a 'post-imperial' model is required. Iain Chambers (1994) and Reebee Garofalo (1993) have both argued that so-called centre-periphery models are not useful for understanding the movement of popular music because there is not simply a 'one-way flow' of music recordings which are then imposed on a passive non-resistant audience. The point I would emphasize here is that the concept of imperialism does not necessarily imply a 'centre-periphery' model in the first place. What it suggests is that there is a dynamic of power struggle which does not rule out the possibility of considerable resistance. This issue is important in light of the way that writers such as Chambers and Garofalo have used 'active audience' theory and followed Dave Laing's argument that the impact of imperialism is undermined by the way that musicians and audiences have 'made use of "imperialistic" music' (1986: 340). As I noted in Chapter 1, making use of music recordings in various ways is not the same as having the power and influence to direct the circulation of music products and recordings. As Edward Said has written, it was never the case that the 'imperial encounter pitted an active Western intruder against a supine or inert non-Western native' (1994: xii). Said argues that there has always been resistance to imperialism and in a vast number of cases this eventually won out. Imperialist domination, therefore, is not simply imposed on hapless victims but is exerted as a consequence of a struggle between the dominant nations and corporations. During this process music does not simply 'flow' in an unchanging way; instead a process of mediation occurs which involves struggles and relations of unequal power. Hence, the music *is* actively transformed, but within the context of particular power struggles, and it is these dynamics which theories of imperialism seek to highlight and explain.

Feeling the effect: cultural imperialism and globalization

While cultural imperialism has sometimes been used as a term to indicate how patterns of 'cultural dependency' (Mohammadi, 1995; Reeves, 1993) are established through media technologies, systems of organization, values and particular products (Boyd-Barrett's modes), it has also been presented as an argument that these have a *direct impact* on indigenous cultures and musical practices. This adds a further inflection to some of the claims made so far. The claim here is that the distribution of media products is contributing to a process of cultural imperialism, whereby – depending on where you are standing in the world – Western or North American, US, British, French, Japanese, Spanish or Chinese media forms, cultural practices and social activities are replacing and forcing out of existence those that are variously described as local, traditional or indigenous. So, for example, Coca Cola, saki or claret replaces local drinks; hamburgers, pasta or tofu replace the traditional food of specific localities; jeans, T-shirts, trainers or business suits replace local clothing styles and the sounds of Janet Jackson, Phil Collins or Luciano Pavarotti have a detrimental impact on local musical practices.

Those who take issue with theories of cultural imperialism (Tomlinson, 1991; Tracey, 1985) do not usually dispute the details about structures of ownership and products which are distributed. Nor do they contest the widespread dominance of specific media technologies. Neither do they usually challenge the statistical figures about which products are moving where or question the way that the same cultural forms (food, music, clothes, films) are becoming widely distributed around the world. The disputes start to occur when the argument is extended to a model of *cultural effects* – the claim that local culture is suffering and being 'battered out of existence' (Tunstall, 1977).

A critical point that has often been raised here concerns the content of the *dominating* culture (Tomlinson, 1991; Tunstall, 1977; Tracey, 1985). If we take it, as writers such as Herbert Schiller (1991) have argued, that one of the most dominant imperialist forces over a large part of the twentieth century has been the United States and its corporations, then a question arises about the characteristics of the 'culture' that is being used to dominate (a question that in turn is as applicable to German, French or Japanese companies and culture). In what ways do films like *Casablanca* or *Jurassic Park*, or cartoon characters such as Donald Duck or the Pink Panther, embody or communicate US values? How does *Dallas*, *Star Trek* or *Roseanne* contribute to US cultural imperialism? In what ways do Madonna, Michael Jackson or Bruce Springsteen embody or communicate 'American' values?

As a number of writers have pointed out (Goodwin and Gore, 1990; Laing, 1986; Negus, 1993), there is not simply one homogenous US culture. The sounds and images of US musical entertainment contain important contributions from numerous groups, such as the Eastern European Jewish influence on the formation and development of Hollywood, television comedy and Tin Pan Alley songwriting or the African-American and Latino influence on the development of jazz, blues, salsa, rap and hip-hop styles. It is difficult and misleading, therefore, simply to view cultural forms emanating from the United States as a unified 'dominant culture'. The situation becomes even more complicated because this 'US' material is also being distributed by Japanese-, German- and British-based corporations.

Such an argument has led to the claim that theories of cultural imperialism are no longer relevant because it is not possible simply to equate the 'culture' that is being distributed by a company with its national origins (Laing, 1986). In an era of 'polycentric corporations' (Morley and Robins, 1995) owned and financed through an alliance of Japanese, European and North American interests (Garofalo, 1993) it is increasingly difficult to locate the 'source' of this culture in national terms.

However, we should be wary of jumping to the conclusion that this means that there is no longer *any* 'dominant culture' and that the world is simply patrolled by 'global' companies which are distributing a variety of 'global' products. Major corporations may present themselves as 'global' in their annual reports and advertising literature, but their operations are global only in a partial sense. Corporations might like to announce that they have no nation, but they do not operate above but in *relation to* nation states. Major corporations continually lobby specific national governments and have registered offices and headquarters in quite specific places. Major music corporations increasingly adopt 'transnational practices', but these are worked out in and implemented from quite specific national bases (Sklair, 1991; Negus, 1993). One way of approaching such 'transnational practices' would be to follow Schiller (1991), who has suggested that cultural imperialism needs to be understood less in terms of national characteristics and more in terms of patterns of 'transnational corporate culture domination' (1991: 15).

In writing elsewhere (1993, 1996) I have argued that one way in which patterns of dominance are maintained is through the organization of working practices and repertoires in a particular manner which privileges what is euphemistically called 'international repertoire'. This is a category that refers to a music that is 'international' in one specific sense: it has become a music business euphemism for the recordings of Anglo-American artists singing conventional rock/pop songs in English (the occasional non-Anglo artist *is* admitted to this category, provided they sing in English). The record industry's own statistics and a number of media scholars have highlighted how this Anglo-international repertoire has dominated sales charts and radio play-lists throughout the world for a number of years (Hung and Morencos, 1990; Laing, 1992; Negus, 1993; Robinson, Buck and Cuthbert, 1991; Wallis and Malm, 1984). Drawing on Stuart Hall's remark that the global is the 'self-presentation of the dominant particular' (Hall, 1991: 67), I have characterized international repertoire as a 'dominant particular' against which other sounds are assessed and around which the world production and consumption of music became organized in the early 1990s (Negus, 1993, 1996). This dominant particular has been inscribed into and constituted within what Schiller (1991) has referred to as a dominant 'transnational corporate culture', a term which refers to ways of working that have been increasingly adopted and advocated by all of the major entertainment corporations.

Yet, this dominant particular has not simply been imposed – either within the corporations or in specific localities. Instead, such transnational practices have provoked a number of reactions and responses from entrepreneurs, music industry staff, audiences and musicians (Negus, 1993, 1995). Such dynamics raise a further series of questions about the content of the *dominated* culture in any locality that might be subject to these dominant particulars. Jeremy Tunstall (1977) makes the point that the characteristics of 'traditional' or 'indigenous' cultures are often assumed with very little research. He argues that it is often the elites and highly educated members of many poor countries who are the most active consumers of media products, while the poor rural dwellers who are short of land, food, literacy, income and life expectation are the main consumers of 'traditional culture'. This argument is borne out by statistical figures which show that the distribution of radios, televisions, telephones and musical equipment tends to correspond to existing patterns of social and economic inequality across the world (Golding, 1994). In many parts of the globe, people are simply not listening to recorded music or viewing music videos. Such a situation might invalidate claims about the direct 'effect' of cultural imperialism (Tunstall, 1977), but these circumstances also indicate how the domination of communication networks and media systems by major companies, which target markets that are viable in terms of profitability and ignore those which are not, is contributing to significant world-wide 'information imbalances' (Hamelink, 1995). The 'effects' of imperialism on culture are numerous and need not be thought of in terms of stimulus–response models of behaviour (the absence of certain technologies and cultural products in some places is as much a consequence of imperialist patterns of domination as is their presence in other locations).

A number of writers have also pointed out that many so-called indigenous or traditional musical cultures, which are often revered for their purity or authenticity, are actually 'hybrid' forms that have been created from continual interactions between 'Western' and 'third world', dominant and subordinate nations or between centre and periphery – the terminology varies: the point is that neat distinctions become blurred at the level of cultural practices (Goodwin and Gore, 1990; Reeves, 1993). One of the implications of this argument is that it is not only difficult to identify what the dominant and subordinate culture might be; these are then becoming mixed up in a way that is leading to new forms of 'global culture'.

Such an argument has been made about 'world music', a term first introduced as a marketing category by record companies (in the UK, France, North America, Japan and Australia) to lump together a vast amount of music that had previously been categorized as 'traditional', 'ethnic' or 'roots' music, particularly music from Africa, South America and Asia. The category world music (or sometimes world beat) has also been used to refer to the music of various artists who have tried to synthesize different types of music (whether Paul Simon, David Byrne, Peter Gabriel, Youssou n'dour or Cheb Khaled).

Judgements about this category of music have often been divided between those who celebrate it as an indication of new forms of 'global culture' and those who argue that this is yet more of the same imperialist exploitation. For Rick Glanvill (1989), world music involves exploitation and builds on a long practice whereby the music industries of Europe and North America have been 'revitalizing artistic forms' (Reeves, 1993) by drawing on musicians and styles from the third world. Not only has music been appropriated, removed from its context and packaged in a way that will make the most money, it has often been taken from musicians who have little copyright protection and who frequently receive no financial recompense. Glanvill (1989) has drawn an analogy between the production of world music and colonial trade patterns, arguing that the music of South America, Africa and Asia has been mined as a 'raw material' and then appropriated, used, repackaged and sold back.

As Andrew Goodwin and Joe Gore (1990) have pointed out, it is misleading to view music as a 'raw material' that is simply mined. Glanvill neglects the processes of mediation, the way in which music is always being transformed as it is made and travels among musicians and between audiences. Some writers have taken up this point and suggested, extending models of Anglo-American active audiences onto a more global stage, that this is an example of the 'margins' or 'periphery' fighting back against the 'centre' or global 'mainstream' (Chambers, 1994; Garofalo, 1993; Wallis and Malm, 1992). According to one version of this argument, the use of explicitly African elements does not involve the mining of scarce resources or exploitation, but a 'reuniting of rock with its roots'. For Sam Steele and Stephen Dalton, 'when musicians such as Peter Gabriel, Paul Simon and David Byrne and cutting-edge dance boffins scour Africa for inspiration – they are not engaging in cultural imperialism so much as reuniting rock with its roots' (1994: 20). Hence, it has been argued that new types of global culture are being made as new cosmopolitan, hybrid and multicultural forms which are contributing to both diverse and converging patterns of cultural practice across the world (Chambers, 1994; Lipsitz, 1994).

This is an important point because it again highlights that cultural activities in any one place cannot simply be interpreted as a response to or 'reflection' of the practices of imperial nations or corporations. There is no simple correspondence between the international movements of musical commodities in production and the way cultural forms are circulated through practices of consumption (Negus, 1996). However, from this premise (that the productive power of imperial corporations cannot directly determine consumption) a further claim has then been made: that the appearance of the same cultural forms around the world is not due to the activities of imperial powers (whether nations or corporations) but is a consequence of processes of 'globalization' in which various patterns of difference and the convergence of cultural practices and social activities are making it difficult to identify any power that might be directing such movements. The globalization argument, in its various forms, tends not to identify any form of overt exploitation or imposition, but is employed to emphasize processes of 'transculturation' whereby various forms of musical expression are continually interacting with one another, in the process generating a variety of musical styles that might be leading to a 'transnational music' or a converging 'nationless culture' (Wallis and Malm, 1984, 1992).

Drawing on the theories of Anthony Giddens (1990), John Tomlinson has argued that globalization can be distinguished from imperialism due to the way in which it is a 'far less coherent or culturally directed process . . . globalization suggests the interconnection and interdependency of all global areas which happens in a far less purposeful way' (1991: 175). As an explanation of the movement of cultural forms and musical commodities across the planet, globalization is a more benign theory. No one is really responsible. Power relations cannot be identified so easily, if at all. Change just seems to be happening as 'modernity' trundles like a 'juggernaut' across the world (Giddens, 1990).

Such an argument can then lead to a type of universalism – for example, that the thousands of people listening to Madonna and Michael Jackson, dancing to their music and reaching out their hands towards them at concerts are sharing in a universal musical language which touches a common chord across humanity and which transcends cultural differences. According to Michael Tracey, in his argument against cultural imperialism, the 'genius of American popular culture [is] to bind together better than anything else common humanity' (1985: 40) For Tracey, US culture is not offering exploitation, but a 'service'. Garofalo comes very close to implying the same thing when speculating about the world-wide popularity of Michael Jackson, suggesting that the 25 million people outside of the USA who purchased Jackson's *Thriller* album were not 'unwitting dupes of imperialist power' but responding to an album that 'resonated with the cultural sensibilities of a broad international audience' (1993: 25).

The people who have bought Michael Jackson albums may not feel that they have been duped, and US music clearly contains many different elements from 'non-Western traditions' (Goodwin and Gore, 1990). However, this type of argument tends to assume that a cultural form is universal because it appears to be universally popular. It does not connect the widespread appeal of the artist with the systems of production and distribution that have put a Madonna or

a Michael Jackson in the position *to be* universal in the first place.
There may be many cultures around the world that have produced
cultural forms that could be universally enjoyed. But some are more
likely to get to a position *to be* enjoyed than others.

A question that needs to be asked here, and one which requires
more research to answer, is how and through what processes did
Michael Jackson become a 'dominant particular'? What are the his-
torical-geographical dynamics of his success? While part of the
answer would concern the qualities and characteristics of Michael
Jackson's apparently universal appeal (i.e., what his music means
for various audiences), there is a further question here about who
has access to the technologies and techniques of cultural production
and distribution. This leads me back to Lenin's point about the
international dynamics of capitalist imperialism: apparently universal forms of human behaviour have frequently become popular
through relations of power and domination. Cultural imperialism
does not need to imply that audiences are dancing to Madonna
because they have rather passively absorbed cultural values from
elsewhere. As I discussed in Chapter 1, audiences can make their
own meanings, develop their own uses and gratifications and use
cultural products in a variety of ways. But, making meanings,
actively using technologies and interpreting texts is not the same
as having the power and influence to distribute cultural forms.

Although crude versions of cultural imperialism have been criti-
cized for positing a rather passive, gullible and easily manipulated
audience absorbing values from outside (Laing, 1986; Garofalo,
1993; Tomlinson, 1991), it seems to me that there is still much more
to be written about imperialism before the world can be characterized as post-imperial. On this point it is important to bear in mind
that processes of cultural imperialism have not simply and straightforwardly come about as a direct result of the culture industries or
modern mass media technologies. The introduction of modern media forms was facilitated by patterns of domination and relationships of dependency that were established under colonial
administrations. As Mohammadi (1995) has argued, when the colonial powers packed their bags and removed their national people
from administrative positions and from running governments
directly, it was not the end of their influence. They left behind
many European values and attitudes. These were encoded within
religious practices (taken by missionaries, for example), styles of
politics, forms of education and professional training, as well as

clothing styles and habits that did not exist before colonial domination. On this point, Annabelle Sreberny-Mohammadi (1996) has suggested that the dynamics of 'cultural imperialism' should be understood in relation to the way this has been facilitated by the 'cultures *of* imperialism', a dynamic that has a longer historical trajectory than the appearance of electronically recorded and transmitted media in the twentieth century.

My general point is that theories of imperialism may still provide important insight for further research into the movement and mediation of music around the world. Research into three issues in particular might significantly improve our understanding of such cultural dynamics.

- First is the continuing competition between dominant capitalist nations and their corporations. The fact that Sony (Japan), MCA (Canada and Japan), EMI (Britain), Bertelesmann (Germany) and Time Warner (USA) have been competing with each other by distributing cultural products that are not necessarily produced in the same region as their corporate headquarters should not necessarily lead to the conclusion that 'we are seeing the emergence of truly global, decentred, corporations' (Morley and Robins, 1995: 32). While the dynamics of corporate competition (for new markets, consumers and potential commodities) are changing, it may not yet be a post-imperial global era (Schiller, 1991). According to Ambalavaner Sivanandan, what is occurring is not globalization but changes to the 'circuits of imperialism'; rather than trade following the flag, now the 'flag follows trade' (1990: 184). Just as the motor industry can manufacture a car from components made in factories 'spread over Europe across the Atlantic through to the Pacific before being assembled in any given city' (Sivanandan, 1990: 171), so a song can now be composed on an Adornian musical assembly-line that is stretched across a network of studios in various locations which are connected by digital cables and satellite beams. In the process some locations are privileged above others. Further research could contribute much to our understanding of how patterns of music distribution are related to competition between the major capitalist nations and companies and provide insights into the dynamics of power in such relationships.
- Boyd-Barrett's model of 'modes of imperialism' and my own tentative work on the international music industry (Negus, 1993,

1996) could be developed further to examine how music production is organized in quite specific ways across different regions and to what extent patterns of organization are 'globalized' or translated into very specific practices in particular locations. The issue here concerns the key characteristics of the 'dominant particulars' of the music industry in terms of repertoires, working practices, methods of promotion and performance and technologies of reception. A further question concerns the type of responses or resistance that this might generate in specific localities.

• Jan Fairley has argued that there is also a need to understand cultural imperialism as an experience before the concept can be entirely dismissed. As she has pointed out, 'cultural imperialism is lived, experienced, struggled with, ideologically, emotionally, psychologically and physically; it is not an intellectual argument to be shot down by statistics' (1994: 116). Fairley's observations are drawn from studying in Latin America, where she argues that the distribution of cultural forms and broadcasts are often experienced in terms of clear sources of imperial power. While many intellectuals in Europe and North America seem to have been experiencing the 'globalization' of cultural forms and practices, for many other people across the world the same sounds, words, images and activities are daily associated with repression, exploitation and what is frequently experienced and labelled as 'cultural imperialism'. The *experience* of cultural imperialism, as Fairley argues, needs to be taken seriously before the *theory* can be fully rejected.

The local and the importance of places

Jocelyne Guilbault (1993b) has observed that, as writers have begun to identify various 'world' and 'global' musics, so defining the 'local' has become a preoccupation in many parts of the world. In the 'traditionally dominant cultures', defining the characteristics of local culture has increasingly become a focus for debates about national distinctiveness and difference, while for 'small and industrially developing countries' discussions of local culture have often emerged as a reaction to the fear of losing cultural identity in the face of globalization, conceived as either global homogenization or cultural imperialism or both (Guilbault, 1993b).

Debates about local distinctiveness, in contrast to the idea of emergent transcultural global forms, rest on the assumption that there is a connection between an actual place and the characteristics of the cultural forms that are produced there. The idea that certain musical sounds are associated with particular geographical places is a familiar one that has been used by the music industry in marketing campaigns and by audiences and artists when establishing a sense of identity for their music. Music has been constantly 'placed' as it has been produced, promoted and listened to, whether as the sound of Strauss's Vienna, Elgar's England, Satie's Paris, the Mersey sound, the Manchester sound, the house sound of Chicago, the Delta Blues, the sound of merengue from the Dominican Republic or grunge from Seattle.

Many cities in the United States have been associated with distinct musical sounds. At different moments the map has resonated with the sounds of Miami, Nashville, New Orleans, Philadelphia, San Francisco and Austin. This has sometimes been ephemeral when a city has become identified with a particular style for a short length of time (Seattle with grunge in the late 1980s and early 1990s or flower power with San Francisco in the 1960s) or it may be more long term – for example, the way that Nashville has become a metonym that stands for country music (Curtis and Rose, 1983).

While such everyday connections between musical sound and geographical place are frequently taken for granted, they raise a number of intriguing but often theoretically vague questions about how the meaning of a place might be created, constructed and conveyed. Where, for example, is the Seattleness of grunge or the Frenchness of Satie, and how do we recognize it when we hear it? Do you have to come from Chicago to produce a 'Chicago sound'? Such questions raise similar issues to those that were addressed in Chapter 4 in discussions of identity (e.g., concerning the gayness of gay disco music or the blackness of black music). Here I will try to build on what I have written in this previous chapter by indicating how this sense of locality might inform music making and be produced through musical practices.

For a number of writers who have been concerned with this issue (Wallis and Malm, 1984, 1992; Robinson, Buck and Cuthbert, 1991) there has frequently been an assumption that 'local' music has something valuable that connects it to a particular place – something that 'global' or 'international' music does not have. However, it is often very unclear what this might be. In Roger Wallis and Krister Malm's work, for example, the local is central to their study yet seems to be a particularly elusive and also very malleable concept. At one point they offer a definition of the local as a term that 'is used to denominate the level of music activity of the common man in society' (Wallis and Malm, 1992: 22). Apart from the sexism of such a definition, this vague category is then used with very little precision to refer to various types of music. Although formulated as a concept for music 'below the national level' (a household, village, town or county), the local soon becomes a synonym for a range of 'national' musics identified as Jamaican, Kenyan, Canadian, Swedish and Welsh (1992: 236–52).

Robinson, Buck and Cuthbert also use the concept of 'local music' in a very malleable way, offering the following definition: 'By local we refer to a country or community, whichever represents the salient culture of a particular musician. In terms of individuals, we call all musicians who live and work within a specific place "local" musicians for that place; Michael Jackson is a local musician in New York City' (1991: 30).

Such a definition begs many questions. Would Michael Jackson also be a 'local' musician if he was recording in Tokyo or Berlin? Can a country and community represent the 'salient culture' of a musician in the same way? In what actual sense is such a culture 'local'? Such a definition also sits uncomfortably alongside the authors' reference to 'international popular music' as 'mass culture' and 'local music' as 'folk culture'. The dichotomy here is between a global and homogenous mass culture characterized by formulas, sameness and standardization and local, diverse, pluralistic varieties of music (more innocent, pure and immediate). A similar approach can be found in the writings of Wallis and Malm (1984, 1992), who frequently imply that local music comes from a place, whereas 'international pop music' seems to come from no place.

The point I am perhaps labouring in this semantic nit-picking here is that attempts to 'define' the local can lead to many ambiguities and contradictions. The concept is very loose and malleable and is frequently used in a confusing way over and sometimes against existing concepts (such as nation, community, town). Just as no sound, cultural form or corporation can be 'global' in anything but a partial way, so the characteristics of 'local music' (a country, a community, the sound of a star in a city) are so varied and lead to a rather confusing array of potential 'global–local' musical relationships. The 'local' seems to become as elusive, vague and all-embracing as the 'global'.

In contrast to this approach, it might be more useful to adopt more precise terminology and, instead of trying to *define* the local, to ask how the local is given meaning in specific circumstances. In short, how is a sense of physical place (nation, town, room) represented, conveyed and experienced?

On this point, though, a further potential confusion often arises with the blurring of real and imaginary places. In a book that sets out to address 'the musical construction of place', Martin Stokes does just this when he writes that 'The musical event, from collective dances to the act of putting a cassette or CD into a machine, evokes and organises collective memories and present experiences of places with an intensity, power and simplicity unmatched by any other social activity' (1994: 3).

Stokes is probably right to emphasize the way in which many musical events may produce a profoundly distinctive and particular experience of place for those participating (Woodstock, Live Aid or being at a concert by your favourite artist or dancing to music at a wedding). Stokes is also careful to acknowledge the impact of quite specific material constraints and social relationships on the way that music is created in specific places. However, he makes a highly speculative leap when claiming that 'a private collection of records, tapes and CDs . . . articulates a number of highly idiosyncratic sets of places and boundaries', particularly when he argues that such a 'private collection of records, tapes and CDs illustrates the ways in which music can be used as a means of transcending the limitations of our own place in the world' (Stokes, 1994: 4).

While the imagination is an important element in many musical experiences, this type of anthropo-existential approach to place leads Stokes to suggest that by playing a private collection of CDs an individual can transcend the limitations of his or her own place on the planet and engage in a kind of musical tele-transportation. Although many people may often *feel* that music can transport them, the actual conditions of that experience are somewhat more mediated and grounded in very particular social circumstances. As Richard Barnet and John Cavanagh observed when referring to similar 'global dreams' to those evoked by Stokes: 'A pop song can carry an anxious 12 year old from the slum streets of Rio to a fantasy world of luxury and thrills . . . you can lie on a straw mat on the dirt floor of a Bangkok shanty town listening to Michael Jackson and imagine yourself living another life' (1994: 36–7). The point being, of course, that the straw mat is still there while the music is playing. It is simply a fantasy and, as Tony Mitchell has pointed out, the practices of music consumption which include a feeling of moving across space are complex and contradictory and are just as likely to involve the listener in an 'imagined exotic adventure' (1993: 313) as they are to entail a sympathetic and more constructive engagement with 'other' places.

From my own perspective, gained from teaching communication and media studies for a few years, I would suggest that music is not *that* special and no more enables people to transcend places than novels, films or television programmes (all of which are often produced in a deliberate attempt to make us feel that we are somewhere else). A *place* and a *sense of space* are different – materially, experientially and conceptually. A place as the particular, concrete site of specific social activities does not always coincide with a 'sense of space', the more abstract way in which we might locate ourself in the world, that 'stretched' sense of where we belong in relation to other parts of the planet (Giddens, 1990; Massey, 1994).

My point here is that understanding how music comes to be connected to a particular place involves more than applying a concept of the 'local' or conceptualizing places in an ungrounded way, which confuses quite tangible 'real' things and the imaginings of a listener. To avoid such confusions, it would be useful to analyse how that imagined place and sense of space is produced as a cultural construction and what its relationship to any real existing place might be. This is something that Sara Cohen has attempted to do in her work on the 'Liverpool sound'.

Hearing the music of place: the Liverpool sound

Cohen has approached the relationship between place and music in a case study in which she has conceptualized the 'Liverpool sound' as a complex amalgam:

> Liverpool's popular music incorporates a variety of regional, national and international influences, but is also particular to Liverpool, reflecting

a range of social, economic and political factors peculiar to the city. Local issues of ethnicity, religion and gender, patterns of immigration and intermarriage, kinship networks, and the geographical distribution of musical instruments and equipment, are closely bound up with the production of musical sounds and structures. (Cohen, 1994: 117)

Cohen argues that this complex is 'reflected' in the music of musicians, which in turn then helps to 'construct' particular places and the ways that 'people conceptualize them' (1994: 117). In attempting to unravel such circular connections and interactions, Cohen's methodological strategy takes two routes. One is to focus on the practices and vocabularies of band members who feel that they are somehow capturing the essence of Liverpoolness and 'reflecting' this in their music. The other approach is to attempt to get at how music constructs or is used to represent a place, an example being how The Beatles signified places and associated musical meanings through songs such as *Penny Lane* or *Strawberry Fields Forever*, which in turn have an impact on how people understand these places.

Cohen's research is particularly useful for highlighting how musicians continually 'place' themselves and their music. In this case, musicians in Liverpool construct a sense of spatial rivalry through music by contrasting the characteristics of their own sounds with those from the nearby city of Manchester and against pressures from the industries of the English capital of London. Cohen clearly shows that Liverpool musicians experience music as 'theirs' and impose a meaning on the music that is grounded more in inter-city rivalries than actual sounds. Like much writing about the local, however, Cohen gives little concrete sense of how this is communicated by the music apart from a few song titles and impressionistic metaphors about the feelings music evokes. On this point the 'Liverpool sound' is explained through a series of vague and often mystical quotes from people (usually musicians adopting a characteristically intuitive romantic discourse) talking about how it is related to aspects of the environment (open spaces or the movement of a river or train) which are then filtered through the bodies of the creative artists and manifested as 'Liverpoolness' in the music.

Cohen's study indicates how a sense of 'Liverpoolness' is experienced and employed musically as a means of establishing difference from other cities, but she says little about the more material practices through which a musical sense of place is produced and communicated. On this latter point I would suggest that the relationship between place and music could be pursued further via two distinct characteristics (which Cohen hints at in her work but does not systematically pursue): 1) How the material conditions of musical production in a specific locality provide the possibilities for a particular music sound to be produced and circulated; and 2) how particular instruments and musical elements signify meaning.

Making the music of place: the Miami sound

A useful starting point for developing such an approach is provided by James Curtis and Richard Rose (1983) in a study of the 'Miami sound'. Writing before the large-scale success of Gloria Estefan (and the association of this particular artist with both a sound and a city), Curtis and Rose provide a way of approaching these two analytically distinct but related characteristics – the specific conditions within which the music is produced and distributed and the adoption of particular musical styles of signification.

Curtis and Rose identify a number of the geographical conditions that contributed to the appearance of the Miami sound as a 'place-specific music'.

Migration Following the Cuban revolution of 1959, many Cubans migrated to Florida and, indeed, were actively encouraged and politically welcomed by the US government, aware that this was a highly symbolic act during the Cold War.

Language and cultural forms Cuban immigrants brought with them the Spanish language and a range of Afro-Latin cultural forms, particularly music. In Florida, and particularly in Miami, this interacted with various rock and soul styles, and a variety of hybrid foods, cultural practices and language uses ('Spanglish') emerged and could be found in stores, supermarkets, bars and restaurants.

Entrepreneurial activity Many of those who left Cuba were from the more wealthy classes of the population and hence entered the United States with money that was then invested in recording facilities and in setting up studios. This partly helped to 'define' the musical sound of Miami, but it also attracted Latin musicians from other parts of the United States, the Caribbean and Latin

America. Hence, the setting up of specifically 'Latin' musical production facilities contributed to the production of a particular type of creative environment.

Radio A network of Spanish-language radio stations was gradually established. These provided an immediate outlet for distributing and promoting the music that was being produced in the area and contributed to the local circulation of the music that was being created.

If these specific factors provided the conditions for music to be produced and distributed in specific ways, the cultural interactions in Miami created a particular type of musical signification. The meeting of Latin and US musicians and singers resulted in a cultural fusion during which key elements of rock and disco were combined with specifically Cuban musical styles (the 'Cubanness' of which has been discussed in more detail in Chapter 4). Through this process a 'Miami sound' was created in which very particular musical elements could be identified:

1) a blend of rock-pop song structure (verse, chorus, verse, chorus, middle, chorus, etc.) with the repeated rhythmic chordal patterns and matrices of much Latin music;
2) a rhythm that combined the distinctive off-beat 3/2 clave of Cuban music with the more on-beat 4/4 rhythm of rock and disco;
3) a particular blend of instruments which brought together sounds not usually combined – for example, bongos and conga drums were not usually employed in rock/US pop, but the electric guitar was not often used in Cuban music; the piano was played according to the conventions of Latin music, for rhythm rather than melody, and a bass playing style developed that combined the syncopated off-beat across the bar swinging pattern of salsa and mambo with the on-beat bass pattern of rock and disco;
4) songs were sung in both Spanish and English or Spanglish, with tracks sometimes recorded in English and Spanish (a practice later developed for distributing Gloria Estefan's music to different markets).

Through this discussion, Curtis and Rose argued that all of these aspects contributed to the creation of a distinctive Miami musical sound; particular sounds were connected to and came to signify place identities through quite specific historical circumstances rather than through any essential connections to a people or piece of land. Their study is useful for indicating how music becomes associated with places through both the definite conditions of its production and the adoption of particular musical signifiers. It is within and out of such processes that place can then be experienced through music.

However, Curtis and Rose's study lacks the very elements that were highlighted by Cohen in her research into the Liverpool sound – a sense of the way in which people experience and interpret these sounds (how people 'place' the sounds that they hear). Curtis and Rose demonstrated how the Miami sound came to be created, but gave few clues as to the ways in which people recognized it.

It is perhaps inevitable that as soon as the 'Miami sound' was produced and in circulation, as soon as the music was on the move out from the place of its origins (particularly with the commercial success of Gloria Estefan), it could be pastiched or simulated elsewhere, a practice that has frequently occurred with other types of place-specific music. Hence, the 'Merseybeat' sound has been imitated, pastiched and parodied since the 1960s, and rock, rap, zouk and salsa have all been moving across the world, out from their points of origin. As this occurs, music often signals its geographical sources and is recognized as having an 'origin', but far more frequently it is given new characteristics and meanings as it is remade within new geographical dialogues (see, for example, Guilbault, 1993a; Román Velázquez, 1996). Both the historical roots and the geographical routes of particular musical forms become increasingly hard to trace as they echo back across space and time. Yet, at the same time, musical labels are continually introduced to place music anew (e.g., Swedish Latin jazz, Brazilian death metal and French funk).

Conclusion – geographical musical tracks

In the first part of this chapter I devoted some space to a discussion of imperialism to argue that the geographical movement of music takes place within very specific power struggles and social-political relationships. In doing this, I indicated how theories of imperialism

(I employed the specific theory formulated by Lenin and elaborated this with Boyd-Barrett's modes of media imperialism) are potentially useful for identifying the dynamics and power struggles through which musical and cultural changes are occurring across the world. In contrast, I pointed to how theories of globalization tend to propose a far less coherent, motivated or culturally directed process.

Globalization theories (I referred in particular to Giddens and Tomlinson) provide little indication of how specific nations or corporations are directly shaping the international movement of popular music around the world. Bearing in mind the complexity of national relationships and the way that companies are increasingly operating as 'polycentric corporations', I suggested that research into the 'dominant particulars' of international music distribution and their experiential consequences might contribute further to our understanding of the spatial routes of popular music.

In the latter part of this chapter I have moved from the 'global' and considered in more detail what is sometimes referred to as 'the local' or the relationship between music and place. Here, combining the insights of studies carried out by Cohen in Liverpool and Curtis and Rose in Miami, I have suggested that a useful way of approaching 'place-specific music' is to consider three distinct features: first, how the material circumstances in particular places (such as the characteristics of the population, entrepreneurial activity and communication networks) provide possibilities for and hence contribute to the production of specific sounds. Second, I pointed to some of the ways that particular musical instruments, rhythms and voices (using a particular language, accent and words) can be employed to communicate a symbolic sense of the identity of a place. Third, I discussed how listening involves the recognition and interpretation of how a place is signified musically and that this is often related to the way that music can be used to construct a sense of 'spatial rivalry'. These three features draw on and bring together issues I have touched upon in different parts of this book (production, reception and communication of identity). I now want to conclude by considering some of the more overtly political processes within which such mediations occur.

CHAPTER SEVEN
POLITICS

By giving this chapter the title of politics I do not mean to suggest that the 'politics of music' is a subject that can be separated off into a discrete section from other issues in this book. As I have already indicated in previous chapters, studying the sounds, words and images of popular music leads directly towards debates about dynamics of power and influence. In the first two chapters I referred to the views of theorists who have argued that the power to influence the form and meaning of popular music is exercised by entertainment corporations during production, and contrasted this with the counter-claim that active audiences are able to challenge and undermine such influences during consumption. In subsequent chapters I have discussed how the adoption and communication of particular cultural identities can be a political act and how the production of historical knowledge and the uses to which it is put has political implications. I have also pointed to how the movement of music around the world is implicated in struggles for markets, for resources and over representations.

Having mentioned all this, however, in this chapter I want to focus selectively on some specific issues that have been explicitly labelled as 'political' in discussions of popular music. I shall start with the 'message' of popular music and, following discussions in previous chapters, argue that any political content of a song has to be understood in terms of processes of mediation during which it can undergo change and be connected to various political agendas. I shall then consider one of the most overt relationships between music and politics in the twentieth century by discussing the connections between cultural activity and the state.

In this section I will draw on the ideas of theorists who have argued that modern states are not composed of neutral institutions of administration but have structural tendencies which can predispose them towards quite exclusive goals. I shall refer to Nazi Germany as an illustration of a state attempting to control cultural practices and in doing so I will also highlight the problems and dilemmas that can be posed for those seeking to impose political restrictions and ideological constraints upon music. The example of Nazi Germany is used here, not to imply that all state music activity is inevitably fascist or totalitarian, but to highlight, in a stark way, how various issues I have been discussing (systems of production, patterns of consumption, modes of transmission, a sense of history and identity) are not simply of 'academic' interest but can be employed by the modern nation state and used for quite authoritarian and exclusivist ends. Building on what I have written in other chapters of this book, the case of Nazi Germany is also used here as an example of processes of mediation and articulation through which particular styles of music are produced, circulated, experienced and given quite specific cultural and political meanings.

In the final part of the chapter I will move from the 'malevolent' state of control, constraint and exclusivity to attempts to mobilize the potentials of the 'benevolent' state and the possibilities for a more inclusive and democratic form of musical practice. Throughout this chapter I shall highlight how theoretical knowledge about music plays a part in guiding and helping understand musical activities. I will conclude by suggesting that research and study might contribute to the intercultural dialogues that are facilitated by music on its travels around the world.

Imagining: the elusive political message

Academics and journalists have often searched for political meaning in the words, sounds and images of popular music. Likewise, recording artists have often attempted to communicate political ideas through their sounds, lyrics and images. This has led some commentators to ask how music and popular songs encode particular political messages: how do we identify the political content of music? A number of writers have devoted themselves to this task (Orman, 1984; Pratt, 1994; Street, 1986), and I could take up space in this chapter going through the lyrics of songs, the videos of artists and the sounds of particular instruments in search of a 'political message'.

If I start doing this, though, I will be engaging in a process of 'decoding' as part of an audience for the music. In trying to understand the political meaning of any piece of music or song I would have brought all sorts of assumptions and expectations to my interpretation. A process of articulation would have occurred – I would have been connected to, or connected myself with, a particular song, a recorded voice and a range of sounds, words and images. A process of mediation would have occurred – maybe subtle, maybe profound – in which I would have 'finished' a song by giving it a definitive meaning for me that I could then attempt to communicate in these pages.

I don't want to do this because one of the implications of what I have been arguing in this book is that we cannot locate the political meaning of music in any sound text. To search for *the* 'meaning' is probably a waste of time, and it might give more insight into how music communicates to follow the processes of change which occur as the music leaves its point of origins and connects with different bodies across a range of social and technological mediations. It is perhaps the way that music connects with meanings that indicates how it can work and be made to work for particular political agendas, a point I will be illustrating in various ways throughout this chapter.

This point should, I hope, be fairly clear by now, but I want to illustrate this with reference to one song that has been identified as 'political' (there are, of course, countless others). In 1971, a year after The Beatles released their last album, *Let it Be*, John Lennon produced a single and an album with the same name, *Imagine*. The title song is a rather hymnlike ballad which draws on the tradition of the singer-songwriter intimately 'confessing' at the piano and inflects this with some 'soul gospel tinged singing' (Middleton, 1990: 16). The piano is recorded multi-tracked, which gives it a deep and resonant tone. The voice is dreamlike and distant – using an echo effect and relaxed style of delivery that Lennon had developed on many of The Beatles' recordings (such as his *I'm Only Sleeping*, *Tomorrow Never Knows*, *Lucy in the Sky with Diamonds*) and in his solo work.

Since it was first released in 1971 *Imagine* has become one of Lennon's most popular compositions. It has been played, performed, re-recorded and broadcast continually all over the world. One of my reasons for referring to the song here is that it is well known and it is an example of a song that has moved through time and space away from its moments of origins. This means that attempting to understand it in relation to the motives of the composer and original performer (John Lennon) or the conditions of its original production (end of 1960s/beginning of 1970s USA and Britain) will give only a partial version of its 'meaning'. It is such movements, and the ability of music and songs to endure through time and across space and connect with a variety of people, that should make us sceptical of any attempts to interpret any meaning as a 'reflection' of a society or an 'expression' of an artist. This song has actually been given quite different political meanings on its travels.

For John Street (1986), the song *Imagine* was a 'political and musical success' because it avoided the didacticism of some of Lennon's other work (e.g., *Woman is the Nigger of the World*) and imaginatively involved the audience as 'participants in Lennon's dream'. Street argued that the song 'embraces neither the analysis nor the practices of socialism, and yet its socialist sympathies are obvious' (1986: 165). Such sympathies have been 'obvious' to other writers too. Robin Denselow, for example, described the song in similar terms as a 'vision of peaceful global Communism' (1989: 106). In much the same way, Jon Wiener wrote that it 'expressed the New Left position for which Herbert Marcuse was the spokesman; the potential power of the working class is undermined by a repressive culture; restoring the utopian impulse is a key step towards social transformation' (1985: 161). For Wiener, the message of *Imagine* was simple and clear. Yet, he found it 'remarkable how many critics misunderstood it' (1985: 160).

What is it that makes the song have 'socialist sympathies' or a 'vision of global communism'? What is it that gives it a 'simplicity and clarity' and makes its meaning so obvious? And if it is so obvious then why do some people not 'understand' the message? The problem with such formulations is that they are based on a simplistic model of how the meaning of popular music is produced and communicated; they are based on the idea that a song has a straightforward 'message' that is then transmitted, received and understood. Any lack of understanding (or changed meaning) is then viewed as a breakdown in communication rather than an integral part of the processes of mediation, articulation and interpretation through which popular music is understood. By this I do not mean to imply that lyrics can have *any* meaning or that the intentions of the author play no part in shaping how a song is understood. However, I do follow Mike Pickering's argument that the enduring appeal of songs through time should not be understood as 'constant and fixed, not open to an infinite range of interpretations, but as being founded upon acts of appreciation and judgement that occur within definite social relations' (1987: 44). A glimpse of such social relations and judgement becomes clear if we consider some of the movements of this song.

Musically *Imagine* is a rather predictable ballad based on a formulaic song structure, and revolving largely around the repetition of two chords (C major, F major), with a vocal that stays within a narrow melodic range. With its harmonies, strings and slow tempo the song has a rather lazy easy-listening quality (particularly when compared with some of Lennon's other songs such as *Revolution, I Want You* or *Mother*).

Richard Middleton (1990) has also noted the song's soft, ballad style but, in agreement with Street and Denselow, has argued that it comes with a 'radical text'. Where this radical text might be located, however, is open to question. The lyrics are characterized by a vagueness that matches the soft dreaminess of the music and the echoey distance of the voice. The listener is asked to 'imagine' that there are no possessions and that there is no hunger, religion or countries. How these are to be removed or how such a change might occur is never mentioned. If this song is political, then there is a conspicuous gap between the sentiment for change evoked in the lyric and the practical political activity that might be required to bring such change about. The listener – 'you' – is merely invited to 'join us' (presumably the dreamer and his friends) in merely 'imagining' a world as 'one'.

The lyrical sentiments of the song are consistent with the vagueness and simple sloganlike quality that characterized much of Lennon's attempts at social and political commentary. As Denselow has rather melodramatically noted of his politics: 'Lennon's tragedy was that he realised that the sixties dream was collapsing, wanted to escape from the bland, money-making scene that could have trapped him, was instinctively idealistic and political, but had no political framework in which he could operate happily' (1989: 102). Similar points have been made about Lennon by Dave Harker

(1980), who has noted how, like those of many popular songwriters, Lennon's political songs tended to deal with social issues in terms of an 'us' and 'them' – *they* were always doing things to *us*. As Harker has also noted, what was never really clear, though, was who this 'they' were and who this 'us' might be.

Whether or not songwriters should be expected to provide such a coherent political framework (and it seems to me to be asking a lot), the song was subsequently adopted and used to refer to different us's against various thems. In 1987 *Imagine* was collectively sung at a Conservative party conference in Britain to greet Margaret Thatcher – one of Britain's most right-wing leaders, who led one of the governments least sympathetic to social democratic principles since the Second World War. As Middleton (1990) has pointed out, such an occasion was an example of 'articulation in practice' – the song was actively being taken and given additional meanings and connected with a very particular political ideology and social agenda. For Simon Frith, the use of this song at this occasion was an example of 'hegemony at work' (1988a: 203).

In referring to 'hegemony' here Frith was drawing on a particular interpretation of the ideas of Antonio Gramsci, who used this concept to refer to how dominant groups not only seek to maintain power through coercion and persuasion, but also attempt to gain consent for their leadership by adopting a range of cultural symbols and then connecting these with their own political and ideological leadership. Hegemony is actively won and maintained by accommodating and incorporating a range of dissenting or potentially oppositional beliefs and by redefining these in relation to a particular agenda. So, just two years after Street had written that the song's socialist sympathies were obvious, it was being rearticulated to new meanings. It was being claimed and connected with a completely different political agenda. This was not socialism, but a 'market-force version of Lennonism' (Frith, 1988a: 202).

My point here is not simply to suggest that the song was ambiguous and open to interpretation – this might lead us to start searching for unambiguous songs that are somehow not open to different interpretation. My point is not just about interpretation, it is about how songs and music *accumulate* and *connect* with new meanings and beliefs as they pass through time and travel to different places. After all, at the same time that *Imagine* was being articulated *to* a conservative free market agenda in Britain, it was being sung as a call for peaceful change and in an attempt to mobilize people *against* a conservative agenda and the repression and violence that had been wielded by various Stalinist states of Eastern and Central Europe and the former Soviet Union (Ramet, 1994; Ryback, 1990).

A few years later, at the beginning of 1991, when British and US troops were intervening in the conflict between Iraq and Kuwait, this song was again considered to be 'political'. This time the BBC's radio training department circulated a memo to their local radio network on the subject of 'Gulf discs', asking broadcasters 'to think carefully before playing any song of this nature which might upset our listeners' (cited in Cloonan, 1993: 219–20). Alongside Lennon's *Imagine* was Stevie Wonder's *Heaven Help us All* and Bob Marley's *Buffalo Soldier*. Here *Imagine* was heard by a state-regulated broadcasting system as a piece of music that would be too upsetting for listeners who might not want to be reminded of the less glorious aspects of a military conflict. Such an attempt at censorship begins to raise questions about the relationship of the state to popular music and the way in which a very particular agenda of meanings can be articulated to popular music by national governments.

The state and fear of music

The relationship between music making and government has often been discussed in terms of a liberal pluralist conception of political activity whereby state officials are perceived to act autonomously and to arbitrate between different social groups and forces. The assumption guiding such an approach is that government or its appointed officials can in some neutral way allocate resources and represent the common interests of the people or nation. Such an approach informs Roger Wallis and Krister Malm's (1992) study of 'media policy and music activity'.

Wallis and Malm (1984, 1992) conducted research into music making in various 'small' countries across the world and tried to assess how various groups and individuals (such as producers, broadcasters, researchers, company executives, trade and community organizations, educationalists and audience members) could put pressure on governmental bodies that would facilitate greater representation of musical activities and provide a challenge to the monopoly of music making enjoyed by the major entertainment corporations. After a wide-ranging study of music making in various countries (including Jamaica, Kenya, Wales and Sweden) they arrived at the rather pessimistic conclusion that attempts to influence government policies and cultural activities are ultimately impeded, not by any structural aspects of political and economic systems, but due to the foibles of 'politicians':

> Policies, of course, are no better than the people who formulate and implement them. Many politicians pay generous lip-service to ideals of national and/or ethnic cultural identity . . . Politicians hesitate before opening the media to thoughts and statements which could weaken their own position, and musical expression by virtue of its popular appeal can do just that. Politicians also usually have a secret desire to retain guarantees for their own access to the media. (Wallis and Malm, 1992: 256)

Such an argument draws heavily on a type of common-sense reasoning which treats 'politicians' as a universal homogenous category and then views them as ultimately corrupted by egotistical 'secret desires'. The rationality here is little above a type of morbid bar-room pessimism which proposes that governments fail because 'politicians' are not to be trusted.

While there may occasionally be an element of truth in such an assertion (and this may explain the endurance of such a belief), by reducing the failure of attempts to push through more democratic music practices to the idea that politicians are corrupt, and by equating the inadequacy of music policies simply with the disreputable individuals who implement them, this type of conclusion detracts from the way that music policies are being actively shaped by (as well as directed at) governments that are not simply composed of neutral bureaucrats, administrators or representatives of 'the people' (who are then simply corrupted by their own self-interests). For all the value of their research into musical practices in different parts of the world, Wallis and Malm pay little attention to the character of the state, the relationship of government to the state and how states have a quite specific agenda of interests which can decisively thwart or transform the aims of those who are attempting to generate democratic cultural change through government institutions.

One of the points I want to make in this section is that activities of modern government do not (and probably cannot) simply represent 'the people'. I want to suggest that researchers concerned with the relationship between music making and governments need to grapple directly with theoretical arguments about the structural interests and agenda of the state and system of nation states. My argument here draws on quite different ideas about the activities of 'politicians' (and possible reasons for not trusting them). My starting point is that government is a process of rule that is, in the modern age, conducted through the institutions of the state (Hoffman, 1995). Governments should not simply be viewed cynically as collections of untrustworthy individual politicians and bureaucrats. Governments are made up of those who govern (or administer) and usually have limited terms of office; governments may come and go without changing the state and political system.

States are complex, contradictory, historically varying and geographically specific entities that are difficult to understand and as a result have been conceptualized in a variety of ways. This is an important point, because how we make sense of the state theoretically will inevitably have an impact on the type of policies that we might want to promote or how we might critique the way that government and politicians are acting. Here, I am approaching the state as the institutional system through which government has to be carried out. From this perspective, the state could also include the police, the judiciary, the military, the civil service, the monarchy – if any – religious institutions and the education system. As such, states have changed historically and been organized in different ways across the world. What I am concerned with here is not the numerous particularities of and contrasts between individual states, but the theoretical way of understanding how the state operates and the implications of this for studying how music is regulated by governments. As this is intended as an introduction to the topic (and within the context of a book on popular music at that), I shall simplify the issues and debates slightly by identifying two contrasting ways of characterizing the state. These, in turn, imply different ways of thinking about the state's political role and its relationship to cultural forms and practices.

I have already referred to one approach to the state, which is sometimes called the liberal pluralist version. For brevity I will refer to this as the *benevolent* state, the one that provides health care, education and information to all citizens within its jurisdiction. Those who favour this view of the state often argue that benign state control is the best way of guaranteeing that cultural forms will not become an instrument of particular interests; the liberal pluralist state will work in the 'public interest'.

In contrast to this approach is the view that the state does not represent all members of a society, but acts to further the interests of a ruling class or an alliance of dominant ruling groups (these ruling classes may be composed of a particular coalition of the military, the aristocracy, capitalists or religious leaders, depending on where you are located in the world). Although influenced by debates within Marxism, this is not exclusively a 'Marxist' conception of the state. Unlike the view of the state as neutral facilitator, this theoretical approach draws attention to how the state exerts control in order to maintain itself and the position of the classes or elite groups who are most dominant and have a vested interest in keeping the existing system and social relationships as they are. This is a theoretical approach which also draws on the writings of Max Weber to highlight how the state exercises and maintains a monopoly over the legitimate use of force and violence within a particular territory. This is the state of domestic counter-intelligence and external espionage, the state that engages in surveillance at home and deploys police and troops to control dissent and demonstrations. This is the state that has the power to declare war on other states and decide who any internal enemies are. This is what I shall call the *malevolent* state.

These two versions of the state and processes of government can be thought of as contrasting poles (benevolent and malevolent) of a political continuum. Each tends to privilege one aspect of the central tension across which the government of the modern nation is carried out, captured in Anthony Giddens's question 'How might the monopoly of the means of violence on the part of states be reconciled with the established political ideas about the "good society"?' (1985: 295). There is no easy answer to this question, and some of the major ongoing debates in political science have concerned the relationships between these two poles and the gap in between. To what extent, and at which historical moments, can the state of social care and welfare rapidly become a state of internal repression and external aggression? To what degree are different state institutions interrelated and connected together so as to form a unity that represents a united dominant class? In what ways might the secret service, police force, education system, health service and culture institutions be autonomous from each other? These types of question might seem a long way from listening to a recording, dancing in a club or watching a musical performance – but they do become an issue when state authorities consider that such activities are important both culturally and politically. Throughout the twentieth century there have been many occasions when governments have viewed poets, musicians and artists with a degree of suspicion and feared their potential influence.

Such anxieties go back to some of the founding ideas on which the modern state is based and have often been directly related to music. For example, the ancient Greek philosopher Plato argued that the social effects of music often went unnoticed because it appeared to be a rather innocent aspect of 'play'. Plato worried that music might generate lawlessness; new types of song and forms of music that were created within a society, or music that came from outside, could have a direct impact on the entire society. For Plato, 'the music and literature of a country cannot be altered without major political and social changes' (1974: 171). He envisaged a situation whereby music would unobtrusively influence 'morals and manners', affecting people in their everyday lives; it would then undermine the laws and constitution and finally it would 'upset the whole of private and public life' (1974: 192). Music, for Plato, had the potential to unsettle the most stable of social relationships and political structures.

According to Plato, political leaders had to be very careful about the music they allowed to be produced and listened to within the territory of their jurisdiction. Such a view has been shared by numerous state officials since this time and has continued to be asserted throughout the twentieth century, when there have been numerous attempts to ban certain types of music – not for aesthetic reasons, but because of their potential to connect with ideas and struggles for social and political change. So, for example, in the Soviet Union under Stalin stringent restrictions were imposed on composers, with many having their music tampered with or banned from public performance. Music had to communicate the correct message to the workers. Dmitry Shostakovitch, for example, was required to rewrite the endings of his symphonies because they were considered not optimistic enough. His music was judged according to a political ideology which had a particular idea of what pessimistic and defeatist music sounded like. When General Augusto Pinochet seized power in Chile in 1973 and imposed a military dictatorship, one of the first cultural policies of the new regime was to ban the use of Quena flutes and the charango, instruments used in songs that had become associated with the united popular opposition movement. It was not that the music produced by these instruments had any intrinsic meanings, but that in order to assert hegemony the state institutions were employed to break up cultural practices and their meanings (in addition to breaking up people – singer Victor Jara had his hands cut off at the wrists, thus symbolically denying his ability to make music, before being assassinated).

In referring to such incidents I am not arguing that all state activity will inevitably result in the use of cultural forms for oppression. Nor am I suggesting that states cannot and do not often work according to the ideals of the liberal pluralist state. I am also not implying that state power is simply imposed on hapless victims. Power always arises out of and is exercised through particular struggles and relationships. State attempts to erect cultural boundaries have always been challenged and are becoming ever more difficult to maintain as satellites and computer networks are able to beam images and information rapidly across frontiers without the intervention of border guards and customs officers. State attempts to make people play and listen to particular types of music have always led to resistance and opposition. What I am highlighting here, though, are the potentials of the 'malevolent state'.

To pursue this issue in more detail, and as an example of extreme state control of musical activity and how it was challenged, I want to focus on one of the most explicit attempts to regulate culture in Europe during the twentieth century: that of Nazi Germany. While this was a very particular state and way of governing that was established within specific historical and social circumstances, it was also a state that shared many characteristics with other modern nation states. My discussion here is informed by Giddens's argument (and caution) that totalitarianism, as the type of rule which characterized Nazi Germany and the Stalinist Soviet Union, is not a peculiar deviation of government but instead 'is a tendential property of the modern state' (1985: 295).

State repression and the regulation of music in Nazi Germany

In January 1933 the Nazi party seized power in Germany and instituted a fascist dictatorship with Adolph Hitler as leader. In the November of the same year, the Nazis established the Reich Culture Chamber (Reichskulturkammer – RKK), which replaced the cultural organizations, trade unions and various associations within the arts. The coordination and regulation of literature, radio, theatre, music and the arts was brought under the direct control of the Reich Minister of Public Enlightenment and Propaganda, Joseph Goebbels.

In my discussion of this period here I want to highlight how music was not simply subject to irrational propaganda principles that were imposed by a group of thugs (an image sometimes evoked to explain the power of fascism). Instead, I want to emphasize how music was regulated according to a very particular rationality and logic which aimed at quite specific pragmatic and utilitarian goals, which in turn were informed by particular ideas about the importance of music for history and cultural identity, a concern about the impact of music from other geographical places and a belief that such influences could be controlled through the regulation of production and consumption. As Zygmunt Bauman has argued in his study of the Holocaust, what happened in Nazi Germany was not an act of irrationality but was brought about through 'a typically modern ambition of social design and engineering, mixed with the typically modern concentration of power, resources and managerial skills' (1989: 77). As Giddens has also observed in a broader context, 'there is no type of nation state in the contemporary world which is completely immune from the potentiality of being subject to totalitarian rule'. The possibilities for such domination, according to Giddens, depend upon the state's ability to 'successfully penetrate the day-to-day activities of most of its subject population' (1985: 302). This is something that the Nazi state managed to do in a logical and rational manner. The day-to-day musical activities and cultural life of the nation were quite explicitly 'penetrated' and connected directly with the political and economic goals of the state.

Nazi music policy was based on an economic and ideological logic that engaged with and attempted to resolve a number of pre-existing anxieties, concerns and 'problems' that had been identified in the country prior to the rise of the party. The Nazi party had come to power offering two particular solutions for the people who supported them. First, they pledged to solve Germany's economic problems. A particular issue was the considerable unemployment and inflation that had followed the world-wide recession of the 1920s and financial collapse of 1929. Second, the Nazis aimed to restore German pride following the humiliation that had been suffered during and as a result of the imperial struggles that had culminated in defeat and an imposed settlement at the end of the 1914–18 war. Nazi music policy was thus directed to both economic imperatives and cultural values.

Nazi music policy and national musical pride

Having reviewed various German music publications that appeared in the years leading up to 1933, Albrecht Riethmüller found that music criticism and the writings of musicologists had been pervaded by a concern that 'the preservation of German music culture was consistently seen as endangered by a plethora of foreign influences' (1991: 178). These foreign influences were identified mainly as coming from the United States and most frequently labelled as jazz, but they also included the endangering influence of the Wurlitzer organ. After 1933 this concern gained momentum. Instruments and performance styles that were considered 'alien to the German spirit', such as cowbells, mutes and the plucking of strings, were prohibited (Perris, 1985: 56).

In order to save German music from corruption by foreign influences, the Nazi state needed scientific research that would provide knowledge that enabled them to identify the 'Aryan' characteristics that required protecting and promoting. Musicologists were therefore called upon to investigate and identify 'Germanness' in music. One particular figure who loomed large in such a project was the composer Richard Wagner. He had published articles on race, religion and German nationalism which were permeated by an emotive anti-Semitic vocabulary in which Germans were portrayed as a 'race' corrupted by Jews. Wagner also promulgated the 'Führer concept' – the idea of the 'superman' as a heroic saviour of the people. Wagner published his thoughts in articles that provided a meta-context that reinforced some of the meanings in his librettos and operas. These connections were detected in the themes of *The Ring of the Nibelung*, *Lohengrin* and *The Mastersingers of Nuremberg* (Perris, 1985).

Wagner lived before the Nazis came to power and was a composer of music for the stage. But, as has often been observed, his work had striking 'parallels and associations with Hitler's creed' (Perris, 1985). Wagner's music could be quite readily articulated to the Nazi political project. When the Nazis took power on 30 January 1933 the state opera was ordered to give a performance of *The Mastersingers of Nuremberg*. After this event, Goebbels declared that the 'Awake!' chorus had now 'regained its true significance' (Perris, 1985: 55).

This is a very particular example of music and a composer being articulated to a political project and being set up as state-approved and -promoted culture. As Germanness in music was defined and identified, so particular composers and musics were prioritized. At the same time, the state sought to identify foreign influences and purge alien 'non-Aryan' elements from German culture. For example, the music of Jacques Offenbach was banned, whereas Johann Strauss, after detailed investigations, was found to be 'true German' (Wicke, 1985). As Bauman (1989) has pointed out, there is more than simply a coincidental parallel between purging alien elements from music and 'weeding out' alien elements from the society. The rationalization and purification of culture was part of a project that involved the purification of the population.

The struggle against music from the United States

The Nazi party were particularly concerned about the influence of jazz, which was considered to be a 'degenerate music'. Again, this anxiety was in part a response to concerns that had continually been voiced in Germany for many years before the Nazis took power. Peter Wicke has noted that a respected music journal, *Melos*, had castigated jazz in the following terms in an article in 1930: 'The foundations of jazz are the syncopations and rhythmic accents of the Negroes; these have been modernised and given their present form by the Jews, mainly New York Tin Pan Alley Jews. Jazz is Negro music, seen through the eyes of these Jews' (quoted by Wicke, 1985: 152).

It was this belief that jazz was 'Jewish' and 'Negro' music that caused the party so much ideological concern. This was part of a broader concern with the impurity and degeneracy of US cultural forms and a fear that 'Americanization' was sweeping away traditional culture, a belief that was found not just in Germany but held by many intellectuals across Europe during the 1930s. Nazi music policy thus employed ideas about the influence of US music that would lead to debates about cultural imperialism (discussed in Chapter 6) and was also based on assumptions about the essential connection between musical forms and certain 'racial' characteristics (discussed in Chapter 4).

The party immediately sought to regulate this influence by controlling the activities of musicians. All musicians had to be registered and their racial identity and origins were clearly categorized. In this way the party could stop black and Jewish musicians playing jazz in Germany, although many had already begun to flee the country and did not need persuading that this was not a good place to be making music.

Having regulated the actual musicians, the party faced a further dilemma: although black and Jewish musicians were not actually playing jazz, perhaps the degenerate elements might still be present in the music *composed* by black and Jewish musicians but *played* by Germans. The Nazis were suspicious that this might be the case, and to deal with this began further to regulate the repertoire that musicians used in performance and also monitored and controlled the catalogues of songs that were printed and distributed by music publishers. This involved raiding publishing houses and monitoring live performances to check that no 'Jewish' or 'Negro' styles or compositions were being retained in the performances.

The economics of Nazi music policy: industries and jobs

A further attempt was made to purge the US jazz influence through the regulation of radio. In Germany, as elsewhere, the use of radio began increasing dramatically, and between 1932 and 1943 the number of listeners grew from four to 16 million (Kater, 1992). In addition, between 1932 and 1938 the number of hours devoted to broadcasting increased from 13 to 20 (Wicke, 1985). Radio was an important new communication medium that became vital for the distribution of Nazi propaganda. Broadcasting output was therefore carefully scrutinized by the party and jazz broadcasts were banned from 1935.

The Nazi party also attempted to deal with the US influence by trying to control the recording industry. To do this, all recordings and producers had to be registered with the department of commerce and trade, and in 1938 attempts were made to 'Aryanize' the repertoires of the music industry. However, this was not a straightforward process. The Nazi state had to balance its desire to purge alien cultural elements with a recognition of political expediencies and acknowledgement that the German divisions of record companies had long-standing agreements with US companies that could not simply be broken and, crucially, the country was in need of the cash from foreign investment.

Here, Nazi music policy was heavily influenced by a wider aim of reducing levels of unemployment (Meyer, 1991). For to stop the production of certain types of music and to halt investment could result in German workers becoming unemployed. Such dilemmas were partly concealed by the messages promulgated by the RKK that foreign musicians were 'skimming wages of their German employees' (Kater, 1992: 37). Hence, the expulsion of Jewish and black musicians was not simply presented in culturally chauvinistic terms but also justified economically, as providing work for Germans. Many German musicians had been having a particularly hard time since the end of the 1920s, partly due to the introduction of recorded sound in the movies, which had meant that many musicians were no longer required in movie theatres.

The practical problems for Nazi policy: active audiences, creative artists and the international culture industry

Right from the outset, Nazi music policy was beset by various problems. One initial issue concerned the different approaches preferred by Goebbels and Hitler. While Goebbels initially wished to promote new music as a way of elevating and cultivating the minds of listeners, Hitler wanted music that would be emotionally rousing and which could also provide diversion and entertainment (Meyer, 1991). In practice, these two men had to adapt their individual preferences to the changing political circumstances, which in turn necessitated modifications to the music policy, which became increasingly escapist as the Nazis fared badly in the war. Although initially transmitting a blend of rousing marches, national folk tunes and entertaining dance numbers, broadcasters were increasingly encouraged to programme more sentimental music. As Wicke

(1985) notes, crude propagandist inflammatory songs were an exception; the formula which was developed and which became the preferred approach involved a deliberate attempt to 'befog the brain'. Publishers, record companies and broadcasters were encouraged to produce and distribute pathetic and sentimental songs that emphasized ideas about fate and homeland.

However, policy took a further twist after Goebbels decided that entertainment programming was a vital part of the war effort. Listeners' request programmes were set up as a way of encouraging links and a sense of interaction between dispersed people via the medium of radio. In a further move, in 1942 the party formed the German Dance and Entertainment Orchestra with the specific aim of recording jazz on disc and broadcasting jazz performances. Overall, Nazi music policy was a contradictory assortment of the ideologically motivated, economically expedient and pragmatically opportunist. The amount of control and influence that could then be exerted through such policies had to contend with a number of specific challenges.

One challenge came from jazz enthusiasts, who managed to develop networks and circles for the acquisition and distribution of recordings and who often produced their own copies of well-known US recordings on plain inconspicuous labels. In addition, jazz fans tuned into other radio stations such as the BBC from Britain, which were transmitting dance music with propaganda commentary in German and English across much of occupied Europe and Germany. Even after their countries had been invaded and occupied, many Dutch, Belgian, French, Danish and Norwegian people resisted Nazi music policy by broadcasting US jazz from illegal radio stations (Kater, 1992). Radio broadcasts coming over the border into German occupied territories were a constant problem to which the Nazis had to respond. This continually undermined their attempts to develop a radio broadcasting policy that could be kept within the borders of the state.

The people who were broadcasting and listening to these recordings comprised an audience that were *active* in a far more explicitly political way than the acts of interpretation and appropriation I discussed in relation to theories of audiences in the first chapter of this book. This audience activity involved listening to music in a way that avoided surveillance and raids. In Nazi Germany and the occupied territories the penalty for listening to enemy jazz broadcasts could be jail or the concentration camp (Kater, 1992).

Musicians also resisted Nazi policies. In addition to contributing to the distribution of illicit recordings, a number of bands would play the jazz that was deemed to have 'degenerate syncopations' but then resort to performing officially sanctioned songs when Nazi party officials were present at a theatre or club. This 'degenerate' music was in turn illicitly recorded and circulated. As Wicke (1985) has noted, The Peter Kreuder Dance Symphony Orchestra had a successful recording out in 1937, released on Deutsche Grammophon Gesellschaft, titled *Karawane*. The disc made no reference to the fact that this was a version of Duke Ellington's *Caravan* that had been released in the United States the year before.

The music industry also contributed to the undermining of Nazi cultural policy by providing audiences and musicians with recordings. The corporations were interested in making money before considering any questions about national politics or cultural identity. For example, the Lindström company distributed numerous US versions of recordings by major jazz musicians through its Odeon Swing Masters series. Yet, if companies like Lindström were undermining the Nazis' attempts at purging alien elements by distributing recordings made by Jewish and black producers, they were also supporting the state by distributing officially sanctioned Nazi recordings and providing vital sources of capital for the economy (Kater, 1992; Wicke, 1985).

Hence, even a state with as much apparent political power as Nazi Germany could not control the production and consumption of music in a straightforward or effective manner. Neither were such regulatory regimes established as consistent with an overall programme; cultural practices, political beliefs and economic activity did not simply coincide. The state had to struggle continually with a range of contradictions and dilemmas posed by the character of music as a cultural form, but also due to the way that particular patterns of opposition and resistance were encountered.

Musical practice and the benevolent state: policies and resources

In the above section I have suggested that state attempts to regulate culture in Nazi Germany were unsuccessful because they were ultimately unable to control the activities of musicians, producing organizations and audiences. Similar points have been made about the inability of the Stalinist states of Eastern Europe to control the production of jazz and rock music during much of the twentieth century (Ryback, 1990; Starr, 1983). The implication of this type of argument is that, despite the possibilities that exist for modern states to be used to further authoritarian ends, political power is not so easily exercised and maintained. This may not only pose a problem for those who might attempt to use state institutions to pursue exclusivist goals, it also becomes an issue for those who wish to mobilize the potentials of a 'benevolent' state. In the following sections I will consider this issue in more detail by outlining attempts to influence music making towards more liberal, inclusive and democratic aims through music quota policies and the distribution of local resources.

Protecting and promoting culture: music quotas

One problem that the states of Nazi Germany and the Stalinist Soviet Union encountered was their inability to regulate and control the geographical movement of music into their territories. Such an issue has not only been a concern of malevolent states, but has often been a feature of the activities of more liberal and democratic states. As Jocelyne Guilbault (1993b) has pointed out, more recent approaches to cultural policy that have been adopted during the 1980s and 1990s have often been informed by ideas about 'protecting' and 'promoting' cultural forms. As Guilbault has observed, this has assumed two distinct dynamics. First, protecting and promoting culture has become an issue and arisen as a response to fears that the monopoly over world financial and industrial systems enjoyed by Western nations has gradually been threatened by increasing competition from newly emerging economies and closer contact with cultures from other parts of the world. At the same time, in those places referred to by Guilbault as 'small countries', a concern about protecting and promoting culture has been directly related to fears about 'losing' cultural identity as international products are imported, and these are perceived to replace existing cultural practices and lead to resources flowing out of the country towards the major industrial nations.

In the 1960s and 1970s many of the calls for cultural protection and preservation came from voices in what was called the third world and were far more directly related to arguments about cultural imperialism and more clearly formulated within the context of unequal economic and political power relationships. However, since the end of the 1980s many of the demands have come from the 'smaller countries' of Western Europe, as well as Canada, New Zealand and Australia. As Georgina Born has pointed out, much of the cultural policy that has been formulated and advocated within this context has thus assumed 'a degree of economic well-being and of political strength and autonomy' (1993: 267). The struggle for cultural autonomy and attempts at preserving local culture have not simply been an issue in nations that were previously by convention categorized as the third world.

Attempts at protection have often involved the application of trade restrictions and tariff barriers. More usually, as Wallis and Malm have observed, one of the most frequent policies has involved an attempt to introduce quota controls on the amount of foreign music broadcast. Such a policy has been advocated or adopted in an effort to find a 'means of defending local content against the flood of Anglo-American hit music emanating from the giant media conglomerates' (Wallis and Malm, 1992: 2). And it is worth noting that there are an increasing number of smaller 'floods' in different parts of the world (Robinson, Buck and Cuthbert, 1991). At the same time, particular 'local' or 'indigenous' forms of music, neglected by the music corporations because they have historically provided little profit potential, have been actively financed and promoted by various governmental agencies in France, Australia, Denmark, Canada, Portugal and New Zealand (Castelo-Branco, 1991; Grenier, 1993; Gumbel, 1993; Laing, 1989; Pickering and Shuker, 1992). National state-sponsored organizations (particularly from France and Australia) have also supported their own national artists overseas in an attempt to raise the international profile of the country and bring in revenue (Felder, 1991; Tulich, 1992).

Such activities are a far cry from the malevolent state activities of Nazi Germany. These states have been attempting to act in a benevolent way by encouraging a greater range of musical activities than would otherwise be occurring and by preserving the livelihood and life style of particular groups and communities. However, such policies are by no means straightforward and also lead to a number of dilemmas. These have been well illustrated in Mike Pickering and Roy Shuker's (1992, 1994) analysis of the unsuccessful attempt at introducing a national music quota on New Zealand radio. Drawing on debates about this issue in other countries, Pickering and Shuker surveyed the arguments for and against forcing radio stations to broadcast a minimum amount of national New Zealand music and concluded that 'a quota or some such measure is necessary if locally produced popular music in New Zealand is to prosper' (1994: 74). Here I want to draw on their argument to outline how the state can support musicians from a particular locality, but also to highlight some of the dilemmas involved and arguments against such a policy. Pickering and Shuker have identified a number of benefits of radio quotas, which can be focused as four key points.

The nurturing of local talent   Because radio is such an important medium for the distribution of recorded popular music, Pickering and Shuker argue that it can have a significant impact on the fate of musicians. Not only does radio give new artists exposure to audiences (and vice versa), it also contributes to the market success of bands and performers and hence is directly related to a musician's ability to be able to make a living out of playing music. Giving local artists exposure on radio would encourage musical development and facilitate the career prospects of musicians.

The promotion of non-market-oriented aesthetic criteria   Pickering and Shuker argue that quota policies would force broadcasters to provide a distinct national musical aesthetic, which would be a valuable contrast to the unimaginative and safe options that are pursued by commercial radio, driven as it is by the desire to increase ratings. As I discussed in Chapter 3, and as Pickering and Shuker also argue, commercially-run radio tends to fragment audiences into market segments for the benefit of sponsors and advertisers and in the process can stifle creativity by giving little opportunity to new sounds and by not encouraging musical cross-fertilization between different genres of music. Here, quotas can encourage the programming of a greater range of musics and may lead to a broader array of aesthetic practices among musicians and more choice for audiences.

The promotion of local musical production   Pickering and Shuker observe that radio stations in New Zealand (like those in many countries around the world) tend to programme the hits of recognized 'international' artists (usually Anglo-American) that feature regularly in the charts of the US-based trade magazine *Billboard*. This can result in radio stations giving the impression that there is little music of any worth being produced locally, which then sends a negative signal to the major record companies, who have even less interest in producing and promoting the music of local New Zealand artists. The argument here is that radio quotas which force broadcasters to programme more locally produced music would thus benefit the New Zealand music industry by increasing their profile and potential profits.

National economic gains   The protection and promotion of locally produced music by New Zealand artists through radio quotas would result in a concomitant gain for the national economy, according to Pickering and Shuker. Music quotas would actually reduce the revenue that was leaving the country in performance and copyright payments to overseas companies and in turn increase the earnings of New Zealand entrepreneurs and performers. Hence, Pickering and Shuker argue that radio quotas do not simply involve cultural policy at 'home', but 'intervention in the context of an international capitalist market' (1994: 92). Within this context, the building of a strong home repertoire is a prerequisite for enabling artists and composers to compete with performers from other nations in the world.

In summary, Pickering and Shuker present a strong case for supporting music quotas on radio by basing their arguments on the perceived benefits that these will bring to the careers and livelihood of musicians, the diversity of music available to audiences and the gains to the national economy. However, there are a number of ways in which their claims can be challenged. Here I shall highlight just three problems with this version of the quota argument.

Quantity versus quality   Those who are opposed to restrictions on radio often argue that quotas will simply result in a quantitative rather than a qualitative approach to radio programming. Instead of the quality of the music and production being judged, broadcasters will need to assess the origins of the artists, and if there are not enough quality recordings available from a pool of national musicians then tracks will need to be added merely to meet the required quota. In their defence, Pickering and Shuker suggest that this is a smoke screen, pointing out that most commercial radio stations judge tracks by their potential appeal in terms of a series of market-researched audience 'tastes' rather than any intrinsic qualities. For Pickering and Shuker the key issue is about diversity: broadcasters should make a diversity of music available and then allow the audience to make judgements about what is and is not good 'quality'.

Enforcement of quotas   A second argument against quota policies has concerned the issue of enforcement: a government would need to find the funds to enforce such a quota and this would involve personnel carrying out a policing role and imposing sanctions against those who did not conform to such a policy. Pickering and Shuker are aware of the problems here and are particularly concerned to distance the type of state activity that they are advocating from that of the malevolent state seeking to control its citizens (such as occurred in the case of Nazi Germany, for example). As they observe:

> In liberal democratic societies, it is a common requirement of licensing authorities that broadcasting stations and companies adhere to certain principles, such as percentage of content devoted to different areas of output, so that quiz and game shows, for instance, are balanced by news and current affairs coverage. The twenty per cent music quota was intended to introduce a requirement of this kind, rather than manifest the Orwellian bogey of unbridled state power. (Pickering and Shuker, 1994: 77)

Whether the existence of prior regulations by itself justifies the introduction of yet further restrictions is a debatable issue, but an additional problem for music quota policy is connected to this issue due to the way in which such regulatory mechanisms are posited at a national level.

Nationalism   The problem here arises from the need to define who is to be included in the quota and the way in which this can be easily accommodated to a form of petty nationalism. Here, Pickering and Shuker acknowledge that 'insular nationalism seems to us a highly regrettable side of the issue' (1994: 73), but it is one that they tend to evade. The definition that they follow when proposing their argument for a quota is similar to that which has been adopted elsewhere, being 'music composed, arranged, performed or recorded and produced by New Zealand citizens or residents' (Pickering and Shuker, 1994: 75).

From my perspective, this is an issue that has to be taken very seriously and cannot simply be passed over as a rather 'regrettable side' of the debate. As many parts of the world have witnessed an increase in conflicts based on ethnic exclusivity and petty nationalism in the latter part of twentieth century, it is important to highlight the fact that music quota policies involve having to identify what should be promoted as 'ours' and then to classify other musical sounds, or the people producing those sounds, according to the soil on which they were born, the language in which they sing or the ethnic category to which they 'belong'. At the same time, foreign music (and its alien producers) are usually demonized as a 'threat' to the cultural life and economic well-being of the nation (hence, the repeated use of the metaphor of 'swamping' in discussions of this issue).

Yet a further problem is posed by those who actively wish to listen to this foreign music. Presumably they are either gullible victims who are being manipulated and are in need of enlightenment and correction or they are colluding in undermining the cultural life of the nation. This is a particular dilemma for any policy that is drawn up within the constraints of a national agenda. There is an important issue here, that of 'liberal' and 'democratic' governments also being part of nation states.

Discussing the state and nationalism, Anthony Giddens has concisely referred to the nation state as 'a bordered power container' (1985: 120). The nation state maintains an administrative monopoly over a territory that has clearly demarcated boundaries and exists within a complex of other nation states. As Giddens has observed, a state cannot operate on its own but is continually defining itself through its relationship to other nation states. Hence, borders are controlled and maintained, and within these boundaries the state regulates the individuals and things that may enter a territory. The state also regulates the types of information and people that may be imported into the territory. For example, the state maintains and enforces laws about censorship and protects certain types of information through secrecy legislation. Since the first books were published various states throughout the world have attempted to control the publications entering their territory, whether for reasons of obscenity, ideas of religious faith or notions of the 'national interest'. On this issue, although a state may have no formal 'music policy', musical activity can still be regulated in a variety of ways – through the granting of licenses to clubs, venues and radio stations; by stopping certain foreign musicians obtaining work permits and hence performing (Jones, 1993); by banning or restricting particular forms of public music making (busking, street singing and the 're-petitive beats' of rave music – but not muzak in clothes shops).

With this in mind, it is perhaps not surprising that central to the discourse of the nation state is the ideology of nationalism: the belief that a people with common characteristics, such as language, reli-gion or ethnicity, or sometimes simply those people who have been born on a particular piece of soil, constitute a separate and distinctive political community. The state attempts to use a range of symbols and beliefs (flags, anthems, festivals, icons, historical nar-ratives, etc.) in order to encourage a sense of psychological affilia-tion and emphasize and maintain a shared sense of belonging to what for most people, who will only ever meet a small number of their compatriots, will be an 'imagined community' (Anderson, 1983). Within this context the discourse of those in authority within state institutions is frequently against foreign or alien elements, which are often seen as a threat to the way of life of the nation.

Hence, while protectionism and quota policies are not necessarily motivated by nationalistic beliefs, they can be easily accommodated to such an agenda. However, a further caveat should be added to disrupt this argument further: the influence of the nation state can be challenged through the processes that occur over and *across* the system of nation states. As James Anderson has argued (referring to some of the 'global' processes that were discussed in Chapter 6), the power and influence of the nation state is changing as 'it is interacting with a plethora of other, different kinds of political institutions, organizations, associations and networks. Contempo-rary globalization is overlaying the mosaic of nation-states and national communities with other forms of political community and non-market social relations' (Anderson, 1995: 103). This leads me on to two further issues with which I shall conclude this chapter: first, the possibility for more local and city-based activities, and second, the potential for transnational musical activity across the borders of nation states.

The state as provider of local resources

In addition to attempts at protecting and promoting music, various local state agencies have also made efforts to provide resources for musicians and audiences. Unlike the protectionist policies which have been advocated for or operated at a national level, these have more often been introduced within the context of a neighbourhood or city. In Britain, for example, city councils in Liverpool, Sheffield and London have made resources available to subsidize the production, distribution and promotion of particular types of music by funding studios, rehearsal rooms and venues and by supporting events. This has been done with the aim of both creating jobs and providing more leisure facilities. Local governments have also attempted to help musicians gain deals with record companies, a practice that acknowledges the tendency of record companies to ignore certain locations when seeking new talent (Cohen, 1991b; Frith, 1993). Local city councils in various parts of Europe have also considered using or have used music making as part of a strategy for regenerating neglected urban areas and to try and bring people back to city centres, particularly during the night (Bianchini and Parkinson, 1993). Such efforts, far from being driven by a clear ideological agenda, have often been pursued in a more diffused and pluralistic way. This has often involved a variety of state organizations and interests in responding to pressure from audiences for venues and repertoire and lobbying from musicians for a livelihood.

Simon Frith (1993) has argued that such local initiatives have often been more effective than national policies. Through the allocation of resources, local councils have been able to support a diversity of different interest groups which have in turn been able to create their own momentum and generate alternative types of cultural practice on a small scale. In contrast, national governments, faced with the pressures of the nation-state system, have often been far more exclusivist (nationalistic) in orientation. However, this is not to imply that local councils can simply operate autonomously from national government. One issue that has often preoccupied activists in Britain since the 1980s has concerned the extent to which cultural policies can be effectively implemented at a regional, city or neighbourhood level and the degree to which such activity may challenge the agendas and aims of centralized national government. After all, any major attempt by a city council to push through policies that do not have the approval of national government will often have to confront legal challenges and economic sanctions, as well as direct political constraints. As those of us in Britain saw during the 1980s, when a radical metropolitan authority, the Greater London Council, began supporting cultural practices and giving a voice and resources to social groups that posed a challenge to the political ideology of the national government, it was promptly abolished.

Plurality, policy and the production of music knowledge

Drawing inspiration from the Greater London Council's support, albeit brief, for a variety of community groups and cultural practices during the 1980s, and noting city-based and neighbourhood initiatives in other parts of Europe, Born has argued for what she has called a 'postmodern cultural policy' – one which does not take the nation state as the 'unit of analysis' and which, by implication, would involve 'support for aesthetic pluralism' both within and across national borders. Born has proposed that such a policy should 'encourage aesthetic experiment and diversity within different extant genres' (1993: 279).

This argument for aesthetic pluralism is attractive, particularly in light of the constraints and limitations that are imposed on creative activity and musical diversity by the procedures and institutional systems of the music industry (as discussed in Chapter 2). However, a difficult question for such a policy is not about the goal of aesthetic diversity, but the practices through which it might be achieved. On this point, Born has proposed that, as 'musical-aesthetic judgements must be made', it would be necessary to create 'a diverse, plural and volatile set of genre-specific panels, made up of elected musical "experts"'(1993: 281). These experts will be accorded the task of establishing 'non-market social forms of aesthetic judgement' which will then guide their decision to support a certain selection of musical-aesthetic practices.

In proposing this, Born has raised an important issue about alternative ways of making aesthetic judgements. Her suggestions have been presented in a deliberately tentative manner with the aim of encouraging further debate, and in attempting to extend this debate I want to highlight how this issue leads directly on to the question of why we are producing a particular type of knowledge about popular music and how this might be used. For the call for panels of 'experts' to make musical-aesthetic judgements is an explicit argument for producing knowledge about popular music as a legislating intellectual. As Bauman (1987, 1992) has argued in his discussion of intellectual activity, this is an approach whereby knowledge production is seen as contributing to a type of 'social gardening'; difficult decisions may well have to be made, but some music and people will inevitably be judged as more worthy, while others will be weeded out and rejected. In this way, such an approach has the potential to lead to popular music studies as a type of cultural engineering.

Yet, as the authority of the legislating intellectual has been increasingly questioned, so the 'validity claims' of such a position have been challenged by both philosophical ideas and political events, which have shown that questions of truth and aesthetic judgement are grounded in particular culturally specific, geographically varying and historically changing circumstances. As a consequence, rejecting the 'authority' of the legislator, there has been a tendency for an alternative intellectual activity to be adopted – that of the 'interpreter' (Bauman, 1987). This is the person who recognizes that claims about intellectual authority, truth, value and the legitimacy of knowledge are relative. In contrast to the actions of the policy-making legislator, however, such an approach can then lead to a hermeneutics of resignation, a nothing-can-be-done-to-change-things type of attitude or merely disinterested aestheticism.

At this point, by drawing on the ideas of Bauman, I have set up another dichotomy: a stark choice between legislator or interpreter. If the first type of activity can manage to avoid nationalistic agendas, then it may still face the problem of creating cultural hierarchies: if the 'market' is not to decide what is produced and listened to then some other criteria or policy formulas will have to be produced to authorize the range of music to be made available. There is a question here that goes back to the discussion of radio quotas in this chapter, and further back to early debates about independent record companies (Chapter 2). What would a 'non-market' music sound like? Could it be encouraged without forming committees to stand in aesthetic judgement over practising musicians (and direct the choices of audiences)? Could diversity be encouraged through the distribution of resources or by providing a quantitative space within the broadcast media, without the policing of aesthetics or 'quality'?

Unlike the legislating policy maker who must grapple with these types of issues in the belief that the benefits will outweigh the problems, however, the adoption of the stance of 'interpreter' can lead to a type of disengaged popular music studies in which there is an avoidance of any attempt to bring about change and an embracement of the plurality of the market place. Here, value judgements are to be avoided and the different meanings of musical commodities are just there to be analysed and interpreted for their intrinsic 'academic' interest.

I want to conclude by tentatively suggesting an additional route to the choices offered by this dichotomy. It is one that is not so clearly mapped out, but one that might embrace the dynamism and transformative potentials of music as it connects with people on its movements. It is an approach, already hinted at in the work of various writers I have been discussing in this book, whereby music is treated less as an artefact with particular aesthetic qualities (which need to be identified and approved) or a polysemantic commodity open to various pleasurable uses and gratifications, and more as a medium of communication (Lull, 1992) and form of public knowledge with potentials to bring people together in new dialogues and social relationships.

Conclusion: for a politics of music as public knowledge and affective communication

In the first part of this chapter I focused on *Imagine* to illustrate how popular songs do not simply have one political meaning but can be connected to different political agendas in quite specific circumstances. I then considered how the modern nation state, in both its benevolent and malevolent guises, can be used to give particular meanings to music and musical activity. In this discussion I referred to specific processes of mediation (when the meanings of music are actively transformed) and articulation (when these meanings are connected to a particular political agenda). It is such transformative potentials that provide illustrations of how music can be both tied down to particular authoritarian agendas and claimed for specific interest groups, but which also indicate how music can be continually disconnected from its meaning and functional importance for states and industries.

This point has also been highlighted in studies of music making in various countries around the world by Wallis and Malm, who have referred to the way that vast amounts of music are produced and consumed 'below the national level of government and corporate activities' (Wallis and Malm, 1992: 22). As Ruth Finnegan (1989) has also observed, such everyday musical activities do not confine themselves to specific localities, but carve out and follow a number of 'pathways'. Some of these have been traced by Mike Pickering (1987) when following the movement of specific songs through time and across the spaces of everyday life between the seventeenth and nineteenth centuries in Britain. Hints of the variety of contemporary routes that are taken by music have been registered as the sounds of a collective of amateur musicians from the small English city of St Albans were exchanged in solidarity with those of Romanian musicians immediately after the fall of the Ceauşescu regime during 1990; were apparent in the mutual visits, exchanges of recordings and combined performances which involved musicians from Ireland and Turkey in exploring the Arabic influences on both musics (Stokes, 1994); and are evident through the ways in which Welsh musical enthusiasts have been distributing recordings, paying visits to and forming links with other Celtic regions across Europe for a number of years (Wallis and Malm, 1992).

These examples provide only the merest hint of the activities engaged in by amateur musicians and their audiences. Such practices frequently do not correspond to the interests of the entertainment industry or fit in with the agenda of the nation state. For this reason they are often ignored and remain invisible and inaudible (Finnegan, 1989; Fornäs, Lindberg and Sernhede, 1995). Yet, it is here, in the often hidden world of everyday music making, where sounds can move beyond simply being a form of aesthetic expression or commercial commodity and when music can take on a political significance as a medium of transnational knowledge and affective communication which moves across the borders of nation states and out from the generic categories of the music business.

In putting this argument, I am drawing on Lawrence Grossberg's (1992) observation that music works 'at the intersection of the body and emotions', and in so doing can generate 'affective alliances' between people, which in turn can create the energy for social change that may have a direct impact on politics and culture. Such affective alliances do not operate according to the assumptions of orthodox political theory and nor do they correspond to the rationale of conventional party politics. For this reason they are often disregarded or dismissed as 'romantic' or 'utopian'. Yet, the 'affective empowerment' that is generated can provide the potential for hope and political change. This does not simply involve utopian dreaming. As Grossberg has argued, such empowerment is 'increasingly important in a world in which pessimism has become common sense, in which people increasingly feel incapable of making a difference . . . affective relations are, at least potentially, the condition of possibility for the optimism, invigoration and passion which are necessary for any struggle to change the world' (Grossberg, 1992: 86).

A number of writers have identified this potential energy emerging on an everyday level, as music escapes its narrow definition as a commodity and provides a number of opportunities for creative activity and 'border dialogues' (Chambers, 1990, 1994; Gilroy, 1993b). Such possibilities have also been identified during more dramatic and revolutionary political struggles and social changes, as I discussed in Chapter 5 when referring to how rock music played an important part during the events in the former GDR that led up to the dismantling of the Berlin Wall.

In his discussion of these changes in Germany, Wicke had observed that 'music is a medium which is able to convey meaning and values which – even (or, perhaps, particularly) if hidden within the indecipherable world of sound – can shape patterns of behaviour imperceptibly over time until they become the visible background of real political activity' (1992a: 81). It is this 'intangible' presence of music as a form of affective communication that has so often been acknowledged in everyday discourse but frequently neglected in studies of politics and the communication media and culture industries due to the apparent non-referentiality of music and the way it seems to operate at the level of the 'phatic and the ineffable' (Gilroy, 1993a). In previous chapters I have already discussed how music can be made to encode and communicate quite specific cultural meanings; here I want to extend this idea by emphasizing how music works as a public form of knowledge and mode of understanding which is shared by vast numbers of people across the world, those of us who know that, while music is not a 'universal language', the meanings of musical sound are not *that* 'indecipherable'. As Raymond Williams (1965) once wrote when referring to how music and rhythm can provide ways of 'describing and communicating':

rhythm is a way of transmitting a description of experience, in such a way that the experience is re-created in the person receiving it, not merely as an 'abstraction' or an 'emotion' but as a physical effect on the organism – on the blood, on the breathing, on the physical patterns of the brain. We use rhythm for many ordinary purposes, but the arts . . . comprise highly developed and exceptionally powerful rhythmic means, by which the communication of experience is actually achieved . . . The dance of the body, the movements of the voice, the sounds of instruments are, like colours, forms and patterns, means of transmitting our experience in so powerful a way that the experience can literally be lived by others. This has been felt, again and again, in the actual experience of the arts, and we are now beginning to see how and why it is more than a metaphor; it is a physical experience as real as any other. (Williams, 1965: 40–1)

It is this potential of music that is so often neglected when it is treated simply in terms of its aesthetics, commodity form or practical utility and not in terms of its knowledge-producing, transformative and communicative potentials. Such qualities have also been highlighted by Paul Gilroy (1993a), who has traced how, for many years, music has operated beyond the boundaries of the nation state and borders of commercial markets as a transnational, pan-regional form of cultural communication. It has provided diverse populations of black people with a vision of the future based on the 'politics of fulfilment' (rather than the 'rational' teleologies of orthodox liberal politics). Music has provided an affective form of communication that has not simply been subjective, intuitive and irrational, but which has been used to produce forms of 'counter-rationality' which in turn have created affiliations, alliances and understanding amongst dispersed and diverse groups of people. In his writing, Gilroy has illustrated how, across the routes that connect Africa, the Americas, the Caribbean and Europe, music and rhythm has been a significant means of articulating and communicating experiences within a black diaspora. Gilroy's work is suggestive of the way that musical forms directly contribute to what he has called 'intercultural conversations', yet such dialogues have often received little serious acknowledgement in contemporary debates about politics, cultural production and public processes of communication (for a further discussion of this point, see Negus, 1996).

These potentials take on a particular significance at a time when increasingly important questions are being raised, in various countries, about the nature of education and what it is for (i.e., specific vocational training or general intellectual development?) and when the reason for doing academic research is being debated (i.e., providing pragmatic information for governments and industries or pursuing an independently defined scholarly agenda?). As various national governments are applying pressure with the aim of making academic activities and teaching less autonomous and more oriented towards, and financially dependent upon, private industry and government agencies, I want to conclude in an open way by suggesting that those of us involved in researching and writing about popular music might contribute to a web of knowledge, critical dialogue and intercultural conversation that is doing more than simply offering proposals to governments and making contributions to the well-being of national music industries.

Of course, we remain connected to states and industries, both inside and outside the academy, and it is important that we critically assess and inform people about how these states and industries are operating. Much *can* be achieved by researchers and writers supporting and engaging with various types of music making, creating dialogues with practitioners and subjecting the institutions of government and cultural production to critique. Those pursuing musical careers and who are daily subject to industry pressures and the regulatory mechanisms of nation states often require the type of comprehensive information and reasoned independent judgements that academic researchers can provide. However, this does not need to set limits to our 'pragmatic' choices, research and writing. One thing I have found from my own experience of and research into music making and from talking to numerous people I have met through many years of playing, listening to, studying and teaching about music is that musical practices continually refuse and move across the attempts to lock them into neat national boxes and political boundaries. At the same time, musical activity frequently does not correspond to the market segments of the industry and is always moving out and away from its containment within age, life style, national, ethnic, class, gendered, sexualized and racialized categories.

Perhaps future research and the study of popular music should build on such potentials and aim at producing a type of knowledge and informative discourse that does more than serve the interests of governments or industries, and which is not confined to the training of and discussions among 'experts' in seminars and at conferences:

this would be a type of public knowledge, open to question, discussion and critique, which might contribute to the creation of dialogues between people who are continually moving, performing and listening to music across cultural boundaries, geographical borders and social divisions.

BIBLIOGRAPHY

Abercrombie, N., Hill, S. and Turner, B. (1988) *Dictionary of Sociology*. Harmondworth: Penguin.

Adorno, T. (1945) 'A Social Critique of Radio Music', *Kenyon Review*, 11, pp. 2208–2171.

Adorno, T. (1967) 'Perennial Fashion – Jazz', in *Prisms*, trans. S. and S. Weber. London: Neville Spearman.

Adorno, T. (1973) *The Philosophy of Modern Music*. New York: Seabury Press.

Adorno, T. (1976) *Introduction to the Sociology of Music*, trans. E. B. Ashton. New York: Seabury Press.

Adorno, T. (1989) 'On Jazz', *Discourse*, 12, 1, pp. 44–69 [first published 1936].

Adorno, T. (1990) 'On Popular Music', in S. Frith and A. Goodwin (eds), *On Record, Rock, Pop and the Written Word*. London: Routledge.

Adorno, T. (1991) *The Culture Industry: Selected Essays on Mass Culture*, ed. J. Bernstein. London: Routledge.

Adorno, T. and Horkheimer, M. (1979) *Dialectic of Enlightenment*. London: Verso.

Ainley, R. and Cooper, S. (1994) 'She Thinks I still Care: Lesbians and Country Music', in D. Hamer and B. Budge (eds), *The Good, the Bad and the Gorgeous: Popular Culture's Romance with Lesbianism*. London: Pandora.

Ala, N., Fabbri, F., Fiori, U. and Ghezzi, E. (1985) 'Patterns of Music Consumption in Milan and Reggio Emilia', in D. Horn and P. Tagg (eds), *Popular Music Perspectives*, 2. Exeter: IASPM.

Allen, L. (1994) *kd lang and the White Lesbian Body*. Paper given at the British Sociological Association Conference 'Sexualities in Social Context', Preston, 28–31 March.

Andermahr, S. (1994) 'A Queer Love Affair? Madonna and Lesbian and Gay Culture', in D. Hamer and B. Budge (eds), *The Good, the Bad and the Gorgeous: Popular Culture's Romance with Lesbianism*. London: Pandora.

Anderson, B. (1983) *Imagined Communities*. London: Verso.

Anderson, J. (1995) 'The Exaggerated Death of the Nation-State', in

J. Anderson, C. Brook and A. Cochrane (eds), *A Global World?*. Oxford: Oxford University Press.

Anthias, F. and Yuval-Davis, N. (1992) *Racialized Boundaries*. London: Routledge.

Barnard, S. (1989) *On the Radio: Music Radio in Britain*. Milton Keynes: Open University Press.

Barnet, R. and Cavanagh, J. (1994) *Global Dreams: Imperial Corporations and the New World Order*. New York: Simon and Schuster.

Bauman, Z. (1987) *Legislators and Interpreters*. Cambridge: Polity Press.

Bauman, Z. (1989) *Modernity and the Holocaust*. Cambridge: Polity Press.

Bauman, Z. (1992) *Intimations of Postmodernity*. London: Routledge.

Becker, H. (1973) *Outsiders: Studies in the Sociology of Deviance*. Glencoe, IL: Free Press.

Becker, H. (1974) 'Art as Collective Action', *American Sociological Review*, 39, pp. 767–76.

Becker, H. (1976) 'Art Worlds and Social Types', in R. Peterson (ed.), *The Production of Culture*. London: Sage.

Bennahum, D. (1993) *k.d.lang*. London: Omnibus Press.

Bennett, T., Frith, S., Grossberg, L., Shepherd, J. and Turner G. (1993) 'Introduction', in T. Bennett, S. Frith, L. Grossberg, J. Shepherd and G. Turner (eds), *Rock and Popular Music: Politics, Policies, Institutions*. London: Routledge.

Berland, J. (1993a) 'Contradicting Media: Toward a Political Phenomenology of Listening', in N. Strauss (ed.), *Radiotext(e)*, Semiotext(e). New York: Columbia University Press.

Berland, J. (1993b) 'Sound, Image and Social Space: Music Video and Media Reconstruction', in S. Frith, A. Goodwin and L. Grossberg (eds), *Sound and Vision: The Music Video Reader*. London: Routledge.

Bianchini, F. and Parkinson, M. (eds) (1993) *Cultural Policy and Urban Regeneration: The West European Experience*. Manchester: Manchester University Press.

Bilby, K. (1985) 'The Caribbean as a Musical Region', in S. Mintz and S. Price (eds), *Caribbean Contours*. Baltimore: Johns Hopkins University Press.

Boggs, V. (1992) 'Salsa's Origins: Voices from Abroad', *Latin Beat*, 1, 11, pp. 26–31.

Booth, M. (1981) *The Experience of Songs*. New Haven, CT: Yale University Press.

Born, G. (1993) 'Afterword: Music Policy, Aesthetic and Social Difference', in T. Bennett, S. Frith, L. Grossberg, J. Shepherd and B. Turner (eds), *Rock and Popular Music: Politics, Policies and Institutions*. London: Routledge.

Bourdieu, P. (1986) *Distinction: A Social Critique of the Judgment of Taste*. London: Routledge.

Bourdieu, P. (1993) *Sociology in Question*. London: Sage.

Boyd-Barrett, O. (1977) 'Media Imperialism: Towards an International Framework for the Analysis of Media Systems', in J. Curran, M. Gurevitch and J. Woollacott (eds), *Mass Communication and Society*. London: Edward Arnold.

Bradley, D. (1992) *Understanding Rock 'n' Roll*. Milton Keynes: Open University Press.

Bruner, G. (1990) 'Music, Mood and Marketing', *Journal of Marketing*, 54, 4, pp. 94–104.

Burnett, R. (1990) *Concentration and Diversity in the International Phonogram Industry*. Gothenburg: University of Gothenburg Press.

Butler, J. (1990) *Gender Trouble: Feminism and the Subversion of Identity*. London: Routledge.

Cable, M. (1977) *The Music Industry Inside Out*. London: W. H. Allen.

Calvo Ospina, H. (1995) *Salsa! Havana Heat, Bronx Beat*. London: Latin American Bureau.

Castelo-Branco, S. (1991) 'Cultural Policy and Traditional Music in Portugal Since 1974', in M. Bauman (ed.), *Music in the Dialogue of Cultures: Traditional Music and Cultural Policy*. Wilhelmshaven: Florian Noetzel Verlag.

Chambers, I. (1985) *Urban Rhythms, Pop Music and Popular Culture*. London: Macmillan.

Chambers, I. (1990) *Border Dialogues*. London: Routledge.

Chambers, I. (1994) *Migrancy, Culture, Identity*. London: Routledge.

Chapman, R. (1992) *Selling the Sixties: The Pirates and Pop Music Radio*. London: Routledge.

Chapple, S. and Garofalo, R. (1977) *Rock 'n' Roll is Here to Pay: The History and Politics of the Music Industry*. Chicago: Nelson Hall.

Clarke, G. (1990) 'Defending Ski Jumpers: A Critique of Theories of Youth Subcultures', in S. Frith and A. Goodwin (eds), *On Record: Rock, Pop and the Written Word*. London: Routledge.

Clarke, J., Hall, S., Jefferson, T. and Roberts, B. (1981) 'Sub-Cultures, Cultures and Class', in T. Bennett, G. Martin, C. Mercer and J. Woollacott (eds), *Culture, Ideology and Social Process*. Milton Keynes: Open University Press.

Cloonan, M. (1993) *Banned: Popular Music and Censorship in Britain, 1967–1992*. PhD thesis, University of Liverpool.

Cohen, S. (1991a) *Rock Culture in Liverpool: Popular Music in the Making*. Oxford: Clarendon Press.

Cohen, S. (1991b) 'Popular Music and Urban Regeneration: The Music Industries of Merseyside', *Cultural Studies*, 5, 3, pp. 332–46.

Cohen, S. (1994) 'Identity, Place and the "Liverpool Sound"', in M. Stokes (ed.), *Ethnicity, Identity and Music*. Oxford: Berg.

Cohen, S. (1995a) 'More than The Beatles: Popular Music and the Production of the City'. Paper presented to 'Contested Cities', Conference of the British Sociological Association, University of Leicester, 10–13 April.

Cohen, S. (1995b) 'Sounding out the City: Music and the Sensuous Production of Place', *Transactions of the Institute of British Geographers*, 20, winter, pp. 433–46.

Crafts, S. D., Cavicchi, D. and Keil, C. (1993) *My Music*. Middletown, CT: Wesleyan University Press.

Crisell, A. (1994) *Understanding Radio*, 2nd edition. London: Routledge.

Cubitt, S. (1991) *Timeshift: On Video Culture*. London: Routledge.

Curran, J. (1990) 'The New Revisionism in Mass Communication Research: A Reappraisal', *European Journal of Communication*, 5, 2, pp. 135–64.

Curtis, J. and Rose, R. (1983) 'The Miami Sound: A Contemporary Latin Form of Place-Specific Music', *Journal of Cultural Geography*, 4, pp. 110–18.

Dannen, F. (1990) *Hit Men: Power Brokers and Fast Money Inside the Music Business*. New York: Times Books, Random House.

Denisoff, R. S. (1975) *Solid Gold: The Popular Record Industry*. New Brunswick, NJ: Transaction Books.

Denselow, R. (1989) *When the Music's Over: The Story of Political Pop*. London: Faber & Faber.

du Gay, P. and Negus, K. (1994) 'The Changing Sites of Sound: Music Retailing and the Composition of Consumers', *Media, Culture and Society*, 16, 3, pp. 395–413.

Duany, J. (1984) 'Popular Music in Puerto Rico: Toward an Anthropology of Salsa', *Latin American Music Review*, 5, 2, pp. 186–216.

Dyer, R. (1988) 'White', *Screen*, 29, 4, pp. 44–65.

Dyer, R. (1990) 'In Defence of Disco', in S. Frith and A. Goodwin (eds), *On Record: Rock, Pop and the Written Word*. London: Routledge.

Eisen, J. (1969) *The Age of Rock*. New York: Vintage.

Fabbri, F. (1982) 'A Theory of Musical Genres: Two Applications', in P. Tagg and D. Horn (eds), *Popular Music Perspectives*. Exeter: IASPM.

Fairley, J. (1994) 'Essay Review of Rockin' the Boat: Mass Music and Mass Movements, Edited by Reebee Garofalo', *Popular Music*, 13, 1, pp. 111–17.

Felder, R. (1991) 'France Looks to Conquer the US', *Music Business International*, May, pp. 20–1.

Finnegan, R. (1989) *The Hidden Musicians: Music Making in an English Town*. Cambridge: Cambridge University Press.

Fornäs, J., Lindberg, U. and Sernhede, O. (1995) *In Garageland: Rock, Youth and Modernity*. London: Routledge.

Fox, B. (1993) 'Danger in Downloading the Perfect Digital Copy', *Music Business International*, 3, 5, pp. 13–15.

Frith, S. (1978) *The Sociology of Rock*. London: Constable.

Frith, S. (1981) 'The Magic that Can Set You Free: The Ideology of Folk and the Myth of the Rock Community', *Popular Music*, 1, pp. 159–68.

Frith, S. (1983) *Sound Effects: Youth, Leisure and the Politics of Rock 'n' Roll*. London: Constable.

Frith, S. (1986) 'Art Versus Technology: The Strange Case of Popular Music', *Media, Culture & Society*, 8, pp. 263–79.

Frith, S. (1987) 'Copyright and the Music Business', *Popular Music*, 7, 1, pp. 57–75.

Frith, S. (1988a) *Music for Pleasure*. Cambridge: Polity Press.

Frith, S. (1988b) 'Introduction' and 'Video Pop: Picking up the Pieces', in *Facing the Music*. New York: Pantheon.

Frith, S. (1990) 'Afterthoughts', in S. Frith and A. Goodwin (eds), *On Record: Rock, Pop and the Written Word*. London: Routledge.

Frith, S. (1991) 'The Good, the Bad, and the Indifferent: Defending Popular Culture from the Populists', *Diacritics*, 21, 4, pp. 102–15.

Frith, S. (1993) 'Popular Music and the Local State', in T. Bennett, S. Frith, L. Grossberg, J. Shepherd and B. Turner (eds), *Rock and Popular Music: Politics, Policies and Institutions*. London: Routledge.

Frith, S. and Horne, H. (1987) *Art into Pop*. London: Methuen.

Frith, S. and McRobbie, A. (1978) 'Rock and Sexuality', *Screen Education*, 29, pp. 3–19.

Garofalo, R. (1986) 'How Autonomous is Relative: Popular Music, the Social Formation and Cultural Struggle', *Popular Music*, 6, 1, pp. 77–92.

Garofalo, R. (1993) 'Whose World, What Beat: The Transnational Music Industry, Identity and Cultural Imperialism', *The World of Music*, 35, 2, pp. 16–32.

Gendron, B. (1986) 'Theodor Adorno Meets the Cadillacs', in T. Modeleski (ed.), *Studies in Entertainment*. Bloomington: Indiana University Press.

George, N. (1988) *The Death of Rhythm & Blues*. New York: Pantheon.

Giddens, A. (1985) *The Nation State and Violence*. Cambridge: Polity Press.

Giddens, A. (1990). *The Consequences of Modernity*. Stanford, CA: Stanford University Press; Cambridge: Polity Press (1991).

Gill, A. (1993) 'Going Belly up with Suede', *The Independent*, 25 March, p. 16.

Gill, J. (1995) *Queer Noises: Male and Female Homosexuality in Twentieth-Century Music*. London: Cassell.

Gillett, C. (1983) *The Sound of the City*. London: Souvenir Press.

Gilroy, P. (1987) *There Ain't no Black in the Union Jack*. London: Hutchinson.

Gilroy, P. (1993a) *The Black Atlantic, Modernity and Double Consciousness*. London: Verso.

Gilroy, P. (1993b) *Small Acts: Thoughts on the Politics of Black Cultures*. London: Serpent's Tail.

Girard, B. (1992) 'Introduction', in B. Girard (ed.), *A Passion for Radio, Radio Waves and Community*. Montreal and New York: Black Rose Books.

Glanvill, R. (1989) 'World Music Mining: The International Trade in New Music', in F. Hanly and T. May (eds), *Rhythms of the World*. London: BBC.

Glasser, R. (1990) 'Paradoxical Ethnicity: Puerto Rican Musicians in Post-World War 1 New York City', *Latin American Music Review*, 11, 1, pp. 63–71.

Golding, P. (1994) 'The Communications Paradox: Inequality at the National and International Levels', *Media Development*, 41, 4, pp. 7–9.

Goldman, A. (1982) *Elvis*. Harmondsworth: Penguin.

Goodman, F. (1993) 'Future Shock: How the New Technologies Will Change the Music Business Forever', *Musician*, December, pp. 32–49.

Goodwin, A. (1992) *Dancing in the Distraction Factory: Music Television and Popular Culture*. Minneapolis: University of Minnesota Press.

Goodwin, A. and Gore, J. (1990) 'World Beat and the Cultural Imperialism Thesis', *Socialist Review*, 20, 3, pp. 63–80.

Gorbman, C. (1987) *Unheard Melodies: Narrative Film Music*. London: BFI; Bloomington: Indiana University Press.

Gorman, P. (1995) 'Enter the Dragon', *Music Business International*, June, pp. 11–15.

Gottlieb, J. and Wald, G. (1994) 'Smells Like Teen Spirit: Riot Grrrls, Revolution and Women in Independent Rock', in T. Rose and A. Ross (eds), *Microphone Fiends: Youth Music and Youth Culture*. London: Routledge.

Grenier, L. (1993) 'Policing French-Language Music on Canadian Radio: The Twilight of the Popular Record Era?', in T. Bennett, S. Frith, L. Grossberg, J. Shepherd and B. Turner (eds), *Rock and Popular Music: Politics, Policies and Institutions*. London: Routledge.

Gronow, P. (1983) 'The Record Industry: The Growth of a Mass Medium', *Popular Music*, 3, pp. 53–75.

Grossberg, L. (1987) 'The Politics of Music: American Images and British Articulations', *Canadian Journal of Political and Social Theory*, 11, 1/2, pp. 144–51.

Grossberg, L. (1992) *We Gotta Get out of this Place*. London: Routledge.

Grossberg, L. (1994) 'Is Anybody Listening? Does Anybody Care? On the State of Rock', in A. Ross and T. Rose (eds), *Microphone Fiends: Youth Music and Youth Culture*. London: Routledge.

Guilbault, J. (1993a) *Zouk: World Music in the West Indies.* Chicago: University of Chicago Press.

Guilbault, J. (1993b) 'On Redefining the "local" through World Music', *The World of Music*, 35, 2, pp. 33–47.

Gumbel, A. (1993) 'Patriotic MPs Insist on Le pop français for Radio Listeners', *The Guardian*, 29 December, p. 3.

Hall, S. (1974) *A 'Reading' of Marx's 1857 Introduction to the Grundrisse.* Occasional Paper. Brimingham: Centre for Contemporary Cultural Studies.

Hall, S. (1980) 'Encoding-Decoding', in S. Hall, D. Hobson, A. Lowe and P. Willis (eds), *Culture, Media, Language.* London: Hutchinson.

Hall, S. (1986) 'On Postmodernism and Articulation, An Interview with Stuart Hall, Edited by Lawrence Grossberg', *Journal of Communication Inquiry*, 10, 2, pp. 45–60.

Hall, S. (1991) 'Old and New Identities: Old and New Ethnicities', in A. King (ed.), *Culture, Globalization and the World-System.* London: Macmillan.

Hall, S. (1994) 'Reflections upon the Encoding/Decoding Model: An Interview With Stuart Hall', in J. Cruz and J. Lewis (eds), *Viewing, Reading, Listening: Audiences and Cultural Reception.* Boulder, CO: Westview Press.

Hall, S. and Jefferson, T. (eds) (1976) *Resistance through Rituals: Youth Subcultures in Postwar Britain.* London: Hutchinson.

Hall, S. and Whannel, P. (1964) *The Popular Arts.* London: Hutchinson.

Hamelink, C. (1995) 'Information Imbalances across the World', in J. Downing, A. Mohammadi and A. Sreberny-Mohammadi (eds), *Questioning the Media*, 2nd edition. London: Sage.

Hardy, D. and Laing, D. (1990) *The Faber Companion to 20th-Century Popular Music.* London: Faber & Faber.

Harker, D. (1980) *One for the Money: Politics and Popular Song.* London: Hutchinson.

Harker, D. (1985) *Fakesong: The Manufacture of British 'Folksong', 1700 to the Present Day.* Milton Keynes: Open University Press.

Harker, D. (1992) 'Still Crazy after all these Years: What was Popular Music in the 1960s', in B. Moore-Gilbert (ed.), *Cultural Revolution? The Challenge of the Arts in the 1960s.* London: Routledge.

Harker, D. (1994) 'Blood on the Tracks: Popular Music in the 1970s', in B. Moore-Gilbert (ed.), *The Arts in the 1970s: Cultural Closure?* London: Routledge.

Hatch, D. and Millward, S. (1987) *From Blues to Rock: An Analytical History of Pop Music.* Manchester: Manchester University Press.

Hayward, P. (1990) 'Industrial Light and Magic: Style, Technology and Special Effects in the Music Video and Music Television', in P. Hayward (ed.), *Culture, Technology and Creativity in the Late Twentieth Century.* London: John Libbey.

Hebdige, D. (1977) 'Reggae, Rastas and Rudies', in J. Curran, M. Gurevitch and J. Woollacott (eds), *Mass Communication and Society.* London: Edward Arnold.

Hebdige, D. (1979) *Subculture: The Meaning of Style.* London: Methuen.

Hebdige, D. (1981) 'Towards a Cartography of Taste, 1935–1962', *Block*, 4, pp. 39–56.

Hebdige, D. (1987) *Cut 'n' Mix: Culture, Identity and Caribbean Music*. London: Routledge.

Helmreich, S. (1992) 'Kinship, Nation and Paul Gilroy's Concept of Diaspora', *Diaspora*, 2, 2, pp. 243–9.

Hennion, A. (1982) 'Popular Music as Social Production', in D. Horn and P. Tagg (eds), *Popular Music Perspectives*, 1. Exeter: IASPM.

Hennion, A. (1983) 'The Production of Success: An Anti-Musicology of the Pop Song'. *Popular Music* 3, pp. 158–93.

Hennion, A. (1989) 'An intermediary between Production and Consumption: The Producer of Popular Music', *Science, Technology and Human Values*, 14, 4, pp. 400–24.

Hesmondhalgh, D. (1996) 'Is This What You Call Change? Post-Fordism, Flexibility and the Music Industries', *Media, Culture and Society*, 18.

Hill, D. (1986) *Designer Boys and Material Girls: Manufacturing the 1980s Pop Dream*. Poole: Blandford Press.

Hind, S. and Mosco, S. (1985) *Rebel Radio: The Full Story of British Pirate Radio*. London: Pluto Press.

Hirsch, P. (1970) *The Structure of the Popular Music Industry: The Filtering Process by which Records are Preselected for Public Consumption*. Ann Arbor: Institute for Social Research, University of Michigan.

Hirsch, P. (1972) 'Processing Fads and Fashions: An Organizational Set Analysis of Cultural Industry Systems', *American Journal of Sociology*, 77, 4, pp. 639–59.

Hoffman, J. (1995) *Beyond the State: An Introductory Critique*. Cambridge: Polity Press.

Hollander, E. and Stappers, J. (1992) 'Community Media and Community Communication', in N. Jankowski, O. Prehn and I. Stappers (eds), *The People's Voice: Local Radio and Television in Europe*. London: John Libbey.

Hung, M. and Morencos, E. (1990) *World Record Sales, 1969–1990: A Statistical History of the World Recording Industry*. London: International Federation of the Phonographic Industry.

IASPM-Japan (1991) *Popular Music in Japan*. International Association for the Study of Popular Music, Japan.

IFPI (1993) 'Electronic Delivery', *IFPI for the Record*, April, pp. 1, 4–5.

Jensen, J. (1984) 'An Interpretive Approach to Cultural Production', in W. Rowland and B. Watkins (eds), *Interpreting Television*. London: Sage.

Jensen, J. (1992) 'Fandom as Pathology: The Consequences of Characterization', in L. Lewis (ed.), *The Adoring Audience: Fan Culture and Popular Media*. London: Routledge.

Jones, L. (1965) *Blues People: Negro Music in White America*. London: MacGibbon & Kee.

Jones, S. (1993) 'Who Fought the Law? The American Music Industry and the Global Popular Music Market', in T. Bennett, S. Frith, L. Grossberg, J. Shepherd and B. Turner (eds), *Rock and Popular Music: Politics, Policies and Institutions*. London: Routledge.

Jones, S. and Schumacher, T. (1992) 'Muzak: On Functional Music and Power', *Critical Studies in Mass Communication*, 9, pp. 156–69.

Kalinak, K. (1992) *Settling the Score: Music and the Classical Hollywood Film*. Madison: University of Wisconsin Press.

Kaplan, E. A. (1987) *Rocking around the Clock: Music Television, Postmodernism and Consumer Culture*. London: Methuen.

Kater, M. (1992) *Different Drummers: Jazz in the Culture of Nazi Germany*. Oxford: Oxford University Press.

Koestler, A. (1964) *The Act of Creation*. London: Hutchinson.

Koestler, A. (1978) *Janus: A Summing Up*. London: Picador.

Kofsky, F. (1970) *Black Nationalism and the Revolution in Music*. New York: Pathfinder.

Kogawa, T. (1993) 'Free Radio in Japan: The Mini FM Boom', in N. Strauss (ed.), *Radiotext(e)*. Semiotext(e). New York: Columbia University Press.

Laing, D. (1969) *The Sound of our Time*. London: Sheed & Ward.

Laing, D. (1985) *One Chord Wonders: Power and Meaning in Punk Rock*. Milton Keynes: Open University Press.

Laing, D. (1986) 'The Music Industry and the Cultural Imperialism Thesis', *Media, Culture and Society*, 8, pp. 331–41.

Laing, D. (1989) 'Moving away from US Influence', *Europe Etc*, in *Music Week*, January, pp. 14–15.

Laing, D. (1992) "Sadeness", Scorpions and Single Markets: National and Transnational Trends in European Popular Music', *Popular Music*, 11, 2, pp. 127–39.

Lanza, J. (1994) *Elevator Music*. London: Quartet.

Lee, S. (1995) 'Re-Examining the Concept of the "Independent" Record Company: The Case of Wax Trax! Records', *Popular Music*, 14, 1, pp. 13–32.

Lennon, J. (1964) *In His Own Write*. London: Jonathan Cape.

Lennon, J. (1965) *A Spaniard in the Works*. Harmondsworth: Penguin.

Lewis, G. (1991) 'Who Do You Love? The Dimensions of Musical Taste', in J. Lull (ed.), *Popular Music and Communication*, 2nd edition. London: Sage.

Lewis, L. (1990) *Gender Politics and MTV: Voicing the Difference*. Philadelphia: Temple University Press.

Lewis, L. (ed.) (1992) *The Adoring Audience: Fan Culture and Popular Media*. London: Routledge.

Lewis, P. and Booth, J. (1989) *The Invisible Medium: Public, Commercial and Community Radio*. London: Macmillan.

Lipsitz, G. (1990) *Time Passages, Collective Memory and American Popular Culture*. Minneapolis: University of Minnesota Press.

Lipsitz, G. (1993) 'Foreword' to S. D. Crafts, D. Cavicchi and C. Keil, *My Music*. Middletown, CT: Wesleyan University Press.

Lipsitz, G. (1994) *Dangerous Crossroads: Popular Music, Postmodernism and the Poetics of Place*. London: Verso.

Longhurst, B. (1995) *Popular Music and Society*. Cambridge: Polity Press.

Lull, J. (1992) 'Introduction', in J. Lull (ed.), *Popular Music and Communication*, 2nd edition. London: Sage.

McClary, S. (1991) *Feminine Endings: Music, Gender and Sexuality*. Minneapolis: University of Minnesota Press.

MacDonald, I. (1994) *Revolution in Head: The Beatles' Music and the 1960s*. London: Fourth Estate.

MacDougald Jr., D. (1941) 'The Popular Music Industry', in P. Lazarsfeld and F. Stanton (eds), *Radio Research 1941*. New York: Dewell, Sloan and Pearce.

McLaughlin, T. (1970) *Music and Communication*. London: Faber & Faber.

MacLeod, B. (1979) 'Facing the Muzak', *Popular Music and Society*, 7, 1, pp. 18–31.

McRobbie, A. (1980) 'Settling Accounts with Subcultures: A Feminist Critique', *Screen Education*, 34, pp. 37–49.

McRobbie, A. (1994) *Postmodernism and Popular Culture*. London: Routledge.

McRobbie, A. and Garber, J. (1991) 'Girls and Subcultures', in A. McRobbie (ed.), *Feminism and Youth Culture*. London: Macmillan.

Manuel, P. (1985) 'The Anticipated Bass in Cuban Popular Music', *Latin American Music Review*, 6, 2, pp. 249–61.

Manuel, P. (1986) 'Marxism, Nationalism and Popular Music in Revolutionary Cuba', *Popular Music*, 6, 2, pp. 161–78.

Manuel, P. (1991) 'Salsa and the Music Industry: Corporate Control or Grassroots Expression?', in P. Manuel (ed.), *Essays on Cuban Music*. Lanham, MD: University Press of America.

Marcus, G. (1992) *Dead Elvis: A Chronicle of Cultural Obsession*. Harmondsworth: Penguin.

Martin, G. (1994) *Summer of Love: The Making of Sergeant Pepper*. London: Macmillan.

Martins, C. A. (1987) 'Popular Music as Alternative Communication: Uruguay, 1973–82', *Popular Music*, 7, 1, pp. 77–94.

Marx, K. (1954) *The Eighteenth Brumaire of Louis Bonaparte*. Moscow: Progress.

Marx, K. (1973) *Grundrisse*. Harmondsworth: Penguin.

Massey, D. (1994) *Space, Place and Gender*. Cambridge: Polity Press.

Mellers, W. (1973) *Twilight of the Gods: The Beatles in Retrospect*. London: Faber & Faber.

Mercer, K. (1994) *Welcome to the Jungle: New Positions in Black Cultural Studies*. London: Routledge.

Meyer, M. (1991) *The Politics of Music in the Third Reich*. Peter Lang.

Middleton, R. (1990) *Studying Popular Music*. Milton Keynes: Open University Press.

Miller, J. (ed.) (1980) *The Rolling Stone History of Rock 'n' Roll*. New York: Random House.

Miller, J. (1994) 'Should Phone Companies Make Films?' *New York Times*, 2 January, p. 11.

Milliman, R. (1982) 'Using Background Music to Affect the Behaviour of Supermarket Shoppers', *Journal of Marketing*, 46, pp. 86–91.

Mitchell, T. (1993) 'World Music and the Popular Music Industry: An Australian View', *Ethnomusicology*, 37, 3, pp. 309–38.

Mohammadi, A. (1995) 'Cultural Imperialism and Cultural Identity', in J. Downing, A. Mohammadi and A. Sreberny-Mohammadi (eds), *Questioning the Media*, 2nd edition. London: Sage.

Moore, A. (1993) *Rock: The Primary Text*. Milton Keynes: Open University Press.

Morley, D. (1992) *Television, Audiences and Cultural Studies*. London: Routledge.

Morley, D. (1993) 'Active Audience Theory: Pendulums and Pitfalls', *Journal of Communication*, 43, 4, pp. 13–19.

Morley, D. and Robins, K. (1995) *Spaces of Identity: Global Media, Electronic Landscapes and Cultural Boundaries*. London: Routledge.

Negus, K. (1992) *Producing Pop: Culture and Conflict in the Popular Music Industry*. London: Edward Arnold.

Negus, K. (1993) 'Global Harmonies & Local Discords: Transnational Policies and Practices in the European Recording Industry', *European Journal of Communication*, 8, 3, pp. 293–316.

Negus, K. (1995) 'Where the Mystical Meets the Market: Commerce and Creativity in the Production of Popular Music', *Sociological Review*, 43, 2, pp. 316–41.

Negus, K. (1996) 'Globalization and the Music of the Public Sphere', in S. Braman and A. Sreberny-Mohammadi (eds), *Globalization, Communication and the Transnational Public Sphere*. Derby: Hampden Press.

Ong, W. (1971) *Rhetoric, Romance and Technology*. Ithaca, NY: Cornell University Press.

Orman, J. (1984) *The Politics of Rock Music*. Chicago: Nelson Hall.

Padilla, F. (1989) 'Salsa Music as a Cultural Expression of Latino Consciousness and Unity', *Hispanic Journal of Behavioural Sciences*, 11, 1, pp. 28–45.

Padilla, F. (1990) 'Salsa: Puerto Rican and Latino Music', *Journal of Popular Culture*, 24, pp. 87–104.

Palacios, J. (1995) 'The Rock 'n' Roll Experience in Mexico During the 1960s'. Paper presented at the 7th IASPM International Conference, 'Music on Show: Issues of Performance', Strathclyde University, 1–6 July.

Pekacz, J. (1994) 'Did Rock Smash the Wall? The Role of Rock in Political Transition', *Popular Music*, 13, 1, pp. 41–9.

Perez, B. J. (1986) 'Political Facets of Salsa', *Popular Music*, 6, 2, pp. 149–60.

Perris, A. (1985) *Music as Propaganda: Art to Persuade, Art to Control*. Westport, CT: Greenwood Press.

Peterson, R. (1976) 'The Production of Culture: A Prolegomenon', in R. Peterson (ed.), *The Production of Culture*. London: Sage.

Peterson, R. (1982) 'Five Constraints on the Production of Culture: Law, Technology, Market, Organizational Structure and Occupational Careers', *Journal of Popular Culture*, 16, 2, pp. 143–53.

Peterson, R. (1990) 'Why 1955? Explaining the Advent of Rock Music', *Popular Music*, 9, 1, pp. 97–116.

Pickering, M. (1987) 'The Past as a Source of Social Aspiration: Popular Song and Social Change', in M. Pickering and T. Green (eds), *Everyday Culture: Popular Songs and the Vernacular Milieu*. Milton Keynes: Open University Press.

Pickering, M. (1990) 'Recent Folk Music Scholarship in England: A Critique', *Folk Music Journal*, 6, 1, pp. 37–64.

Pickering, M. and Green, T. (1987) 'Towards a Cartography of the Vernacular Milieu', in M. Pickering and T. Green (eds), *Everyday Culture: Popular Songs and the Vernacular Milieu*. Milton Keynes: Open University Press.

Pickering, M. and Shuker, R. (1992) 'Radio Gaga: Popular Music and the Radio Quota Debate in New Zealand', *New Zealand Sociology*, 8, 1, pp. 21–59.

Pickering, M. and Shuker, R. (1994) 'Struggling to Make Ourselves Heard – Music, Radio and the Quota Debate', in P. Hayward, T. Mitchell and R. Shuker (eds), *North Meets South: Popular Music in Aotearoa/ New Zealand*. Perfect Beat Publications.

Plato. (1974) *The Republic*, trans. D. Lee. Harmondsworth: Penguin.

Pratt, R. (1994) *Rhythm and Resistance*. Washington, DC: Smithsonian Institution.

Quintero Rivera, A. and Manuel Alvarez, L. (1990) 'La libre combinacion de las formas musicales en la salsa', *David & Goliath: Revista del Consejo Latinoamericano de Ciencias Sociales*, 19, 57, pp. 45–51.

Ramet, S. (ed.) (1994) *Rocking the State: Rock Music and Politics in Eastern Europe and Russia*. Boulder, CO: Westview Press.

Reeves, G. (1993) *Communications and the 'Third World'*. London: Routledge.

Riesman, D. (1990) 'Listening to Popular Music', in S. Frith and A. Goodwin (eds), *On Record: Rock, Pop and the Written Word*. London: Routledge.

Riethmüller, A. (1991) 'German Music from the Perspective of German Musicology after 1933', *Journal of Musicological Research*, 11, 3, pp. 177–87.

Robbins, J. (1990) 'The Cuban Son as Form, Genre and Symbol', *Latin American Music Review*, 11, 2, pp. 182–200.

Roberts, J. S. (1979) *The Latin Tinge: The Impact of Latin American Music on the United States*. Tivoli, NY: Original Music.

Roberts, J. S. (1992) 'The Roots', in V. Boggs (ed.), *Salsiology: Afro-Cuban Music and the Evolution of Salsa in New York City*. New York: Excelsior.

Robinson, D., Buck, E. and Cuthbert, M. (1991) *Music at the Margins: Popular Music and Global Cultural Diversity*. London: Sage.

Roe, K. (1985) 'Swedish Youth and Music: Listening Patterns and Motivations', *Communication Research*, 12, 3, pp. 353–62.

Roe, K. (1990) 'Adolescents' Music Use', in K. Roe and U. Carlsson (eds), *Popular Music Research*. Sweden: Nordicom.

Roe, K. and von Feilitzen, C. (1992) 'Eavesdropping on Adolescence: An Exploratory Study of Music Listening Among Children', *Communications*, 17, 2, pp. 225–43.

Román Velázquez, P. (1996) *The Construction of Latin Identities and Salsa Music Clubs in London: An Ethnographic Study*, PhD thesis, Leicester University.

Rose, T. (1994) *Black Noise: Rap and Black Culture in Contemporary America*. Middletown, CT: Wesleyan University Press.

Ryan, J. (1985) *The Production of Culture in the Music Industry: The ASCAP-BMI Controversy*. Lanham, MD: University Press of America.

Ryan, J. and Peterson, R. (1982) 'The Product Image: The Fate of Creativity in Country Music Songwriting', in J. Ettema and D. Whitney (eds), *Individuals in Mass Media Organizations: Creativity and Constraint*. London: Sage.

Ryback, T. (1990) *Rock Around the Bloc: A History of Rock Music in Eastern Europe and the Soviet Union*. Oxford: Oxford University Press.

Said, E. (1994) *Culture and Imperialism*. New York: Vintage.

Savage, J. (1991) *England's Dreaming: Sex Pistols and Punk Rock*. London: Faber & Faber.

Scannell, P. and Cardiff, D. (1991) *A Social History of British Broadcasting*, Vol. 1: *1922–1939: Serving the Nation*. Oxford: Blackwell.

Schiller, H. (1991) 'Not Yet the Post-Imperial Era', *Critical Studies in Mass Communication*, 8, pp. 13–28.

Scott, A. (1994) 'Latin America and the Focus in the Nineties Swings South', *Music Business International*, December, pp. 11–13.

Seidman, S. (1981) 'On the Contributions of Music to Media Productions', *Educational Communication and Technology*, 29, 1, pp. 49–61.

Shepard, L. (1962) *The Broadside Ballad*. London: Herbert Jenkins.

Shore, L. (1983) *The Crossroads of Business and Music*. PhD thesis, Stanford University.

Shuker, R. (1994) *Understanding Popular Music*. London: Routledge.

Silverstone, R. (1994) *Television and Everyday Life*. London: Routledge.

Singer, R. L. (1988) 'Puerto Rican Music in New York City', *New York Folklore*, 14, 3–4, pp. 139–50.

Sivanandan, A. (1990) *Communities of Resistance*. London: Verso.

Sklair, L. (1991) *Sociology of the Global System*. London: Harvester Wheatsheaf.

Sklar, R. (1984) *Rocking America: How the All-Hit Radio Stations Took Over*. New York: St Martins Press.

Sreberny-Mohammadi, A. (1996) 'The Many Cultural Faces of Imperialism', in P. Golding and P. Harris (eds), *Beyond Cultural Studies*. London: Sage.

Starr, S. (1983) *Red and Hot: The Fate of Jazz in the Soviet Union*. Oxford: Oxford University Press.

Starr, V. (1994) *k.d.lang: All You Get is Me*. New York and London: Harper Collins.

Steele, S. and Dalton, S. (1994) 'Global Village People', *New Musical Express*, 12 February, pp. 20–1.

Stephens, G. (1991) 'Rap Music's Double-Voiced Discourse: A Crossroads for Interracial Communication', *Journal of Communication Inquiry*, 15, 2, pp. 70–91.

Steward, S. (1994) 'Dancing with the Saints: The International Sound of Salsa', in S. Broughton, M. Ellingham, D. Muddyman and R. Trillo (eds), *World Music: The Rough Guide*. Harmondsworth: Penguin.

Steward, S. and Garratt, S. (1984) *Signed, Sealed and Delivered: True Life Stories of Women in Pop*. London: Pluto Press.

Stokes, M. (1994) 'Introduction: Ethnicity, Identity and Music', in M. Stokes (ed.), *Ethnicity, Identity and Music*. Oxford: Berg.

Stratton, J. (1982a) 'Reconciling Contradictions: The Role of the Artist & Repertoire Person in the British Music Industry', *Popular Music and Society*, 8, 2, pp. 90–100.

Stratton, J. (1982b) 'Between Two Worlds: Art and Commercialism in the Record Industry', *Sociological Review*, 30, pp. 267–85.

Straw, W. (1991) 'Systems of Articulation, Logics of Change: Communities and Scenes in Popular Music', *Cultural Studies*, 5, 3, pp. 368–88.

Street, J. (1986) *Rebel Rock: The Politics of Popular Music*. Oxford: Blackwell.

Szemere, A. (1992) 'The Politics of Marginality: A Rock Musical Subculture in Socialist Hungary in the Early 1980s', in R. Garofalo (ed.), *Rockin' The Boat: Mass Music and Mass Movements*. Boston: South End Press.

Tagg, P. (1989) 'Open Letter: "Black Music", "Afro-American Music" and "European Music"', *Popular Music*, 8, 3, pp. 285–98.

Taylor, J. and Laing, D. (1979) 'Disco-Pleasure-Discourse: On "Rock and Sexuality"', *Screen Education*, 31, pp. 43–8.

Thornton, S. (1995) *Club Cultures: Music, Media and Subcultural Capital*. Cambridge: Polity Press.

Tomlinson, J. (1991) *Cultural Imperialism*. London: Pinter.

Tosh, J. (1984) *The Pursuit of History*. London: Longman.

Tracey, M. (1985) 'The Poisoned Chalice? International Television and the Idea of Dominance', *Daedalus*, 114, 4, pp. 17–56.

Trondman, M. (1990) 'Rock Tastes – On Rock as Symbolic Capital', in K. Roe and U. Carlsson (eds), *Popular Music Research*. Sweden: Nordicom.

Tulich, K. (1992) 'Nine Acts to Hit LA in Unprecedented Effort to "Kick Start" US Awareness and Return Home with Deals', *Billboard*, 9 May, pp. A4/10.

Tunstall, J. (1977) *The Media are American*. London: Constable.

Van Der Merwe, P. (1989) *The Origins of Popular Style: The Antecedents of Twentieth-Century Popular Music*. Oxford: Oxford University Press.

Vignolle, J. (1980) 'Mixing Genres and Reaching the Public: The Production of Pop Music', *Social Science Information*, 19, 1, pp. 79–105.

Vila, P. (1992) 'Rock Nacional and Dictatorship in Argentina', in R. Garofalo (ed.), *Rockin' the Boat: Mass Music and Mass Movements*. Boston: South End Press.

Vincent, D. (1989) *Literacy and Popular Culture: England, 1750–1914*. Cambridge: Cambridge University Press.

von Feilitzen, C. and Roe, K. (1990) 'Children and Music', in K. Roe and U. Carlsson (eds), *Popular Music Research*. Sweden: Nordicom.

Vulliamy, G. (1977) 'Music and the Mass Culture Debate', in J. Shepherd, P. Virden, G. Vulliamy and T. Wishart (eds), *Whose Music? A Sociology of Musical Languages*. London: Latimer New Dimensions.

Wallis, R. and Malm, K. (1984) *Big Sounds from Small Peoples*. London: Constable.

Wallis, R. and Malm, K. (1992) *Media Policy and Music Activity*. London: Routledge.

Walser, R. (1992) 'Review of Origins of Popular Style by Peter Van Der Merwe', *Journal of Musicological Research*, 12, 1/2, pp. 123–32.

Walser, R. (1993) *Running with the Devil: Power, Gender and Madness in Heavy Metal Music*. Middletown, CT: Wesleyan University Press.

Weeks, J. (1986) *Sexuality*. London: Routledge.

Whiteley, S. (1992) *The Space between the Notes: Rock and the Counter-Culture*. London: Routledge.

Wicke, P. (1985) 'Sentimentality and High Pathos: Popular Music in Fascist Germany', *Popular Music*, 5, pp. 147–58.

Wicke, P. (1987) *Rock Music: Culture, Aesthetics and Sociology*. Cambridge: Cambridge University Press.

Wicke, P. (1991) 'The Role of Popular Music in World Changes'. Opening Keynote Address to 'Popular Music and Social Reality', 6th International Conference of the International Association for the Study of Popular Music, Humboldt University, Berlin, 15 July.

Wicke, P. (1992a) 'The Times They are a-Changing: Rock Music and Political Change in East Germany', in R. Garofalo (ed.), *Rockin' the Boat: Mass Music and Mass Movements*. Boston: South End Press.

Wicke, P. (1992b) 'The Role of Rock Music in the Political Disintegration of East Germany', in J. Lull (ed.), *Popular Music and Communication*, 2nd edn. London: Sage.

Widgery, D. (1986) *Beating Time*. London: Chatto & Windus.

Wiener, J. (1985) *Come Together: John Lennon in his Time*. London: Faber & Faber.

Williams, R. (1965) *The Long Revolution*. Harmondsworth: Penguin.

Williams, R. (1976) *Keywords: A Vocabulary of Culture and Society*. London: Fontana.

Williams, R. (1990) *Television, Technology and Cultural Form*. London: Routledge.

Willis, P. (1977) *Learning to Labour: How Working-Class Kids Get Working-Class Jobs*. Farnborough, Hants: Saxon House.

Willis, P. (1990) 'The Golden Age', in S. Frith and A. Goodwin (eds), *On Record: Rock, Pop and the Written Word*. London: Routledge.

Wise, S. (1990) 'Sexing Elvis', in S. Frith and A. Goodwin (eds), *On Record: Rock, Pop and the Written Word*. London: Routledge.

INDEX